POLITICAL SCIENCE AND HISTORY

GLOBAL INTELLIGENCE PRIORITIES

(FROM THE PERSPECTIVE OF THE UNITED STATES)

POLITICAL SCIENCE AND HISTORY

Additional books and e-books in this series can be found on Nova's website under the Series tab.

POLITICAL SCIENCE AND HISTORY

GLOBAL INTELLIGENCE PRIORITIES

(FROM THE PERSPECTIVE OF THE UNITED STATES)

JOHN MICHAEL WEAVER
AND
JENNIFER YONGMEI POMEROY
EDITORS

Copyright © 2019 by Nova Science Publishers, Inc.

All rights reserved. No part of this book may be reproduced, stored in a retrieval system or transmitted in any form or by any means: electronic, electrostatic, magnetic, tape, mechanical photocopying, recording or otherwise without the written permission of the Publisher.

We have partnered with Copyright Clearance Center to make it easy for you to obtain permissions to reuse content from this publication. Simply navigate to this publication's page on Nova's website and locate the "Get Permission" button below the title description. This button is linked directly to the title's permission page on copyright.com. Alternatively, you can visit copyright.com and search by title, ISBN, or ISSN.

For further questions about using the service on copyright.com, please contact:
Copyright Clearance Center
Phone: +1-(978) 750-8400   Fax: +1-(978) 750-4470   E-mail: info@copyright.com.

NOTICE TO THE READER

The Publisher has taken reasonable care in the preparation of this book, but makes no expressed or implied warranty of any kind and assumes no responsibility for any errors or omissions. No liability is assumed for incidental or consequential damages in connection with or arising out of information contained in this book. The Publisher shall not be liable for any special, consequential or exemplary damages resulting, in whole or in part, from the readers' use of, or reliance upon, this material. Any parts of this book based on government reports are so indicated and copyright is claimed for those parts to the extent applicable to compilations of such works.

Independent verification should be sought for any data, advice or recommendations contained in this book. In addition, no responsibility is assumed by the Publisher for any injury and/or damage to persons or property arising from any methods, products, instructions, ideas or otherwise contained in this publication.

This publication is designed to provide accurate and authoritative information with regard to the subject matter covered herein. It is sold with the clear understanding that the Publisher is not engaged in rendering legal or any other professional services. If legal or any other expert assistance is required, the services of a competent person should be sought. FROM A DECLARATION OF PARTICIPANTS JOINTLY ADOPTED BY A COMMITTEE OF THE AMERICAN BAR ASSOCIATION AND A COMMITTEE OF PUBLISHERS.

Additional color graphics may be available in the e-book version of this book.

Library of Congress Cataloging-in-Publication Data

ISBN: 978-1-53615-836-6
Library of Congress Control Number:2019943458

Published by Nova Science Publishers, Inc. † New York

CONTENTS

Preface ix

Chapter 1 Introduction to the National Security Issues
Confronting the United States 1
John M. Weaver

Chapter 2 Making America Secure Again:
A Qualitative Assessment of the United States'
Homeland Security Front 13
Ben Hinkel, Stephen Strausser and Matt Nelson

Chapter 3 The Dragon's Ascension - China's Rise
and Challenge to the American Hegemony:
A Qualitative Assessment 51
*Josie Gardner, Christopher DeJesus, Max Vargo
and Nicole Wightman*

Chapter 4 Postmodern Imperialism:
A Qualitative Assessment of the Aggressive
Spread of Russian Influence 81
*Kyra Shoemaker, Mitchell Forrest,
Jennifer Ohashi and Rachele Tombolini*

Chapter 5	A Qualitative Assessment of Iran: Middle Eastern Threats, Nuclear Ambition, State Sponsored Terrorism, and More *Stephanie M. Savage and Michael Richardson*	113
Chapter 6	East Asia's Formidable Foe: North Korea *Joseph D. Hurd, Joseph Soreco and Gunnar Nemeth*	141
Chapter 7	Sorting Out the Syrian Conflict; Impacts on United States National Security: A Qualitative Assessment *James Simmons, Austin Cullember and Brendan McDonough*	171
Chapter 8	Turkey - Friend or Foe of the United States: A Qualitative Assessment *Christopher Geer, Jaiden Moul, Jordan Sowers and Vivian Ferris*	193
Chapter 9	Is India a U.S. Ally to "The China Threat"? A Qualitative Assessment *Jason Guo*	225
Chapter 10	Monsters of the Middle East: ISIL's Perpetual Pursuit for Power (A Qualitative Assessment) *Alexis Hart and Brielle Schultz*	259
Chapter 11	Prominent Cyber Security Issuesfor the United States: A Qualitative Assessment *Nathan McDowell, Ethan Walker and Matthew Meyers*	287
Chapter 12	Challenges of the U.S. National Security and Moving Forward *Jennifer Yongmei Pomeroy*	315

About the Editors	**329**
Index	**331**
Related Nova Publications	**339**

Preface

The United States is seemingly confronted with more global issues now than it has ever experienced. The U.S., under a relatively new presidential administration, is looking to depart from globalization though there are still inextricable linkages among all countries in the world; in 2018 both the Defense Department and State Department have provided updates to their strategies and security plans. This book provides an open source intelligence analysis of regions, countries and non-state actors from around the world that could have an impact on the United States. These areas and actors are dissected using predominately qualitative analysis techniques focusing on secondary data sources in order to provide an open source intelligence look at threats as seen by the United States using two models (the York Intelligence Red Team Model and the Federal Secondary Data Case Study Triangulation Model). The key audience for this book includes the 17 members of the U.S. intelligence community, members of the U.S. National Security Council, governments of other countries that share the United States' assessment of current threats, nongovernmental organizations (NGOs) looking to provide support abroad, and private sector companies considering expanding their operations overseas.

Chapter 1 - Since Donald Trump has been elected president, there have been a lot of changes in the political landscape and world security. Transnational terrorism has continued to burgeon. Europe continues to be vulnerable and has seen several attacks in recent years like in France, the United Kingdom, and elsewhere; terror organizations have altered their tactics, techniques, and procedures (TTPs) to include the use of easily obtainable items like knives and vehicles to bring to fruition these attacks.

State actors have also exerted greater assertiveness. Russia, comes to the forefront when looking at this country's cyber influences into the elections in the United States, United Kingdom, France, The Netherlands, and elsewhere.

Many countries in the world are now more right leaning to include such nations as the United States, Norway, Great Britain and others. In many cases, this has led to a constriction in economic liberalization whereby countries are now more enthralled with pulling out of trade arrangements that have traditionally been more globalized.

The U.S. National Security Strategy (NSS), is still relatively new. The authors in this publication looked to the latest version to see Trump's priorities (NSS 2017). It provides a brief overview of what is relevant to the United States in an effort for the country to hold onto its position as the world leader in terms of its economic and military might. The NSS served as the point of departure from which the U.S. Departments of State and Defense created their own strategies in 2018. Moreover, this book looks at the latest documents in order to guide the researchers into understanding priorities from which they assessed external threats to the United States. The NSS, is a top down document; it serves as a compass for the executive branch, to provide an azimuth for other federal departments and agencies to use in their role supporting the United States' security interests. It is both relevant and timely, has budgetary implications, and also helps narrow the focus to contribute to national security especially to those in the Intelligence Community (IC) of the United States, and the leaders of the Departments of Homeland Security, Defense, State, and more.

There are implications beyond the United States. The NSS and other complementary U.S. strategies and plans make a cogent argument for why issues are concerns for this nation and even though they are relatively brief, do signal the priorities of this nation to its allies and potential belligerents where American focus will be directed as it moves forward in the years to come.

Accordingly, this document is used by the Defense Department, the Departments of Homeland Security, as well as the State Department as the center of gravity from which they look to work backwards to plan, request resourcing, to allocate manpower and effort, and assign missions towards those ends. At the time of this publication, both the DOD and DOS have updated their plans. The Defense Department's National Defense Strategy (NDS) and the State Department's Joint Strategic Plan (JSP) provide amplification into how the likes of hard power and soft power will work in concert (and in a complementary fashion) to the NSS to help the president obtain his goals (NDS 2018 and NSP 2018). The 17 members of the United States' IC vis-à-vis the National Intelligence Priority Framework (NIPF) and the unclassified version of the Worldwide Threat Assessment (WTA) constantly look at requirements and the subsequent tasking of collection platforms and efforts and provide updates on global threats respectively.

This book looks at 10 prevailing threats either explicitly stated or implicitly derived through a read of the NSS. These include seven sovereign state countries, a regional issue, and two that pertain to non-state actors (cyber space and terrorism).

The homeland will always be at the forefront of U.S. efforts. Domestically, these authors see the security of the homeland as the epicenter of this nation's concerns. Hinkel, Nelson, and Strausser look at the primary threats confronting the United States.

Chapter 2 - Maintaining a global hegemony is not an easy task for the United States. The nation is constantly besieged by threats to its homeland security from hostile nation states, lone wolf style attacks, and gang violence. The authors analyzed these three distinct threat issue areas using secondary government sources such as the National Security Strategy and the Joint Strategic Plan in conjunction with the Federal Qualitative Secondary Data Case Study Triangulation Model. A conclusion about threats to the homeland was drawn through the implementation of the York Intelligence Red Team Model (YIRTM) which is based upon the four instruments of national power.

Chapter 3 - China, the second leading economic power in the world, has had a steady incline in international power through its economic prowess and governmental strength. The current trade wars with the United States (U.S.) prove China's economic stability and independence from U.S. influence while simultaneously using their massive funds to sway other sovereign nations. As the world's most populous nation in the world, China's ascendance from an agrarian society to the second largest economy on the planet has attracted much speculation and debate, especially surrounding its potential to contest or even surpass the United States as the sole superpower. Though China has claimed that it does not seek to alter or disrupt the international system, its actions, both overt and covert, contradict this claim on several different levels. Using a qualitative assessment approach, this chapter examines how and why China is pursuing actions to undermine U.S. influence in both East Asia specifically and the world more broadly in the divided four instrumental dimensions, threatening the U.S. world hegemony.

Chapter 4 - As President Trump entered the White House in January of 2017, he inherited a presidency that faced numerous world issues in the form of foreign and domestic threats. His National Security Strategy (NSS) drafted during his first year as president listed Russia, or the Russian Federation, as a political actor that must be continuously monitored while reducing their threat level to the national security of the United States. Taking an approach of a qualitative methodology, this study investigated those processes Russia has engaged in elevating its position as a world superpower using the four instruments of national power to weaken America's hegemony. Framed by using the logic model, this chapter concludes what, how, and why Russia's actions would weaken the United States' influence by examining the 2014-2018 period.

Chapter 5 - Complex bilateral relations exist between the U.S. and Iran. With the Trump Administration, the relations between the two are even more tumultuous. This chapter explores and analyzes how Iran through the use of the instruments of national power in the context of the York Intelligence Red Team Model (YIRTM) could potentially degrade the security of the United States as a world hegemony. It concludes that the U.S. continues to monitor

Iran as it stands as a significant Middle Eastern power house and is a destabilizing force within the region. Through comprehensive examinations of Iran's activities after the U.S. withdrawal from the Joint Comprehensive Plan of Action (JCPOA), patterns and processes of state sponsored terrorism were identified, historic and current diplomatic turmoil with the United States was acknowledged, and Iran's strengthening cyber capabilities were revealed. The chapter also explores Iran's illicit financial activity to bolster terrorism, human rights abuses, environmental exploitation and even cyber and naval threats. It suggests that Iran will continue to be a destabilizing force throughout the Middle East as well as a national security threat to the United States because of its ever-growing terrorist capability from state sponsorship, a strengthening offensive and defensive cyber military, proliferated aggression through both governmental and religious ideologies, and potential nuclear capabilities and its ambitions in the future.

Chapter 6 - The debate on North Korea is one of most divisive foreign policy issues for the United States. In the latest National Security Strategy (NSS), Trump and his administration identify that one major threat comes from the Democratic People's Republic of Korea (DPRK) and their possession of nuclear weapon and cyber capabilities which is the focus of this study. Employing a qualitative research approach, this chapter takes in-depth investigation using the four instruments of national power and investigate how North Korea in particular has utilized these instruments and is threatening the United States. The chapter also assesses what the current North Korea's activities mean to future regional peace. It concludes that much of North Korea's strategy in the region has been decisively defensive due to its governmental mission and economic structure, putting the country in a situation without many options to gain greater influence in the region and nearly no contribution to the world economy. The nuclear proliferation in North Korea has opened a new door for the country to negotiate a more and better position of power. North Korea has been and further plans to utilize their nuclear capabilities in the context of D.I.M.E to weaken the United States as the world's hegemony. Additionally, the chapter finds that nuclear proliferation has also greatly boosted their military power in the region and is a direct threat to the United States and her influence in the region. North Korea also has been using information technology on platforms such as twitter to hopefully gain more support from the world stage.

Chapter 7 - "Terrorists and criminals thrive where governments are weak, corruption is rampant, and faith in government institutions is low" (NSS 2017, 49). The conflict in Syria arose after the Arab Spring. Bashar al-Assad, the leader of the Syrian regime, began using military force in order to hold onto control of the country. Consequently, more people rebelled, and Syria was thrust into a civil war. The Regime has been accused of using chemical weapons on his own people. This alerted the United Nations (UN) and global powers to these inhumane acts. Subsequently, the UN responded with various diplomatic acts including UN Resolution 2254. At the same time, terror organizations, specifically the Islamic State of Iraq and Syria (ISIS) and Hezbollah, began finding footholds in Syria. This led to the involvement of the United States (U.S.) in this country, fighting against the extremist groups and the Assad regime. While these groups are the face of the Syrian conflict, international actors such as Iran and Russia enable them to survive against the forces of peace. This study uses qualitative research to interpret trends and findings of official press releases, government documents, and plans in place for Syria to make sense of the situation. The fight in Syria is not only enabled through military tools and tactics, but also through diplomacy and other instruments on the global battlefield.

Chapter 8 - Turkey's unique geographic location allows it to exert a greater presence in the European and Middle Eastern regions despite the recent military coup that resulted in instability and shook up its national political regime. Although being a North Atlantic Treaty Organization (NATO) ally, Turkey has not been a reliable one to the United States in the past decade. Set forth in the Integrated Country Strategy by the United States Department of State, the Turkish government is supposed to be improving on their views of human rights and treating individuals with fairness; this investigation found it to be otherwise. The evidence from triangulation of data sources suggests that Turkey has been acting in defiance of these humanitarian ideas. Using the D.I.M.E. model, the analysis revealed how Turkey has been using a modified model to be able to adversely impact the national security of the United States through the instruments of diplomacy, information, military, and economics. Despite its distance from the continental United States, Turkey poises itself in a unique way to the homeland in that its movements with its own ideas and actions directly affect the national security and hegemony of U.S. interests in the Middle East and Europe. With President Erdoğan at the helm, one can follow recent trends in a decline in pro-U.S. and western relations and an incline with its neighbors, Iran and Russia.

Chapter 9 - The China challenge is considered by the current Trump administration as a top national security issue. In order to contain China, the U.S. has been searching for strategies to counterbalance China's power, so it can continue to be the global hegemony. One of strategies is to have a partner located within the broad geographic region. The U.S. has long hoped for India to be its ally in the region especially as India is the world's largest democracy located nearby China. Would India be an ally of the U.S. in the coming years hedging against Chinese influence? Using a qualitative research approach and collected data from unclassified sources, this chapter focused on the two current "hot spot" issues standing between the U.S. and China: the "Belt and Road Initiative" (BRI) and the South China Sea as case studies and investigated complex spatial-temporal relationship among the trio entities – the U.S., China, and India. It was concluded that an ally like India will most likely not succeed because of its long historical pattern on its foreign relations. Despite of India's recent leaning toward to the U.S., India's "non-alignment" tenet of foreign policy has played an important role that will dictate the nation state of India stands at a neutral standpoint in the newly dubbed Indo-Pacific region. In addition, this chapter also outlines the strategies that China has been exercising to undercut India's role as a regional competitor.

Chapter 10 - The United States still regards the Islamic State of Iraq and the Levant (ISIL) as a prominent threat to its national security and has come up with priority actions for its defeat of Jihadist terrorists. With the help of its strong intelligence department and its contemporary recruitment tactics, ISIL is able to spread its influence with little effort. Although they do not have any formal diplomatic connections with outside countries, they are able to still perform at their highest level without having to rely on other people. ISIL also directs their attention to creating a brotherhood which in turn attracts the people who are classified as lone wolves to gain control of the territories that they lost. The United States has become accustomed to other terrorist groups who were not as economically advanced making ISIL a harder target. The United States' goal by 2022 is to contribute to the defeat of ISIL and its branches through the mobilization of a Global Coalition. Although the United States has made efforts in trying to prevent ISIL's influence, the terrorist group continues to adapt to challenges or policies that prevent them from growing. ISIL has proven to be a deadly force that will go to extremes for its cause. ISIL's overall purpose is to gain enough power to be recognized as a formidable group that has taken over a nation and will stop at no end to spread their extremist views across the world.

Chapter 11 - The United States is seen to be not only defending itself constantly from cyber-attacks but also falling behind in the cyber security world. Several definitions from accredited organizations define cyber-attack as a form of a computer virus that can perplex financial records, shut off power grids, or even damage nuclear reactors. The research conducted made use of the Federal Qualitative Secondary Data Case Study Triangulation Model to ensure the use of viable sources in order to help comprehend and demonstrate how cyber-attacks threaten the cyber world of the United States. Within the United States, both public and private networks are deemed as vulnerable targets to these types of attacks from both state and non-state actors (Trump 2017). The two state actors heavily focused on, North Korea and Russia, have earned their titles for their past and frequent cyber-attacking events that occurred during the study's time period examined in this chapter. In conclusion it is found that both state actors, North Korea and Russia, exploit cyber-attacks on the United States to obtain mainly information but also economical gains. The likelihood of a decrease in cyber-attacks on the United States is highly improbably. With the election of the current President of the United States, Donald J. Trump has taken many new actions to emphasize cyber security (Trump 2017). The overall concept of cyber security in this chapter will be focusing on the diplomatic, informational, military, and economic impacts that affect the national security of the U.S. and how Russia and North Korea play major roles in the world of cyber.

Chapter 12 - The National Security Strategy (NSS) is a mandatory document required by Congress to provide strategies to the U.S. national security. The "America First" policy stated in the 2017 Trump Administration's NSS shifts to a domestic economic growth and a strong border setting a different strategic direction than the previous administrations have. The release of it in Trump's first year of his presidency gets much attention and has been debated. For example, Cordesman (2017) thinks that the document is too vague because there is no actual strategy provided, though it does carry on those traditional themes of a U.S. strategy. Feaver (2018) argues that, although the 2017 NSS is not as good as it could be, it does contain a workable foundation by providing "an effective framework for American engagement around the world" and "by choosing to abide by his own commitments, Trump could restore America's global influence."

While it may be too soon to assess the impact of this critical document, this book focuses on the cross-sections of nine "hot spots" identified in this document and conducted systematic assessments on national power. Mostly, these systematic assessments are conducted in the dyad form - the U.S. against either a state-actor such as North Korea, Russia, Iran, and Turkey, or a non-state actor including the Islamic State (ISIL) and cyber space, except in Chapter 11 where the author investigated the trilateral relationships among U.S.-China-India. Collectively, all authors use diplomacy, information, military, and economic instruments, also known as the D.I.M.E. in conjunctions with the York Intelligence Red Team Model, known as YIRTM, as the conceptual framework and investigated how those state actors and non-state actors have been using the four instruments creating and projecting their power. All authors together also addressed another central overarching question which is why those adversaries of the U.S. have undermined the U.S. hegemony in global affairs in the context of the YIRTM and will continue to do so.

Starting from the homeland, each chapter generated a variant model of the D.I.M.E. logic model. These models were derived from extensive data extraction and cross-coding of frequency. Table 1 shows these models. If an actor has the same frequencies for two instruments, then this actor is characterized with additional models – see the columns of "Model 2," "Model 3," and "Model 4." For example, in the case of China, the coding frequencies for diplomatic and information are the same, therefore, China has been emphasized using these two models for its national power building.

In: Global Intelligence Priorities ISBN: 978-1-53615-836-6
Editors: John Michael Weaver et al. © 2019 Nova Science Publishers, Inc.

Chapter 1

INTRODUCTION TO THE NATIONAL SECURITY ISSUES CONFRONTING THE UNITED STATES

John M. Weaver[*]
York College, York, Pennsylvania, US

INTRODUCTION

Since Donald Trump has been elected president, there have been a lot of changes in the political landscape and world security. Transnational terrorism has continued to burgeon. Europe continues to be vulnerable and has seen several attacks in recent years like in France, the United Kingdom, and elsewhere; terror organizations have altered their tactics, techniques, and procedures (TTPs) to include the use of easily obtainable items like knives and vehicles to bring to fruition these attacks.

State actors have also exerted greater assertiveness. Russia, comes to the forefront when looking at this country's cyber influences into the elections

---

[*] DPA.

in the United States, United Kingdom, France, The Netherlands, and elsewhere.

Many countries in the world are now more right leaning to include such nations as the United States, Norway, Great Britain and others. In many cases, this has led to a constriction in economic liberalization whereby countries are now more enthralled with pulling out of trade arrangements that have traditionally been more globalized.

The U.S. National Security Strategy (NSS), is still relatively new. The authors in this publication looked to the latest version to see Trump's priorities (NSS 2017). It provides a brief overview of what is relevant to the United States in an effort for the country to hold onto its position as the world leader in terms of its economic and military might. The NSS served as the point of departure from which the U.S. Departments of State and Defense created their own strategies in 2018. Moreover, this book looks at the latest documents in order to guide the researchers into understanding priorities from which they assessed external threats to the United States. The NSS, is a top down document; it serves as a compass for the executive branch, to provide an azimuth for other federal departments and agencies to use in their role supporting the United States' security interests. It is both relevant and timely, has budgetary implications, and also helps narrow the focus to contribute to national security especially to those in the Intelligence Community (IC) of the United States, and the leaders of the Departments of Homeland Security, Defense, State, and more.

There are implications beyond the United States. The NSS and other complementary U.S. strategies and plans make a cogent argument for why issues are concerns for this nation and even though they are relatively brief, do signal the priorities of this nation to its allies and potential belligerents where American focus will be directed as it moves forward in the years to come.

Accordingly, this document is used by the Defense Department, the Departments of Homeland Security, as well as the State Department as the center of gravity from which they look to work backwards to plan, request resourcing, to allocate manpower and effort, and assign missions towards those ends. At the time of this publication, both the DOD and DOS have updated their plans. The Defense Department's National Defense Strategy (NDS) and the State Department's Joint Strategic Plan (JSP) provide amplification into how the likes of hard power and soft power will work in concert (and in a complementary fashion) to the NSS to help the president obtain his goals (NDS 2018 and NSP 2018). The 17 members of the United States' IC vis-à-vis the National Intelligence Priority Framework (NIPF) and the unclassified version of the Worldwide Threat Assessment (WTA) constantly look at requirements and the subsequent tasking of collection platforms and efforts and provide updates on global threats respectively.

This book looks at 10 prevailing threats either explicitly stated or implicitly derived through a read of the NSS. These include seven sovereign state countries, a regional issue, and two that pertain to non-state actors (cyber space and terrorism).

The homeland will always be at the forefront of U.S. efforts. Domestically, these authors see the security of the homeland as the epicenter of this nation's concerns. Hinkel, Nelson, and Strausser look at the primary threats confronting the United States.

When moving across the Atlantic, Europe has shifted to a position of increasing importance for the United States. Consider Russia and its activities in recent years. Forest, Ohashi, Tombolini, and Shoemaker conducted an analysis of Russia. As one of five permanent members of the United Nations Security Council (UNSC), compounded with its nuclear arsenal and formidable military, and its capability to execute cyber activities, Russia continues to demonstrate to the world the influence it still wields. Specifically, these authors looked into Russia's assertiveness of power on the world stage and in its ability to conduct military operations elsewhere as a way to look for its continued rise in power.

Dejesus, Gardner, Vargo, and Wightman looked at another major player in the world and one that could become a concern for the United States. These authors conducted research on China and what it hopes to gain as the United States is relegated to a lesser position with regards to trade initiatives in the Indo Pacific region. They provide amplification into China's buildup of the Spratly Islands, influence in the South China Sea, and the country's continuously growing cyber capabilities.

China's northeast neighbor, the Democratic People's Republic of Korea (DPRK), commonly known as North Korea, has risen as an emerging world player with significant regional influence. Kim Jong-un's North Korea had appeared resolute on his nuclear weapons program, but has since softened his stance. Nevertheless, his authoritarian regime still presents a challenge to Northeast Asia especially since it still possesses the fourth largest military in the world. More pointedly, Hurd, Nemeth, and Soreco look at threats to see what Kim hopes to achieve in this region.

When moving to the Middle East, one just needs to turn to Iran to see that it has significant influence in the region. It would like to emerge as the Shiite counterbalance to the Sunni dominated Saudi Arabia for influence in this region and as one has seen since the disintegration of European sanctions, is increasingly becoming more capable at presenting itself as a potent actor. Richardson and Savage provide elaboration into what is occurring and the likely direction that Iran will pursue for the future.

Syria continues to be a hotbed in the Middle East and is one where many state and non-state actors are vying for power and this has been a primary concern of efforts by the United States in recent years. Also at play are opposition forces exerting influence contrary to what the U.S. would like to see and include such antagonist to the U.S. (namely Iran and Russia). Cullember, McDonough, and Simmons looked at the multi threats at play in this specific country.

One contemporary threat that has emerged as the major actor regarding transnational threats is terrorism and more specifically the Islamic State. Though much has transpired in recent years with military operations launched against terror organizations, threats emanating from terrorism still is a significant threat that targets U.S. interests at home and abroad. Hart and Schultz provide insight into their perspective on this threat and enumerate on what has occurred in recent years.

Turkey has surfaced as an interesting player in recent years. This country has been a member of the North Atlantic Treaty Organization (NATO) for decades. However, in recent years it has made overtures to Russia contrary to NATO's desires and has served as an impediment to the interests of the United States in the Middle East over the last few years, most notably with regards to Syria and Iran. Geer, Ferris, Moul, and Sowers provide analysis on this country.

Jason Guo analyzed how and why China uses its political influence, economic strength, and its military in the context of the York Intelligence Red Team Model to diminish U.S. influence in the Indo-Pacific region. He investigates how India as an important player has been recruited as a counter-balance by the U.S. in the changing global geopolitical landscape.

Finally, cyber incursions present the United States with a significant asymmetric threat that could affect this county's position as a hegemony. At present, no nation possesses the capability to adequately confront the U.S. military directly and win. Yet, other nations have invested in cyber TTPs as a way to exploit weaknesses in this country's networks and infrastructure. McDowell, Meyers, and Walker provide analysis on what cyber threats exist at the present time.

Consistency in research is important. To maintain this and to help better realize standardization to make sense of what is occurring, most of the authors used a logic model incorporated extensively in other research that is predicated on the four instruments of national power (JP 1-02 2010, 112). These instruments include diplomacy, information, military, and economic (hereafter referred by the acronym D.I.M.E.) means; these instruments have been used by leaders of the United States to better exert influence throughout the globe. When returning to the National Security Act of 1947 all but information have been used as a way to apply influence by the United States (Brantly 2016). Other publications have used D.I.M.E. as a way to analyze worldwide threats (Weaver 2015 and Weaver2 2015). Clearly, these instruments of national power have been important to all presidential administrations. Moreover, is that these instruments of national power have been used by instructors and faculty at the mid-grade and senior level staff and war colleges in the United States to foster a strong appreciation for making use of all available resources when working to shape outcomes throughout the world.

More pointedly, the chapters that follow look at the redirection of these instruments. The authors in this book explore just how state and non-state actors use or will use diplomacy, information, military, and economic means to better extend pressure back towards the United States to weaken its strategic power and influence throughout the planet. Moreover, this study looked at these instruments in order to see just how potential foes could make use of them against the United States as a way to weaken its security.

The authors also used the York Intelligence Red Team Model (YIRTM) shown in Figure 1; it visualizes intervening relationships. Directionality along with temporal precedence can lend greater credence to the relevance of a logic model (Warner 2012, 17). This particular ordering of elements is useful; however, by no means could these specific variables be the only factors one considers for helping establish an understanding of influences leading to shaped outcomes.

This model begins with the strategic direction of the actor driven to the weakening of the national security position of this country.

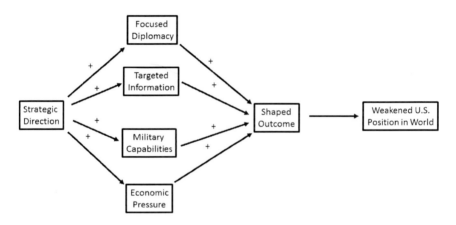

Figure 1. The York Intelligence Red Team Model (YIRTM).

It begins with guidance and direction by a leader (either from within a state or a non-state actor) who provides basics on the "who," "what," "when," "how," "why," and "where." It is through this direct corollary of the guidance and direction provided by the leadership (looking at "who") to see "what" they are doing, and "when" to better understand "how" they are doing it, "why" and "where" in order that one can then look at the four instruments of power as a way to implement their TTPs in direct support of one's cause to ultimately lead to the weakening of the United States.

Diplomacy is the first one. This instrument in particular involves leaders that engage others to bring to fruition conditions favorable to what one wants to achieve. It considers not only the application to one specific country but should also look regionally or globally at outcomes that decisions will have in surrounding countries and well beyond to undermine interests of the United States.

Information is an enabler of power and the application of its use could more aptly effect influence activities throughout the world. Message targeting is often very useful as a way to sway popular opinion to help promote a cause all while delegitimizing the messaging of another country or non-state actor at the same time. Likewise, adversaries can make use of information particularly through social media conduits as a way to inexpensively sell others to their cause to acquire greater support as the non-state actor or country expands its position and influence. This instrument includes the use of cyber as a weapon to exploit weaknesses of a country and more specifically, how it can be used to expose vulnerabilities in the United States. It is often seen as the least expensive of the instruments of power; it is available to all countries and non-state actors and is a formidable TTP.

Conventionally, the instrument that is probably most known throughout the world is the military. The chapter authors looked at military capabilities of state actors, militant TTPs and their competence (non-state actors) and vulnerabilities to U.S. Department of Defense related activities.

Money is a necessity for action and it underpins most activities and has always been associated with power. Economically, nations can exert influence by using their economic position to coerce others to change behavior. What's more is that state and non-state actors can look for opportunities to weaken a nation's economy by identifying vulnerabilities and in the case of this study, looking at how to weaken the United States' economy.

METHODOLOGY

Specifically, this book used data that came solely from secondary unclassified open sources. More pointedly, these authors made use of qualitative techniques to triangulate in on results (Remler & Van Ryzin 2010). Specific to this research, the authors looked at the most prevalent threats confronting the United States in the context of the NSS, NDS, and JSP. Creswell (2008) also provides his perspective into understanding of qualitative techniques. Specifically, this author writes on the strength in using this methodology to more aptly explore the interconnectedness among variables in the pursuit of answering research questions (Creswell 2008).

Accordingly, modern research has also shown why secondary data is relevant and the need to ensure the high quality of the data one uses (Remler & Van Ryzin 2010, 180). Triangulation of data increases comprehension into what is occurring. Additionally, using this data is relatively low in cost when compared to pursuing primary data acquisition and often is quite accessible; practitioners and those who engage in research alike in the social science and policy fields have turned to these sources in order to leverage the data for the purpose of conducting research (Remler & Van Ryzin 2010, 180).

The authors also selected a model previously covered in other research to help balance sources and their approach to problem dissection. The model used throughout this work is the Federal Qualitative Secondary Data Case Study Triangulation Model found in Figure 2 (Weaver 3 2015).

The model used is a Venn diagram and is made up of three concentric components. The first includes plans and systems and the subsequent assessments. The model also affords consideration to a variation of credible written works; these include the following: government documents, legislation, scholarly reports and more. Often these are seen as the most credible in the eyes of a majority of researchers. The final component has more of an oral feel; it turns to transcripts of testimony, press statements coming from official government agencies, speeches, interviews, and information covered by key leaders.

All scholarly research is concerned with validity. Accordingly, this book addressed the topic of validity; it considered two aspects. First, variable checks were performed. These included efforts to ensure that variables measured what they were supposed to measure.

Secondly, face validity was utilized to ensure that models and variables inherently made sense (Creswell 2008). Likewise, face validity techniques evaluated the logic model, variable directionality and purpose to help ensure that what the authors covered was not counterintuitive to what one would reasonably consider when looking at shaped outcomes.

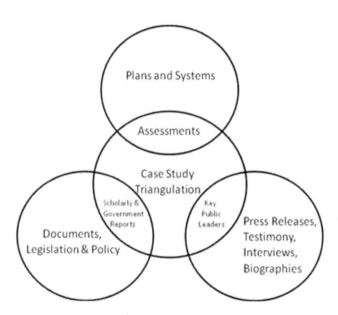

Figure 2. Federal Qualitative Secondary Data Case Study Triangulation Model.

The authors throughout this book used the logic model to better frame contemporary issues while also looking at just how state and non-state actors might consider the D.I.M.E. against the United States to weaken its strategic position in the world; the book also looked at why they would want to do this. Moreover, the Federal Qualitative Secondary Data Case Study Triangulation Model, which has been vetted and used in other studies, provided these authors the opportunity to ensure a balanced approach when considering data sources.

Consideration was afforded to reliability. Consistency in research approaches looked to similar projects to contribute to reliability (Creswell 2008, 190). Likewise, Remler and Van Ryzin (2010, 118) have also underscored the necessity of achieving consistency in measures when looking to bring about reliability when conducting research. Facilitating this was fostered by the consistency of the D.I.M.E. as instruments of power and the use of the YIRTM and the Federal Qualitative Secondary Data Case Study Triangulation Model to analyze the data sources. To better corroborate information, the authors considered multiple sources.

REFERENCES

Brantley, Aaron, F. 2016. Cyber Actions by State Actors: Motivation and Utility. *International Journal of Intelligence and Counterintelligence*, 27 (3): 465-484.

Creswell, J. W. 2008. *Research Design; Qualitative, Quantitative, and Mixed Methods Approaches*, Thousand Oaks, CA: SAGE Publications.

J. P. 1-02. 2010. Department of Defense Dictionary of Military and Associated Terms. *Joint Publication, 1-02*. November 8, 2010.

J. S. P. 2018. *Joint Strategic Plan FY 2018-2022 U.S. Department of State and U.S. Agency for International Development*. https://www.state.gov/documents/organization/277156.pdf. Accessed on April 17, 2018.

N. D. S. 2018. *National Defense Strategy*. https://www.defense.gov/Portals/1/Documents/pubs/2018-National-Defense-StrategySummary.pdf. Accessed on January 20, 2018.

N. S. S. 2017. *National Security Strategy*. http://nssarchive.us/wpcontent/uploads/2017/12/ 2017.pdf. Accessed on January 1, 2018.

Remler, D. K. and Van Ryzin, G. G. 2010. *Research Methods in Practice: Strategies for Description and Causation*, Thousand Oaks, CA: SAGE Publications.

Weaver, John M. 2015. The Perils of a Piecemeal Approach to Fighting ISIS in Iraq. *Public Administration Review*, 75(2) 192-193.

Weaver 2, John M. 2015. The Enemy of My Enemy is My Friend... Or Still My Enemy: The Challenge for Senior Civilian and Military Leaders. *International Journal of Leadership in Public Service*, 11(3-4).

Weaver 3, John M. 2015. The Department of Defense and Homeland Security relationship: Hurricane Katrina through Hurricane Irene. *Journal of Emergency Management*, 12(3) 265-274.

In: Global Intelligence Priorities ISBN: 978-1-53615-836-6
Editors: John Michael Weaver et al. © 2019 Nova Science Publishers, Inc.

Chapter 2

MAKING AMERICA SECURE AGAIN: A QUALITATIVE ASSESSMENT OF THE UNITED STATES' HOMELAND SECURITY FRONT

Ben Hinkel, Stephen Strausser and Matt Nelson
York College, York, Pennsylvania, US

ABSTRACT

Maintaining a global hegemony is not an easy task for the United States. The nation is constantly besieged by threats to its homeland security from hostile nation states, lone wolf style attacks, and gang violence. The authors analyzed these three distinct threat issue areas using secondary government sources such as the National Security Strategy and the Joint Strategic Plan in conjunction with the Federal Qualitative Secondary Data Case Study Triangulation Model. A conclusion about threats to the homeland was drawn through the implementation of the York Intelligence Red Team Model (YIRTM) which is based upon the four instruments of national power.

LITERATURE REVIEW

As the United States faces challenges abroad, it is also inundated with threats on its own soil. Restated in the 2014 Quadrennial Homeland Security Review, the Department of Homeland Security (DHS) adheres to a five-mission structure with the following goals: prevent terrorism and enhance security, secure and manage U.S. borders, enforce and administer American immigration laws, safeguard and secure cyberspace, and strengthen national preparedness and resilience (Fiscal Years 2014-2018 Strategic Plan 2014, 6). Since his inauguration in 2017, President Donald Trump has reaffirmed these goals. The 2017 National Security Strategy devotes one of its three policy pillars to "Protecting the American People, the Homeland, and the American Way of Life" (National Security Strategy 2017, 7). As per the National Security Strategy, America must be "safe, prosperous, and free" if it is to be "an America with the strength, confidence, and will lead abroad" (National Security Strategy 2017, 1).

The most trying moment of the United States' homeland security came on September 11th, 2001. Commonly referred to as the 9/11 terror attacks, this marked the most devastating act of hostility on U.S. soil since the Pearl Harbor attacks on December 7th, 1941. Perpetuated by radical extremists, this attack fueled the growth of the United States' intelligence apparatus and homeland security measures. Since then, the United States has continued its fight against terrorism and radical extremism both at home and abroad.

However, the world has grown increasingly complicated in the time since those attacks. Former Homeland Security Secretary Kirstjen Nielsen outlined several of the changes the Intelligence Community (IC) is making to keep up with the rapid pace of worldwide development during a speech at George Washington University. She notes how lifestyles in the U.S. have grown increasingly digitally dependent, as well as how the nation's enemies continue to evolve their strategies, no longer confined by traditional tactics. Enemies of the United States "don't respect borders, and they aren't constrained by geography" (Nielsen 2018). Social media is now being used as a tool by U.S. adversaries to hurt this nation. Terrorists are using Twitter to recruit foot soldiers. They spread their messages of hate throughout internet chat rooms. Violent acts can be perpetuated anywhere and seen by someone on the other side of the world online, allowing extremist ideology to be disseminated at a much faster rate than ever before.

Cyber-attacks and tactics such as the aforementioned give America's enemies the opportunity to level the playing field. It is no longer enough for the United States to be dominant in the traditional warfare spaces of land, sea, and air. One individual with a computer on the other side of the globe can cripple this country's infrastructure, devastate the economy, or disable communication with their key allies, all without leaving the individual's home. To ward off risks, the National Security Strategy outlines priority actions to keep the homeland safe from those who wish to do harm to America electronically. Washington's priority actions are to identify and prioritize risk, build defensible government networks, deter and disrupt malicious cyber actors, improve information sharing and sensing, and deploy layered defenses (National Security Strategy 2017, 13). America is learning that the country is not adequately prepared for cyber warfare; in fact, the nation is behind the power curve. A massive campaign is soon to begin within the Intelligence Community to prepare in three ways. Firstly, the IC must "improve attribution, accountability, and response." Secondly, the IC will "enhance cyber tools and expertise." Finally, top members of the IC plan to "improve integration and agility" (National Security Strategy 2017, 32). All these actions are meant to streamline U.S. cyber defense networks and processes. The future analysts and other employees of the IC must be well trained in cyber security to ward off hostiles, overcome challenges to intelligence sharing, and implement cyber monitoring and protection tools. However, as America takes these steps to fight an asymmetric war against terrorism, it must continue to be mindful of the physical threats posed by hostile nation states.

Countries such as Iran, North Korea, and Russia, have grown considerably in power in the period following 9/11. The sole-minded focus on non-traditional hostile forces led the United States to ignore the measures nation states have taken to undermine its world power. The IC considers threats to the U.S. from foreign adversaries to be "at the highest levels since the Cold War" (Nielsen 2018). One commonality all these states share is a mix in nuclear capabilities. For the most part, Russia has followed international law regarding its nuclear programs. Unfortunately, Iran and North Korea are less inclined to abide by such institutions as one has seen in the past. These rogue states could represent an existential threat to the security of the United States if North Korea can affix a nuclear warhead on a missile and if Iran is willing to start up its nuclear enrichment program again. Although Iran has no nuclear capabilities, the rogue state could pose as an existential threat to the U.S. if it were ever to restart its nuclear enrichment program. Measures have been taken to reduce the likelihood of nuclear war against these states, but the problems arising from their nuclear aspirations are far from solved.

A substantial step in curbing nuclear proliferation within Iran came from the Joint Comprehensive Plan of Action (JCPOA). As stated in the Joint Strategic Plan, Iran's weapons development "fuels local civil wars, destabilizes the region, and poses imminent threats to international shipping and our closest allies in the Middle East" (Joint Strategic Plan 2018, 24). However, the United States extricated itself from this agreement in 2018 out of concern by President Donald Trump that the deal was unfair to the United States. It has yet to be seen what the implications of leaving will be for the United States and Iran. The President has made it explicit that he will never allow Iran to have access to nuclear weapons, but it is still undetermined how he will ensure this after major U.S. diplomatic relations with the country ended.

Another dangerous nuclear threat to America's homeland, and frequent recipient of the President's ire, is North Korea. This rogue state has "developed an intercontinental ballistic missile (ICBM) with the stated objective of striking the United States. Its unlawful nuclear and ballistic missile programs pose an urgent threat to international security" (Joint Strategic Plan 2018, 24). While there have been efforts among the nations of the United States, China, and South Korea to curb North Korea's aggressive military and nuclear provocations, the threat is still ongoing. Stated within the National Security Strategy, one of the United States' priority actions include enhanced missile defense. To defend against potential threats, "the United States is deploying a layered missile defense system focused on North Korea and Iran" (National Security Strategy 2017, 8). Building upon that priority action, the United States is also enhancing counter proliferation measures with the intention of holding "state and non-state actors accountable for the use of WMD" (National Security Strategy 2017, 8). However, North Korea is not only a threat to the homeland, but to allies of the U.S. worldwide as well. President Donald Trump has singled out North Korea's illegal actions at the United Nations, but it is still unclear what the future holds for North Korea and the chances of them hurting the United States' homeland.

While Iran and North Korea threaten the United States with the possibility of nuclear war, Russia is taking a stealthier approach to undermining American democracy and creating worldwide havoc. Russia has proven to be a dangerous regime with complete disregard for international law multiple times. Recently, Moscow has authorized attacks on private citizens, both in Ukraine and the United Kingdom.

However even more disconcerting than that was their meddling in the 2016 American elections. Vladimir Putin and his team in the Kremlin purposefully weakened this nation's democratic principles through the spread of false information, the infiltration of servers of political institutions, and by intensifying the political polarization between the two prevailing American political parties (President Donald J. Trump Is Standing Up To Russia's Malign Activities 2018). In light of this, election security has risen to the top of the list of priorities within the Department of Homeland Security. The United States' democratic process must march forward, based on a series of free and fair elections. Continuous election interference threatens the very principles which this country was built upon, so it is of vital importance to the security of U.S. homeland that its elections remain free from outside meddling. While Russia was ultimately unsuccessful in altering any actual votes in the presidential election, they did show the world the weakest aspect of America's defenses, cyber-security. As was brought out in the 2016 election, the enemies of the U.S. no longer need to attack the nation physically; its increasing reliance on technology has rendered the nation very susceptible to cyber-attacks. The modern battlefield is no longer just physical, but rather exists in a digital domain as well.

Although there are a great deal of foreign threats jeopardizing the national security of the United States, several of these have arisen from inside the homeland. One such threat includes lone wolf style attacks. Although these lone wolf attacks are rarer and less deadly than terrorist group attacks, that does not make them any less dangerous. Despite the fact that the number of group-based terrorist attacks have declined in the past five years, the amount of solo attacks have been on the rise (Becker 2014). One of the reasons that lone wolf attacks are so dangerous is because these acts of violence (and the offenders committing them) are incredibly difficult for law enforcement officials to track down and outright prevent. Law enforcement is only able to detect and prevent around 60% of lone wolf attacks (Becker 2014). By definition, a lone wolf does not have any need to communicate with a larger terrorist group. Therefore, these attackers can theoretically manifest themselves in any individual, which limits federal law enforcement involvement due to the civil liberties that all Americans enjoy. These solo attackers come from a variety of different backgrounds and ideologies, ranging from right-wing extremists to radical Islamists. They could be psychopaths with nothing to lose or they could be mentally stable (Becker 2014). There have been a variety of solo terrorist attacks in the past five years, which underscores the fact that these lone wolf style attacks are a serious threat to the Homeland's national security.

Some of these lone actors are morally or idealistically driven to conduct acts of terrorism. For example, Robert Lewis Dear shot and killed three people in an attack on the Colorado Springs Planned Parenthood Clinic on November 27, 2015 (Planned Parenthood 2015). After Dear was arrested, he told police that he had committed this act of violence because he was morally against Planned Parenthood performing abortions and that they allegedly sold parts of the fetus' remains (Colorado Judicial Branch 2016). Another example of an idealistically motivated lone wolf attack was committed by Dylan Roof in 2015, who shot and killed nine African-Americans at the Emanuel AME Church in Charleston, South Carolina (Obama 2015). Roof, a white man, had targeted his victims because they were a different race than him and were attending a historically black church.

Some lone wolf actors are galvanized by the actions of another group. For example, Omar Mateen was inspired by the Islamic State of Iraq and the Levant (ISIL) to launch his mass shooting attack on the Pulse Nightclub, a gay bar in Orlando in June 2016. His attack left forty-nine people dead and fifty-three wounded (FBI 2018). ISIL, an Islamic extremist group, follows the anti-gay teachings of the Quran very strictly. The United States is also one of the sworn enemies of ISIL. Therefore, Mateen believed that he was advancing ISIL's radical cause by attacking a gay American nightclub, although he had never received any instructions from the terrorist organization. At the time, the Pulse Nightclub shooting was the deadliest in American history (Nielsen 2018).

Less than two years after the Pulse Nightclub shooting, another mass shooting claimed fifty lives and wounded four hundred twenty-two others (White House Press 2017). On October 1, 2017, Stephen Paddock opened fire on the Route 91 Harvest Festival concert from his Mandalay Bay hotel room in Las Vegas. Paddock had access to high-capacity magazines, and bump stocks attached to his semi-automatic assault rifles, which allowed him to fire the rifles at a near automatic rate. With the assistance of the bump stocks, Paddock was able to rain over one thousand rounds in fifteen minutes down at the crowd below. Paddock committed suicide in the hotel room before he could be apprehended by the police. He left no motive to explain why he committed the carnage (Trump 2017).

Unfortunately, lone wolf attacks aren't the only form of threats from inside U.S. borders. When dangerous individuals organize together, the gangs they form can be more violent than any sole shooter. One of the most prominent gangs in America is the MS-13, or Mara Salvatrucha. MS-13 is comprised of primarily immigrants or descendants of immigrants from the Northern Triangle: El Salvador, Honduras, and Guatemala (ICE 2017). Through crimes such as murder, kidnapping, and drug trafficking, they terrorize neighborhoods in major U.S. cities. Homeland Security Investigations (HSI) in New York has learned MS-13's primary sources of income are extortion, prostitution, membership dues, and illicit trafficking. Different organizations have tried to disrupt MS-13's operations. Special-Agent-in-Charge of New York, Angel Melendez, lays out three critical points in disrupting MS-13. First, by targeting the pathways MS-13 uses through Central and South America, HSI is able to intercept its flow of recruits. Secondly, by working with local law enforcement agencies along the border, HSI has been able to curb MS-13's recruitment and smuggling of young children. Finally, since MS-13 is tied to illicit activities to fund their organization, HSI has revealed MS-13's sophisticated communication and financial network that supports its nefarious activities (ICE 2017). If the flow of money can be stopped or impeded, then gang influence can be reduced in U.S. cities and neighborhoods. Gangs such as MS-13, along with other groups that are involved with drug and human trafficking, sport a vast network of connections they use to conduct their illegal business.

Organizations like U.S. Immigration and Customs Enforcement's (ICE) and Homeland Security Investigations are on the front line in combating these dangerous organizations. As a testament to this, "in 2017 HSI… [made] 4,818 criminal arrests… there were 809 MS-13 arrests. ICE [also] identified and assisted 518 human trafficking victims and more than 904 child exploitation victims… [finally] agents seized almost a million pounds of narcotics" (ICE 2017). Organizations like ICE and HSI are protecting the United States from these criminals and doing their best to seize drugs trafficked by MS-13 and other street gangs. MS-13 and other similar gangs need to move money, weapons, and people across international borders to conduct their operations, but ICE and HSI are necessary structural mechanisms that have the law enforcement ability and possess the right tools for disrupting and intervening these illicit activities.

While gangs and lone wolf shooters receive high volumes of media coverage, a lesser known, but still vitally important, aspect of American homeland security is its critical infrastructure, specifically, the energy sector. America's power grids are among the most vital, and vulnerable, infrastructures in the energy sector. Critical infrastructure sectors are so important to the U.S. that failure in any of these systems would have a devastating effect on homeland security, the economy, and public health. The communications, health, information technology, defense industrial base, nuclear reactors, emergency services, transportation and energy sectors are all deemed to be such "critical infrastructures" (FEMA 2018a). Ever since the 1880s, when electric power started being generated by power stations, electrical technology has been evolving and modernizing. As the system modernized, the U.S. developed a power grid system that utilizes an Industrial Control System (ICS), which relies on communication from intelligence electronic devices (IEDs) to execute operations.

This increased connectivity has posed vulnerabilities for malicious actors to exploit. A basic understanding of how the grid works is necessary in order to understand the threat that is posed. Electric power is first generated through multiple means whether it is nuclear power, coal, or greener methods like wind and solar energy. That power is sent to a transformer which sends it to transmission lines. The transmission lines then send the power to different transformers which then distribute it to homes, businesses, vehicles, and other electronically powered devices.

Cyber-attacks against power grid systems focus their attacks less on financial devastation, but rather seek to cause loss, denial, or manipulation of control and safety of sensors and instruments (Department of Energy 2016). An attack such as this would result in equipment malfunction or failure, physical equipment damage, power disruptions, or blackouts. If the grid were to be shut down through cyber or physical attacks, especially on a national scale, the consequences would be disastrous. Hospitals would lose power, leaving millions to potentially die especially if they lack backup power generation. Food would rot across the nation, and transportation would grind to a halt causing the flow of money and resources wither. While the United States has significantly improved the security of its power grid since 2003, the blackout of that year is illustrative of the damage such an event could have on the American economy. Lasting up to two days in some areas of the Northeast, the event was estimated to have cost an average of $6 billion. This includes approximately $4.2 billion lost in missed income and up to $2 billion lost in affected utilities and spoiled commodities (Electricity Consumers Resource Council 2004).

Also, foreign state actors can cause networked power grid failure. In 2009, Russia and China both made attempts to penetrate the U.S. power grid through the use of sophisticated software programs. This is why the Department of Energy, among others, are constantly evolving their strategies and tactics on how to combat these cyber threats from actors such as Russia, China, Iran, North Korea, and other non-state terrorist organizations (Department of Energy 2016).

The Federal Emergency Management Agency (FEMA) is the U.S. government agency tasked with emergency preparedness and response. On March 1, 2003, FEMA became part of the DHS. FEMA's Office of National Preparedness is responsible for helping to ensure that U.S. responders are trained and equipped to deal with nationwide disasters (FEMA 2018a). One method through which FEMA prepares for disasters is outlined through their annual report on National Preparedness. As described in the infrastructure section of the 2018 report, FEMA details how the U.S. infrastructure systems have been in need of improvement every year since 2012. The core capability of FEMA focuses on stabilizing impacted critical infrastructure during and after a disaster. Damage to critical infrastructure can have catastrophic consequences for response and recovery activities and can lead to other hazards (FEMA 2018a).

RESEARCH QUESTIONS

Following the review of the literature, the authors have generated two research questions. The questions were formed by using the York Intelligence Red Team Model (YIRTM) and the instruments of national power or D.I.M.E (diplomacy, information, military, and economic) as a basis for evaluation. The questions are to be answered from the perspective of those who threaten the United States' homeland. By evaluating the data in relation to the following questions, the United States will have a firmer grasp on what methods need to be improved regarding U.S. national security and how it can better prepare defenses against those who wish to do it harm.

Q1: How are state and non-state actors weakening the United States' homeland security in the context of the YIRTM?
Q2: Why is the hegemonic power of the U.S. being weakened by the state and non-state actors in relation to the YIRTM?

The Logic Model

To assess threats of the national security, the authors evaluated the collected data through the York Intelligence Red Team Model (YIRTM). The YIRTM allowed the authors to best evaluate how adversaries seek to weaken the homeland through their use of the instruments of national power in the four interrelated dimensions of diplomacy, information, military, and economic (known as D.I.M.E.) (JP 1-02 2010, 112). This model is frequently used to conduct research on state or non-state actors in order to provide details on those actors that stand to pose a threat to the United States (Weaver 2015).

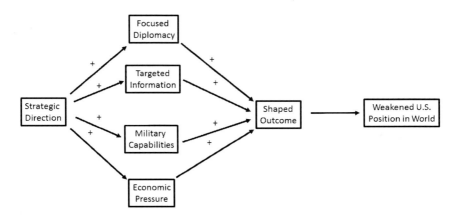

Figure 1. The York Intelligence Red Team Model (YIRTM).

As Figure 1 shows, the YIRTM illustrates a flow process of cause-effect by beginning with strategic direction. Any enemy of the United States is either a state and non-state actor and all take a strategic direction that attempts to weaken the global power of the United States. An enemy can use any combination of the elements of national power to achieve their intended outcome, through the intervening variables of the YIRTM. Once the strategic direction is determined by actors, then an analyst can understand that direction through each instrument of national power (JP 1-02 2010, 112).

Diplomacy is the first instrument of national power. This instrument involves leaders that engage with others to foster conditions favorable to their cause. It entails not just the application to a specific country, but also the regional or even global effects that decisions will have on surrounding countries and beyond to usurp the advancement of the interests of the United States. Often diplomacy can be seen as far less expensive in the long term especially when compared to military options. By developing diplomatic relationships to foster the continuance of a position, more violent (and more expensive) options can often be eliminated (Weaver 2015).

Information is another dimension of national power and it can influence states and organizations around the globe substantially. Targeted messaging can be quite useful to sway popular opinion to promote a cause while simultaneously delegitimizing the story of another country or non-state actor. Misinformation campaigns or propaganda are especially popular methods used to achieve a strategic outcome. An example of information campaigns is how cyber-attacks are used to gather intelligence on the U.S. and other political adversaries (Department of Energy 2016).

The military aspect of D.I.M.E. proves to be the most kinetically oriented instrument of national power. Use of such increases the likelihood for loss of life for both sides and can be a very direct approach to achieve a goal or mission. Throughout the homeland, lone wolves, terrorists, and transnational gangs are not afraid to use deadly force on innocent people to achieve their respective end goal. This chips away at the American illusion of safety and enables these actors to strike fear in the heart of the American citizens.

Finally, the last component of D.I.M.E stands for economics. This instrument of national power looks at how states and non-state actors can benefit themselves economically while adversely affecting the U.S. financially. As the world's leading economy, the United States can often feel threatened by rival emerging economic powers. China maintains the world's second largest economy by nominal Gross Domestic Product (GDP), and is now the largest competitor to the United States. Furthermore, their growing economy has the potential to surpass the United States. Additionally, gangs such as MS-13 benefit economically through their illicit dealings. They make money through drug smuggling, human trafficking, weapons dealing, or any other illicit activity, all which negatively affect the U.S. culturally, socially and economically. The continuous threats or attacks cause the affected country to increase its spending on defense and could have adverse effects economically.

All of the aforementioned elements of D.I.M.E. work in conjunction to create the shaped outcome of the adversary's choosing. These shaped outcomes can result in a weakened U.S. position in the world.

METHODOLOGY

The nature of the two research questions dictated the employment of qualitative approach in this project. To support the researchers' analysis, the sources used were from unclassified, secondary data. Available in the public domain, secondary data proved to be useful in this analysis, as it is a synthesized version of previously collected primary research and firsthand accounts of events. The credibility of sources, as well as their relevance to the analysis, was weighed against the Federal Qualitative Secondary Data Case Study Triangulation Model as seen in Figure 2. The need for a balance among three valuable subsets of secondary data: plans and systems; documents, legislation and policy; and press releases, testimony, interviews, and biographies are all shown in Figure 2. An example of plans and systems would be the United States' Department of State Joint Strategic Plan. Press releases or testimony would be a source such as the transcript of Homeland Security Secretary Kirstjen Nielsen's speech at George Washington University. Finally, an example of documents or legislation would be the National Defense Authorization Act. Through using a combination of all three sections of the Triangulation Model, the authors were able to create a thorough analysis of threats to U.S. homeland security. This model was used in tandem with the YIRTM to focus on methods taken by state and non-state actors to threaten the security of the United States.

Adding to the benefit of secondary data, other than creating a clearer understanding of first-person accounts and individual research, secondary data reduces the cost of gathering information. This factor proved to be a big draw to the authors as they dealt with large quantities of data and sources. The wide array of sources available for secondary, open source data ensured that the authors did not fall into the pitfall of "groupthink," meaning they only referred the sources that confirmed their beliefs (Lowenthal 2015). A variety of secondary sources allow research questions to be tested rigorously, weeding out those that were less sound than others. When the three outer circles of the Federal Secondary Data Case Study Triangulation Model are used in tandem, they support the analysis provided, lending greater credibility to the end result.

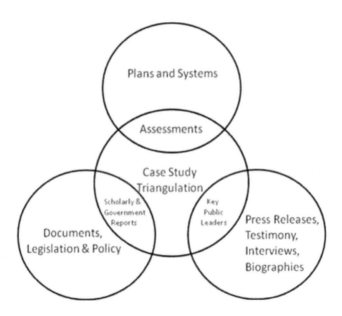

Figure 2. Federal Qualitative Secondary Data Case Study Triangulation Model.

LIMITATIONS

This study was conducted using only secondary data, which can limit the outcome of the research. The temporal scope of this project was limited to a five-year period from 2013 to 2018. While analyzing the data, more weight was assigned to the data collected in recent years as it is more relevant to the current and future state of homeland security. Due to the fact that the world is an ever-changing political, economic, and social landscape, the older information is less likely to be correlated to the future than what has happened more recently (Marchio 2017). Although the YIRTM model had pre-chosen diplomacy, information, military, and economic power as its defining variables, there are other variables that could have an impact on the nation's security.

Another limitation to this study is that primary sources were not considered for this research. Primary sources include personal observations, first-hand accounts from interviews, and surveys conducted by the researchers. Although the researchers in this study have decided to exclude primary sources, future studies might find it beneficial to use these kinds of data to either look for confirmation or build upon the assessments of this research. Primary sources can be very useful in reconstructing and verifying the information in the conclusion (Cheng 2017).

The researchers in this study have chosen to use a triangulation of data sources and a triangulation of interpretation to corroborate their assessment to minimize the limitations inherent in qualitative research. The results of this research can be useful as a guide and a source of information for other studies that might consider quantitative analysis or a mixed methods design. Additionally, more and more information will likely become available over time as the United States' government declassifies it. The results of this study on threats to the United States' homeland security can be used to verify previous research in an effort to help the reader understand domestic threats in the context of the YIRTM.

ANALYSIS

The following is the analysis conducted by the authors to understand the threats posed to the national security of the United States. The analysis was conducted using the York Intelligence Red Team Model, which has been previously discussed. The research also made use of the Federal Qualitative

Secondary Data Case Study Triangulation Model to help strike a balance in the data used and interpretation derived. Specific data sources used to draw the following conclusions can be found in Annex A at the end of this chapter. A total of 24 entries was included. Of which, the frequency codes were ranked as "I" with 16 times, "M" for 12 times, "E" for 10 and "D" for 9, which can be coined as a variant model of the D.I.M.E. – the I.M.E.D. model that emphasizes information and technology, military actions followed next, economic being used as a tertiary tool, and diplomacy being employed last.

Hostile Nation States

As referenced in the literature review, the United States has specifically outlined three nation states as specific threats to its homeland defense: Russia, Iran, and North Korea. Russia has proven to be a hostile state, but not in a similar military capacity as Iran and North Korea. While Iran is not a nuclear power, its nuclear aspirations have worried the United States. Additionally, despite Russia's nuclear capabilities, that is not the main source of consternation for America, but rather its information campaign waged against the United States. Both of these topics will therefore be analyzed in a later section of this chapter. Regarding North Korea and Iran, a nuclear strike on American soil from one of these states would prove to be an existential threat to the American way of life, forcing citizens to change their lifestyles to deal with the dangerous aftermath of a weapon of mass destruction. Focusing specifically on Iran, while the country does not have a nuclear weapon or a delivery mechanism to deliver such a weapon to American soil, the fear of such has led to sanctions against their country. However, in spite of their limited military power, Iranian attacks on American culture have expanded from their borders, and they are now taking actions against individuals in American territory using more conventional means.

Within the past ten years, Iran has backed several attacks against U.S. citizens. Starting with the earliest, in September 2009 "an Iranian operative hired a hitman to assassinate an Iranian-American regime opponent and radio personality" (Iran Action Group 2018, 16). Then in 2011, at a restaurant in Washington D.C., Iranian nationals supported a plan to bomb the establishment as a means to assassinate a Saudi diplomat (Iran Action Group 2018, 16). Most recently, in August 2018, "two Iranian operatives were charged for conducting covert surveillance of Israeli and Jewish facilities in the United States and collecting identifying information about U.S. citizens and U.S. nationals who are members of an Iranian opposition group" (Iran Action Group 2018, 16). Iran has pursued similar means in other regions around the world, proving that these are not isolated incidents, but rather a pattern of strategic maneuvers that they are using to exert their influence around the world. Another method by which Iran seeks to influence the world in its favor is through social media and cyberspace.

The two most prominent social media sites, Twitter and Facebook, have acknowledged that Iran has used their platforms to spread disinformation with the intent of manipulating behavior within the United States. Their attempted influence over American culture was not lost on the corporations, and they are implementing methods to defend against Iranian influence. For example, "in August 2018, Facebook, Twitter, and other U.S. companies reported the removal of more than 1,000 pages, groups, and accounts they assessed were engaged in spreading disinformation on behalf of the regime" (Iran Action Group 2018, 33). These actions, along with human rights abuses, environmental devastation, and the hostility between the Iranian and United States governments gave the latter nation reason enough to pull out of the landmark Joint Comprehensive Plan of Action (JCPOA), which lifted sanctions against the former in exchange for Iran reducing their nuclear program significantly. United States Secretary of State Mike Pompeo is on the record, regarding the withdrawal from the JCPOA, saying that "Our hope is that one day soon we can reach a new agreement with Iran. But we must see major changes in the regime's behavior both inside and outside of its borders" (Iran Action Group 2018, 47). However, while there has been a breakdown of relations between the United States and Iran, there is progress being made between the diplomatic relations of the United States and North Korea.

The long-standing policy of the United States towards North Korea has been the denuclearization of the peninsula. Not only does a growing nuclear capability in North Korea threaten U.S. allies in the region like South Korea, Japan, and Australia, but it has the potential to hurt the United States directly. North Korea has threatened American territories in the past, but progress has been made between the United States and North Korea on the path towards denuclearization. Still, the United States is hesitant to relax its sanctions against the country, as a "nuclear armed North Korea could lead to the proliferation of the world's most destructive weapons across the Indo-Pacific region and beyond" (National Security Strategy 2018, 46). Part of the United States' initiative to deter the North Koreans from attacking its allies or homeland is through joint military exercises in the area surrounding the Korean peninsula. This is done with the intention of remaining "ready to respond with overwhelming force to North Korean aggression... and improve options to compel denuclearization of the peninsula" (National Security Strategy 2018, 47).

In a statement by President Donald Trump, he outlines some of the progress his administration has made thus far. Most notably, "President Trump and Kim Jong Un held a historic summit in Singapore, where Chairman Kim reaffirmed his agreement to complete denuclearization of the Korean Peninsula" (Trump, 2018b). Chairman Kim has shown progress in this commitment; in fact, as of November 2018, it has been ten months without a ballistic missile test from the state. Furthermore, international reporters were invited to North Korea to witness the destruction of several nuclear weapon testing sites. Regardless, sanctions will remain in place on North Korea until it can prove irrefutably that it has completely denuclearized.

Another state actor that has threatened United States' homeland security is Russia. Russia is not only a declared nuclear threat but has damaged the stability of the United States through targeted cyber-attacks, prolonging conflicts in which the United States is involved, and instigating chaos within its allied countries (Coats 2018, 23). The most potentially damaging activity the Russians were embroiled in was their meddling in the 2016 United States' presidential election. While the Russians did not change any physical votes, the extent to which they influenced voter perception of the two primary presidential candidates through targeted social media campaigns is unknown. In fact, the division they sowed by spreading high volumes of misinformation on sites like Facebook, Twitter, and Reddit can still be seen today, as the appointment of new government officials is still incredibly contentious. Measures have been taken against Russia in response to their actions, including "sanctions against 16 Russian entities and individuals for their roles in Russian interference in the 2016 presidential election" as of March 2018, as well as "the closure of two Russian compounds and the expulsion of 35 diplomats" (Trump 2018a). Their election meddling and disinformation campaigns have both proved to be a great danger to the national security of the United States. Washington cannot function as a governing body without a stable government, but what Russia is doing around the world also threatens America's national security.

Similar to what has been done in the United States, Russia has taken nearly identical actions against U.S. allies worldwide, such as their influence in the electoral process of other western democratic nations like the United Kingdom and France. Furthermore, Russia has terrorized their political opponents internationally, including its "attempt to kill a private citizen in the United Kingdom with a military-grade nerve agent" (Trump 2018a). Other international problems the Kremlin is responsible for is their financial and military support to Syrian President Bashar Al-Assad, who has violated international law against his own civilians in the protracted Syrian civil war. Moreover, Putin's regime invaded Ukraine in 2014, with the intention of annexing Crimea. With these aggressive actions, Russia has hurt allies of the United States, leading to a less stable world. Their election meddling actions attempt to prop up nationalistic candidate's platforming on xenophobia. Steps like these weaken the North Atlantic Treaty Organization (NATO), one of the strongest military alliances and the main hedge to Russian aggression on the European continent. When the United States, or any country, can no longer trust its allies that hurts global security. The U.S. strength lies in its alliances; Russia seeks to tear these pacts apart to regain the global power and influence it once had.

To answer the research questions in regard to hostile nation states, the three aforementioned states use different aspects of D.I.M.E. through the YIRTM to erode the hegemonic power of the United States. Starting with Iran, this state is using the first three instruments of national power: diplomacy, information, and military. Their main avenue for diplomatic relations was the JCPOA, however this instrument seems to be weakening with the U.S. withdrawal from the agreement. Conversely, the European Union (EU) is still trying to maintain relations with Iran. They view the deal as "a matter of respecting international agreements and an issue of international security" so the EU is Iran's best option for maintaining diplomatic relations to keep European sanctions lifted (Bruxelles 2018). Regarding information, the prior mentioned social media campaigns were targeted to spread misinformation within U.S. society. Fake news like this weakens faith in American institutions and degrades national unity. Finally, militarily Iran still pursues weapon acquisitions and ballistic missile technology to exert regional power. Most of these actions that Iran is taking to diminish U.S. power is for the purpose of regaining its own strength and rebuild their society. A member of the National Iranian American Council was quoted stating that Iran wants a weaker U.S. and a reduction in sanctions because they are "impoverishing the Iranian middle class, crushing Iranian civil society, and eliminating prospects for peaceful democratic change... creating a destructive situation internally" (NIAC 2018).

North Korea has similar motivations and methods as Iran when combating the United States' power in the context of the YIRTM. However, what North Korea lacks in an information campaign against the United States, they make up for with military power. Through the proliferation of advanced ballistic missile technology, now with capabilities to reach the west coast of the United States and beyond, and a strong and formidable conventional military with the ability to overwhelm South Korea, North Korea has the capacity to weaken the international standing of the United States by hurting its allies. Diplomatically, talks between North Korea and the United States have been beneficial for both parties. However, this is only the latest in a continuous pattern of talks between the two countries. North Korea could obfuscate its nefarious intentions with the United States' demands to have sanctions removed, just to break their promises when they find it convenient to restart their nuclear program. This is not speculation, but rather an emerging trend of the diplomacy between the two countries (Department of State 2018). Furthermore, North Korea is using military means to threaten U.S. allies and diplomatic means to lure this nation into a sense that peace and stability that can be brought into fruition to reach their ultimate goal of unifying Korea under Kim Jong-Un's regime. Members of the IC have assessed that North Korea's ultimate goal is to create a unified, strong Korea that is internationally recognized and welcoming state with enough military and diplomatic force to be respected (Department of State 2018). While it is unlikely that South Korea would ever allow a unified state under the leadership of the North, perhaps over time the two states could come to an agreement, if the North retracts its aggressive military provocations.

Finally, Russia has threatened the United States through mainly military and information means. The information campaign against the United States has been well documented. Special Counsel Robert Mueller indicted 13 Russian official and three Russian organizations in his investigation for their interference in the 2016 presidential election (Department of Justice 2018). The misinformation campaign, under the purview of Russian President Vladimir Putin had a specific goal to "undermine public faith in the U.S. democratic process, denigrate Secretary Clinton, and harm her electability and potential presidency" (Permanent Select Committee on Intelligence 2018). Militarily, Russia is becoming less of a threat, however they still are an aggressor to small, eastern European countries that the United States retains diplomatic ties with. This was especially notable with Russia's annexation of Crimea in 2014. Russia is taking all of the aforementioned actions to "[undermine] Western values and the credibility of Western governments" (Garamone 2018). Ultimately, Russia seeks to regain the world power it had when it was the Union of Soviet Socialist Republics (USSR), by weakening the United States and its homeland security by creating confusion and a lack of faith in the Western lifestyle.

Lone Wolf-Style Attacks

One of the most sinister threats that the United States' homeland faces is lone wolf-style attacks on soft targets. Soft targets are relatively unguarded places, such as grocery stores, movie theaters, banks, medical clinics, and other locations that are common in a civilian's life that are frequented by large swaths of people. These soft assets are easy for lone wolf attackers to launch their acts against because they are often in well-populated areas and lack adequate security protection. Moreover, these attacks also pose a threat because the federal law enforcement agencies often cannot trace and track where and when an attack will occur (Becker 2014). A lone wolf terrorist has no diplomatic sway in order to weaken the U.S. position. Lone wolf actors tend not to utilize diplomacy when taking action against the United States, because diplomacy is not necessary in order to achieve their goals.

In the age of the World Wide Web, all kinds of information are readily available to any individual. Lone wolf actors are able to use the internet to gather necessary information and radicalize themselves. After committing their terror, they are then able to broadcast their actions after causing havoc in the United States. Due to the nature of the internet, these lone wolf terrorists are able to develop and innovate their ideas, forming their plans from prior nefarious individuals (Duke 2017). The fact that this information can be easily spread is incredibly dangerous to the security of the United States. The web is accessible and fairly easy to use anywhere in the world, which allows radical lone wolf actors to communicate globally. Anyone with a computer or phone can communicate with those who also seek to harm the U.S. and obtain the means needed to achieve their goals. In a way, online communication and cooperation are the closest way that a lone wolf actor comes to making use of "terror" diplomacy. While this may not be considered a traditional approach to diplomacy, these actors only take advantage of limited options when it comes to working with others.

Due to the availability of military-grade weapons such as assault rifles in the United States, a lone wolf actor can be a deadly one-man army. These actors tend to use their own kind of individualized hard power that can be associated with the military aspect of the YIRTM. These actors often cause physical harm to others with this hard power in order to carry out their sinister plans. By definition, lone wolf actors are not supported by other organizations or groups of actors (Becker 2014). From an economic standpoint, the funding for their attacks typically comes from their own efforts to earn money. However, lone wolf attacks cause fear and physical damage, which can harm the U.S. economy (START 2017).

Since the attacks on September 11th, 2001, the United States has been facing more lone wolf style attacks than ever before. Federal government agencies, such as the DHS and Federal Bureau of Investigation (FBI), have continued to provide information on the current environment of terrorism to the state and local authorities (National Terrorism Advisory 2017). The federal government also works to help private businesses maintain security by coordinating measures with business owners and by providing risk assessments. Due to the current and constant risks of terrorist and extremist activity, DHS states that law enforcement and security will continue to patrol public places in order to keep the populace safe (National Terrorism Advisory 2017).

In general, lone wolf attacks have been increasing in the amount of damage that they cause over the course of time. Even though many lone wolf actors are provoked into committing their violent acts by their disappointment and disillusionment with their lives, there is no general consensus on why all lone wolves commit their attacks. This complicates the ability of law enforcement agencies such as the police and FBI to locate the violent tendencies of potential shooters (Becker 2014). These attacks are continuing to threaten the American way of life. People no longer feel safe going to everyday and ordinary places such as a church, concert, movie theater, or the doctor's office (Pew Research Center 2017). The DHS reports that the U.S. is facing one of its most serious terror threat environments since the 9/11 attacks. As terrorist organizations continue to exploit the internet to direct, enable, and inspire individuals here in the homeland, the U.S. has been increasing its general security in the wake of these incidents (National Terrorism Advisory 2017).

Gang Violence

Gang culture is the cause of much of the violent crime and drug related felonies in the United States. There is an inextricable link among gangs, gun violence, and drug usage (National Institute of Justice 2018). The FBI has uncovered "that transnational gangs are present in almost every state and continue to grow their memberships, now targeting younger recruits more than ever before" (FBI 2016). In the context of the YIRTM, gangs rely primarily on the military and economic elements of power.

Militarily, gangs use small arms to threaten or perpetuate violence within large cities. There has been an average of nearly 2,000 gang related homicides annually from 2007 to 2012, which is approximately 13 percent of all annual homicides (National Gang Center n.d.). Contrary to the previously analyzed lone wolf style attacks, gang violence does not do as much damage at one time as a lone wolf shooter. However, those types of shootings are infrequent, while gang violence is a commonality within large communities, leading to an overall higher death toll than that of a lone wolf style attack. Economically, gangs pursue a variety of illicit activities to fund their organizations. As mentioned in the literature review, gangs traffic drugs and people into the United States as a primary means of income. The money they make through these endeavors is used to buy the weapons for the purpose of bolstering their territorial power, intimidate rivals, enforce compliance, and spread fear negatively affecting the greater community because of the direct correlations with increased crime rates.

Ultimately, gangs do not wish to see the end of the worldwide dominance of the United States, unlike the hostile nation states that were previously analyzed. The United States is the playground of these gangs. They need this nation to enhance their economic standing, but unfortunately for the gangs, they provide no value to the United States (National Gang Center n.d.). Gangs hurt the homeland security of the U.S. by murdering its civilians, fostering the addiction of the population to drugs, and allowing dangerous individuals to permeate the society. America affords gangs the opportunity to profit off the most vulnerable in the populace.

Protection of Critical Infrastructure

Both state actors and non-state actors have the skills and resources to execute a cyber-attack on the U.S. critical infrastructure. National actors may commit cyber intrusions or espionage, instead of full on attacks, since cyber-attacks could be seen as an act of war. Russia possesses substantial and well-resourced cyber capabilities, for example, block chain technology, in conjunction with China who has been a very active player in the cyber world in recent history. Russia and China are unlikely to execute a cyber-attack resulting in nationwide damage to the U.S. power grid in the short term due to the political and diplomatic consequences, but both have and will most likely continue to probe energy sector networks and remotely access some other assets in order to learn more about U.S. critical infrastructure (Department of Energy 2016, 29).

China has mainly been focused on economic espionage on U.S. companies, and this state actor often uses tools such as network scanners, viruses, and botnets to do so (Department of Energy 2015). They have also aimed more at intellectual property theft and gathering intelligence to boost their own infrastructure. Conversely, Iran and North Korea both have much less sophisticated cyber capabilities but have bolstered their interests in gathering intelligence through cyber warfare against their respective political foes. Terrorist groups have great ambition when it comes to cyber-attacks on the U.S. power grid, but do not possess the skills or tools necessary to do so (Department of Energy 2016, 30). However, due to the interconnectivity of the American critical infrastructure, an attack on one system can have serious reverberations on others.

Over time, critical infrastructure assets have become more interdependent with one another. Critical infrastructure systems often depend upon interlocking systems to function properly, which is beneficial when all systems are working. However, when an adversary strikes, the likelihood of simultaneous disruptions across multiple systems during disasters increases tremendously (U.S. Global Change Research Program 2018). The interconnectivity of critical infrastructure is a double-edged sword. While having the systems tied together, the infrastructure is more efficient, but their coordination also makes the systems more susceptible to attacks and even more devastating to American citizens when one sector fails. Interdependencies within the energy infrastructure have significant implications for response and recovery, since nearly all critical lifeline sectors like healthcare, transportation, communications, and water rely on energy to function (FEMAb 2018, 28).

CONCLUSION

Upon concluding their analysis, the authors agree the greatest threats to the U.S. homeland security come from the information and military dimensions of national power as described in the YIRTM. Diplomacy has been seen to have the least effect in attacking the homeland soil. Furthermore, through the implementation of the Federal Secondary Data Case Study Triangulation Model, the sources used provided high quality of data and thus a well-balanced set of information. Both the YIRTM and the Federal Qualitative Secondary Data Case Study Triangulation Model where useful tools used to assist these authors in answering their research questions. Future studies might want to make use of primary data collected through surveys or interviews to complement the findings of this study.

Restating the research questions, the authors asked, "How are state and non-state actors weakening the United States' homeland security in the context of the YIRTM?" and "Why is the hegemonic power of the U.S. being weakened by the state and non-state actors in relation to the YIRTM?" Each of the four threats analyzed resulted in a different answer to these questions. While each hostile nation state has taken a different path to diminish U.S. security, in general, nations such as Russia, Iran, and North Korea are weakening American homeland security primarily through military force and information campaigns to bolster their own worldwide power (National Security Strategy 2017). Lone wolf shooters use military hardware to achieve their ends, with each motive being different per shooter. It is difficult to ascertain the rationale behind these attackers, since each case is unique, but regardless lone wolf attacks have resulted in a diminished sense of security in the United States (Becker 2014). Gangs also use military measures to weaken the United States' homeland security, but the goal of their military measures is to profit off of the United States' population through the trafficking of drugs or people. Finally, enemies of the United States look for weaknesses to perhaps attack its critical infrastructure to cripple its functionality in the future. The majority of attacks against critical infrastructure come through information means. American adversaries once again attack the critical infrastructure due to its interconnectivity, with an attack on one potentially bringing the whole system down, resulting in a diminished American global hegemony (Department of Energy 2016).

To recap the analysis and reaffirm the conclusions drawn on the research questions, each of the four focus points took a different path to damage the homeland security of the United States. Hostile nation states like Iran, North Korea, and Russia relied on information campaigns waged on this nation's social media sites to undermine faith in its democratic institutions, while simultaneously building their military forces to rival American superior might (National Security Strategy 2017). Lone wolf shooters also rely on military power to pursue their own deranged ends. Violent individuals take advantage of gun rights to acquire military hardware and damage soft targets. The natural rights afforded to these citizens make it very difficult to predict and prevent their next attack especially in the context of civil rights (Becker 2014). Gangs rely on small arms to grow their power. They also engage in illicit activities to enhance their economic security, which feeds their ability to buy military technology, ensuring their regional power from within the United States (FBI 2018). Finally, the critical infrastructure of the U.S is vulnerable to attacks from foreign actors, but agencies like the DOE are working to make sure that the interdependencies of the sectors does not hinder the government's ability to respond effectively (Department of Energy 2016).

The Department of Homeland Security and other government agencies recognize the threats posed to the security of the United States of America.

ANNEX A: LIST OF ALL DATA SOURCES AND THEMATIC CODING SCHEME

How/Why (title)	D.I.M.E.	Source	Source Type (press release, news article, video, etc.)	Date	Page (if applicable)
Acting Secretary of Homeland Security Elaine Duke Discusses Shared Efforts to Combat Terrorism with Foreign Leaders Homeland Security - This source details the efforts of the DHS to use diplomacy and intelligence to combat terrorism	D, I	Department of Homeland Security	Press Release	2017	n/a
Explaining lone wolf target selection in the United States- This source explains how lone wolf actors select their targets by using intelligence, and then carry out the attacks using military-grade weapons	I, M	Studies in Conflict & Terrorism	Article	2014	959-78
Statement for the Record - Worldwide Threat Assessment of the US Intelligence Community- This source explains how the U.S. IC assesses the threats affecting the homeland through the lenses of intelligence and military	I, M	DNI	Testimony	Feb, 2018	n/a
Cyber Threat and Vulnerability Analysis of the U.S. Electric Sector- This source analyzes U.S. intelligence on how vulnerable the U.S. electric grid is from a military attack, which poses a great risk to our own military and economy	I, M, E	Department of Energy	Government Report	2016	n/a

How/Why (title)	D.I.M.E.	Source	Source Type (press release, news article, video, etc.)	Date	Page (if applicable)
Grand Jury Indicts Thirteen Russian Individuals and Three Russian Companies for Scheme to Interfere in the United States Political System- This source provides evidence that Russians had a hand in interfering with U.S. elections, which shows the diplomatic and intelligence aspects of the threat	D, I	Department of Justice	Article	Feb, 2018	n/a
Exposing Russia's Effort to Sow Discord Online: The Internet Research- This source explains how the DHS used intelligence to expose the Russian's actions	I	Permanent Committee on Intelligence	Government Report	n.d.	n/a
Gangs- This source explains how the FBI has an intelligence center to deal with the different gangs, and how gangs threaten the U.S. Economy	I, E	FBI	Article	Oct, 2018	n/a
2018 National Preparedness Report- This report from FEMA shows how well the U.S. is prepared for Natural Disasters that threaten critical infrastructure and the economy	E	FEMA	Report	2018	27-32
NATO Moves to Combat Russian Hybrid Warfare- This source shows how the U.S. military is ready to protect the homeland from foreign attacks	M	DOD	Press Release	29-Sep-18	n/a

Annex A. (Continued)

How/Why (title)	D.I.M.E.	Source	Source Type (press release, news article, video, etc.)	Date	Page (if applicable)
Global Terrorism Index 2017- This source uses intelligence gathered on terrorist groups around the world and how effective their militaries and economies are	I, M, E	Vision of Humanity	Article	2017	n/a
Joint Strategic Plan FY 2018-2022- This source shows how the U.S. government plans to move forward in addressing foreign threats with diplomacy and the military	D, M	DOS, USAID	Strategic Plan	Feb-18	23-33
Gangs and Gang Crime- This source shows how U.S. police gather intelligence on gangs and how gang crime threatens the economy	I, E	Department of Justice	Article	April, 2018	n/a
National Security Strategy- This source goes over how the U.S. is prepared to address threats with diplomacy, the Intelligence Community, and militarily	D, I, M	Office of the President of the United States	Strategic Plan	Dec-17	7-14, 25-32, 45-55
National Defense Strategy- This source outlines how the U.S. is prepared to defend the homeland from diplomatic, intelligence, military, and economic threats	D, I, M, E	DOD	Strategic Plan	2018	n/a
Statement by the President on the Shooting in Charleston, South Carolina- This source shows how President Obama addressed the people of Charleston diplomatically, and how the shooting was caused, in part, by an U.S. Intelligence Community failure	D, I	White House	Press Release	2015	n/a

How/Why (title)	D.I.M.E.	Source	Source Type (press release, news article, video, etc.)	Date	Page (if applicable)
Outlaw Regime: A Chronicle of Iran's Destructive Activities- This source explains how Iran is a military and intelligence threat to the homeland	I, M	DOS	Government Report	2018	4-8, 18-22, 30-34
Planned Parenthood of the Rocky Mountains Response to Colorado Springs Attacks- This statement by Planned Parenthood helped the U.S. Intelligence Community by explaining what took place	I	Planned Parenthood	Press Release	2015	n/a
President Donald J. Trump Is Committed to Countering the Proliferation of Chemical, Biological, and Nuclear Weapons- This source shows how U.S. leadership plans to combat threats to the homeland by means of diplomacy, the military, and economically	D, M, E	Office of the President of the United States	Press Release	26-Sep-18	n/a
President Donald J. Trump is Standing Up To Russia's Malign Activities- This source shows how U.S. leadership plans to combat threats to the homeland by means of diplomacy, the Intelligence Community, the military, and economically	D, I, M, E	Office of the President of the United States	Press Release	6-Apr-18	n/a
Secretary Kirstjen M. Nielsen Remarks: Rethinking Homeland Security in an Age of Disruption- This source explains how the Department of Homeland Security is addressing threats diplomatically, through U.S. Intelligence Agencies, and with the U.S. Military	D, I, M	DHS	Speech	5-Sep-18	n/a

Annex A. (Continued)

How/Why (title)	D.I.M.E.	Source	Source Type (press release, news article, video, etc.)	Date	Page (if applicable)
Statement by President Trump on the Shooting in Las Vegas, Nevada- This source shows how President Trump addressed the people of La Vegas diplomatically, and how the shooting was caused, in part, by an U.S. Intelligence Community failure	D, I	White House	Press Release	2017	n/a
Summary of Homegrown Terrorism Threat- This source shows how the U.S. military and economy are threatened by domestic terrorism, and how U.S. intelligence is combating this threat	I, M, E	National Terrorism Advisory	Bulletin	2017	n/a
The Life Saving Mission of ICE- This source shows how Homeland Security is utilizing intelligence, the military, and economics to address the threats of illegal immigrants	I, M, E	DHS	Article	2018	n/a
Impacts, Risks, and Adaptation in the United States: Fourth National Climate Assessment, Volume II- This source explains how natural disasters threaten the U.S. critical infrastructure and economy	E	U.S. Global Change Research Program	Report	2018	n/a

These departments continue to grow and adapt to the challenges presented to them. Moving forward, several steps need to be taken to ensure to future American security. As referenced throughout this analysis, the United States' greatest weaknesses are in its information and military dimensions. With the majority of threats to the homeland coming from abroad in the cases of hostile nation states through their capacity to attack critical infrastructure and influence American citizens, it would behoove the United States to have greater collaboration between the various departments which defend the state. The Department of State must be staffed with individuals capable of coordinating with the Department of Homeland Security to synchronize efforts to prevent dangerous individuals from entering the country. A similar recommendation is referenced in the Department of Homeland Security's 2013 National Infrastructure Preparedness Plan. The first of seven core tenants states "risks should be identified and managed in a coordinated and comprehensive way across the critical infrastructure community to enable the effective allocation of security and resilience resources" (DHS 2013). This mentality should not be limited to the critical infrastructure community, but rather applied across the entire defense sector. Greater collaboration is the key to greater American security. For now, the United States remains the most powerful country in the world, but its Intelligence Community must be aware of the threats posed to it from inside its borders if the nation wishes to remain the global hegemony.

REFERENCES

Becker, Michael. 2014. "Explaining Lone Wolf Target Selection in the United States." *Studies in Conflict & Terrorism* 37 (11): 959-78.

Bruxelles. 2018. "*Joint Statement on the Re-imposition of US Sanctions Due to Its Withdrawal from the Joint Comprehensive Plan of Action* (JCPOA)." Accessed October 17. https://eeas.europa.eu/headquarters/headquarters-homepage/49141/joint-statement-re-imposition-us-sanctions-due-its-withdrawal-joint-comprehensive-plan-action_en.

Cheng, Hui G.M. 2017. *"Secondary Analysis of Existing Data: Opportunities and Implementation."* Accessed October 16, 2018. https://www.ncbi.nlm.nih.gov/pmc/articles/PMC4311114/.

Coats, Daniel R. 2018, February 13. *"Statement for the Record - Worldwide Threat Assessment of the U. S. Intelligence Community."* Accessed November 19, 2018. https://www.dni.gov/files/documents/Newsroom/Testimonies/2018-ATA-Unclassified-SSCI.pdf.

Colorado Judicial Branch. 2016. *"El Paso - Cases of Interest - People of the State of Colorado vs. Robert Lewis Dear - 04/04/2016 to Present."* Accessed October 17, 2018. https://www.courts.state.co.us/Courts/County/Case_Details.cfm?Case_ID=1625.

Department of Energy. 2016, August. *"Cyber Threat and Vulnerability Analysis of the U.S. Electric Sector."* https://www.energy.gov/sites/prod/files/2017/01/f34/Cyber Threat and Vulnerability Analysis of the U.S. Electric Sector.pdf.

Department of Homeland Security. 2013. *"National Infrastructure Protection Plan 2013- Partnering for Critical Infrastructure Security and Resilience."* https://www.dhs.gov/sites/default/files/publications/national-infrastructure-protection-plan-2013-508.pdf.

Department of Justice - Office of Public Affairs. 2018, February 16. *"Grand Jury Indicts Thirteen Russian Individuals and Three Russian Companies for Scheme to Interfere in the United States Political System."* Accessed November 19, 2018. https://www.justice.gov/opa/pr/grand-jury-indicts-thirteen-russian-individuals-and-three-russian-companies-scheme-interfere.

Department of State. 2018, July 17. *"U.S. Relations with North Korea."* Accessed October 18, 2018. https://www.state.gov/r/pa/ei/bgn/2792.htm.

Duke, Elaine. 2017. *"Acting Secretary of Homeland Security Elaine Duke Discusses Shared Efforts to Combat Terrorism with Foreign Leaders."* Accessed October 16, 2018. https://www.dhs.gov/news/2017/10/21/acting-secretary-homeland-security-elaine-duke-discusses-shared-efforts-combat.

Electricity Consumers Resource Council. 2004, February 9. *"The Economic Impacts of the August 2003 Blackout."* https://elcon.org/wpcontent/uploads/Economic20Impacts20of20August20200320Blackout1.pdf.

FBI. (Federal Bureau of Investigation). *"Gangs."* Accessed October 26, 2018. https://www.fbi.gov/investigate/violent-crime/gangs.

FBI. 2016, November 14. *"FBI Releases 2015 Crime Statistics."* https://www.fbi.gov/news/pressrel/press-releases/fbi-releases-2015-crime-statistics.

FEMAa (Federal Emergency Management Agency). 2018a. https://www.fema.gov/about-agency.

FEMAb. (Federal Emergency Management Agency). 2018. *2018 National Preparedness Report* (pp. 27-32). Accessed on January 18, 2019. https://www.fema.gov/media-library-data/1541781185823-2ae55a 276f604e04b68e2748adc95c68/2018NPRRprt20181108v508.pdf.

Garamone, Jim. 2018, September 29. *"NATO Moves to Combat Russian Hybrid Warfare."* Accessed October 20, 2018. https://dod.defense.gov/News/Article/Article/1649146/nato-moves-to-combat-russian-hybrid-warfare/.

ICE. 2018, August 20. *"The Life Saving Mission of ICE."* Accessed October 26, 2018. https://www.dhs.gov/news/2018/08/20/life-saving-missions-ice.

Iran Action Group - U.S. Department of State. 2018. *"Outlaw Regime: A Chronicle of Iran's Destructive Activities."* Accessed October 7, 2018. https://www.state.gov/documents/organization/286410.pdf.

Joint Strategic Plan - FY 2018-2022. 2018, February. U.S. Department of State and U.S. Agency for International Development. Accessed January 20, 2019. https://www.state.gov/documents/organization/277156.pdf.

JP 1-02. 2010. Department of Defense Dictionary of Military and Associated Terms. *Joint Publication 1-02*. Accessed January 20, 2019. https://fas.org/irp/doddir/dod/jp1_02.pdf.

Lowenthal, Mark M. 2015. *Intelligence: From Secrets to Policy*. 6th ed. CQ Press.

Marchio, J. 2017. "*Analytic Tradecraft and the Intelligence Community: Enduring Value, Intermittent Emphasis.*" Taylor & Francis. Accessed November 16, 2018. https://doi.org/10.1080/02684527.2012.746415.

National Defense Authorization Act. 2018. *House Armed Services Committee Communications.* Accessed January 29, 2019. https://www.congress.gov/bill/115th-congress/house-bill/2810.

National Gang Center. "*National Youth Gang Survey Analysis.*" Accessed October 26, 2018. https://www.nationalgangcenter.gov/surveyanalysis/measuring-the-extent-of-gang-problems.

National Institute of Justice. 2018, April 26. "*Gangs and Gang Crime.*" Accessed October 26, 2018. https://www.nij.gov/topics/crime/gangs/Pages/welcome.aspx.

National Terrorism Advisory. 2017, May 15. "*Summary of Homegrown Terrorism Threat.*" Accessed October 16, 2018. https://www.dhs.gov/sites/default/files/ntas/alerts/National%20Terrorism%20Advisory%20System%20Issued%20May%2015%2C%202017.pdf.

NIAC (National Iranian American Council). 2018, October 18. "*From the Hill: NIAC Asks if the U.S. and Iran are on a Collision Course.*" Accessed October 18, 2018. https://www.niacouncil.org/recap-niacs-brief-hill-u-s-iran-collision-course/.

Nielsen, Kirstjen. 2018, September 5. "*Secretary Kirstjen M. Nielsen Remarks: Rethinking Homeland Security in an Age of Disruption.*" Accessed September 9, 2018. https://www.dhs.gov/news/2018/09/05/secretary-nielsen-remarks-rethinking-homeland-security-age-disruption.

National Security Strategy of the United States of America. December 2017. Accessed October 20, 2018. https://www.whitehouse.gov/wpcontent/uploads/2017/12/NSS-Final-12-18-2017-0905.pdf.

Obama, B. 2015, June 18. "*Statement by the President on the Shooting in Charleston, South Carolina.*" https://obamawhitehouse.archives.gov/the-press-office/2015/06/18/statement-president-shooting-charleston-south-carolina.

Permanent Select Committee on Intelligence. Accessed October 18, 2018. https://democrats-intelligence.house.gov/social-media-content/.

Pew Research Center. 2017. *"Views of Government's Handling of Terrorism Fall to Post-9/11 Low."* Accessed October 16, 2018. http://www.people-press.org/2015/12/15/views-of-governments-handling-of-terrorism-fall-to-post-911-low/.

Planned Parenthood. 2015. *"Planned Parenthood of the Rocky Mountains Response to Colorado Springs Attacks."* Accessed October 16, 2018. https://www.plannedparenthood.org/about-us/newsroom/press-releases/planned-parenthood-of-the-rocky-mountains-response-to-colorado-springs-attacks.

Reidmiller, D. R., C.W. Avery, D. R. Easterling, K. E. Kunkel, K. L. M. Lewis, T.K. Maycock, and B.C. Stewart (eds.) *Fourth National Climate Assessment: Summary Findings.* Accessed January 25, 2019. https://nca2018.globalchange.gov/.

START (National Consortium for the Study of Terrorism and Responses to Terrorism). 2017. *"Global Terrorism Index 2017."* Accessed November 9, 2018. http://visionofhumanity.org/app/uploads/2017/11/Global-Terrorism-Index-2017.pdf.

Trump, Donald J. 2017, October 2. *"Statement by President Trump on the Shooting in Las Vegas, Nevada."* https://www.whitehouse.gov/briefings-statements/statement-president-trump-shooting-las-vegas-nevada/.

Trump, Donald J. 2018a. *"President Donald J. Trump Is Standing Up to Russia's Malign Activities."* Accessed October 15, 2018. https://www.whitehouse.gov/briefings-statements/president-donald-j-trump-standing-russias-malign-activities/.

Trump, Donald J. 2018b. *"President Donald J. Trump Is Committed to Countering the Proliferation of Chemical, Biological, and Nuclear Weapons."* Accessed October 15, 2018. https://www.whitehouse.gov/briefings-statements/president-donald-j-trump-committed-countering-proliferation-chemical-biological-nuclear-weapons/.

U.S. Global Change Research Program. 1970, January 01. *"Impacts, Risks, and Adaptation in the United States: Fourth National Climate Assessment,* Volume II.*"*

Weaver, John M. 2015, March. "The Perils of a Piecemeal Approach to Fighting Isis in Iraq." *Public Administration Review6* Volume 75(2):192-193.

Weaver, John M. May 2018. "Dissecting the 2017 National Security Strategy: Implications for Senior Administrators (the Devil in the Details)." *Global Policy Volume* 9(2):283-284.

In: Global Intelligence Priorities
Editors: John Michael Weaver et al.
ISBN: 978-1-53615-836-6
© 2019 Nova Science Publishers, Inc.

Chapter 3

THE DRAGON'S ASCENSION - CHINA'S RISE AND CHALLENGE TO THE AMERICAN HEGEMONY: A QUALITATIVE ASSESSMENT

Josie Gardner, Christopher DeJesus,
Max Vargo and Nicole Wightman
York College, York, Pennsylvania, US

ABSTRACT

China, the second leading economic power in the world, has had a steady incline in international power through its economic prowess and governmental strength. The current trade wars with the United States (U.S.) prove China's economic stability and independence from U.S. influence while simultaneously using their massive funds to sway other sovereign nations. As the world's most populous nation in the world, China's ascendance from an agrarian society to the second largest economy on the planet has attracted much speculation and debate, especially surrounding its potential to contest or even surpass the United States as the sole superpower. Though China has claimed that it does not seek to alter or disrupt the international system, its actions, both overt and covert, contradict this claim on several different levels. Using a qualitative assessment approach, this chapter examines how and why China is pursuing actions to undermine U.S. influence in both East Asia specifically and the world more broadly in the divided four instrumental dimensions, threatening the U.S. world hegemony.

LITERATURE REVIEW

In December of 2017, President Donald Trump released the first National Security Strategy (NSS) of his presidency where he specifically outlines his concerns about new moves of foreign national powers and how the U.S. should response to such actions. He highlights that Chinese economic policies and their political endeavors are actively attempting to erode the U.S. world hegemony and its ascending stance in the current world hierarchy. Particularly in both military and cyber capabilities, President Trump claims that China could weaken U.S. infrastructure and negatively affect the way of living in the United States which is manifested by the NSS and states "They are determined to make economies less free and less fair, to grow their militaries, and to control information and data to repress their societies and expand their influence" (NSS 2017). The NSS recognizes a working relationship between China and the U.S., unless there is any military advancement by China against the homeland or U.S. allies. The NSS also reclaims the history of China's communist government and the widespread influence China has on its surrounding nations through their communist power backed by their increasing economic capabilities.

In 2019, the Trump Administration set forth the National Defense Authorization Act (NDAA) which focuses on the rebuilding of the U.S. military and its defense priorities against the actor of the threats. The current U.S. administration has strong disagreement on China's investment in new nuclear weapons and views China's rising influence in Southeast Asia, South Asia, Africa, and other regions of the world with concern. Witnessing rapidly growing economic and military capabilities, the Trump administration asserts that China is using its access to the U.S. economy to steal sensitive technology and military information to disadvantage the United States. Furthermore, the NDAA calls for the U.S. to strengthen its foreign investment, military training, equipment, and nuclear capabilities (NDAA 2018).

Chinese President Xi Jinping recently released the transcripts in his 2017 speech at the 19th National Congress of the Communist Party of China, the party he heads. In this speech, President Xi outlines his intentions to continue to spread the power of his party and the influence of China to surrounding nations. During his presidency, President Xi has made steady increases in his own power and that of his party. He also continues to make the claim about the structure of his government, that they are socialists first and foremost, despite the fact that the country is very much communist. Communism and its spread have always been a major concern of the U.S., especially in a powerful country like China (Xi 2017).

The Bureau of East Asian and Pacific Affairs of the U.S. Department of State created a fact sheet in 2018 on China (U.S. Department of State2 2018). The Bureau discusses the foreign and economic relations between the U.S. and China as well as the assistance that the U.S. continues to provide to that nation. The U.S. has a goal of progressing its relationship with China through ending disagreements about its territorial claims in the South China Sea and the country's lack of human rights for its people. The Bureau takes note of China's progression in the world's economy, as it is now the third largest market for exported goods. The U.S. is working towards decreasing the trade deficit in goods with China in order to protect American workers from this country's unfair practices (U.S. Department of State 2 2018).

Researcher Joseph Nye Jr. at Harvard University has published his beliefs on China's economic growth and the possible threat that they pose to U.S. economic dominance. While he finds that China has not shown as much progress on individual economic growth compared to the country's overall economic power, they still pose a threat in the next two decades. He also recognizes that economic strength is important, but military dominance can shift the hands of power. This is where Nye sees China invested more in order to keep up with American superiority. However, he does not see the shifting of power happening anytime soon, with China's economic boom gradually slowing down and the superiority of that the American military possesses (Nye 2019).

On June 18 of 2018, President Donald Trump issued a statement regarding the U.S. trade with China. The President mentioned that the Chinese went against Section 301 of the Trade Act of 1974, by continuing their unfair practices such as acquiring American intellectual property and technology. China is predicted to "raise tariffs on $50 billion worth of U.S. exports" (Trump 2018). The President recognizes China's determination to keep the U.S. in a weaker position regarding trade. The United States has added an additional tariff on $200 billion worth of Chinese goods as retribution for its threatening actions. President Trump reinforces that if it continues to threaten American workers and companies, the U.S. will continue to increase the tariffs on Chinese goods (Trump 2018).

Speaking to the Hudson Institute on October 4th, 2018, Vice President Mike Pence echoed Trump's grievances with China's trade practices but took significant steps in detailing and denouncing China's coercion of nations by recognizing Taiwan's independence. He says that "And since last year, the Chinese Communist Party has convinced three Latin American nations to sever ties with Taipei and recognize Beijing. These actions threaten the stability of the Taiwan Strait – and the U.S. of America condemns these actions" (Hudson Institute 2018). China's growth has given them the ability to influence foreign nations in order to gain more power, including exerting more pressure on Taiwan to conform back to Beijing's control. The U.S. continues to honor the Taiwan Relations Act which dictates the relationship between Taiwan and the U.S. despite it going against Chinese interests (Hudson Institute 2018).

The Joint Strategic Plan (JSP) for the fiscal years 2018-2022 states China as a re-emergence of great power of global competition "which directly challenge the international order based on democratic norms, respect for human rights and peace" (Joint Strategic Plan 2018). With China's increasing economic power since the early 2000s, they have been looking for many ways to protect their rising power and increase their sphere of influence. "China seeks to increase their influence in the Indo Pacific Region" (Joint Strategic Plan 2018). China accomplishes this sphere of influence by creating artificial islands in the South China Sea and arming them with anti-air missile guidance systems and transgressing norms of cyberspace (JSP 2018).

In the Summary of the National Defense Strategy (NDS) of the United States of America, China is named specifically as the primary strategic competitor of the United States. The NDS cites China's predatory economic practices in its attempts to coerce its neighbors along with its militarized posturing in the South China Sea as significant threats to U.S. hegemony in the Indo-Pacific region. These aggressive actions in the Indo-Pacific periphery along with China's growing cyber capabilities paint a clear picture of China's attempt to undermine U.S. strategic interests. Consequently, the NDS specifies that a long-term strategic competition with China is one of the principal priorities of the Defense Department. To gain the advantage in this strategic competition, the NDS outlines several strategies for keeping the Indo-Pacific region stable and prosperous, namely strengthening existing alliances with strategic partners in the region as well as forging new bilateral agreements to deter further Chinese aggression.

Scholar Yuen Foong Khong (2019, 121) highlights the different types of power that can provide a country advantage over another. He specifically analyzes the hierarchy of power between the U.S. and China, and how there has been a shift in recent years directing more world power to Asia. Furthermore, he looks at which powers can provide the most resources, choosing economic power, military power, and soft power as the three largest contributors to influence changes. His claims power resources give credence to the D.I.M.E. (diplomacy, information, military, and economic) elements; this chapter focuses on military and economics. He acknowledges that China has made incredible leaps in both of these categories but argues that there is no way to measure the real power of a country and their threat level without bias or outliers. Khong's (2019, 138) analysis does, however, predict a power struggle in the coming decades with China rapidly approaching the U.S. hegemonic position and the transference of power from West to East.

Finally, a comprehensive report to Congress was created by the Office of the Secretary of Defense, detailing the military capabilities, developments, and limitations of China's combined military forces. The report provides an extensive look at China's military doctrine as well as refreshing the reader on past, present and potential future operations carried out by China's military. In addition to providing context and analysis to certain Chinese disputed areas, the report also looks at China's military in relation to its neighbors, most notably Taiwan and North Korea (Office of the Secretary of Defense 2018).

Given the literature review above, this chapter focuses on the following two research questions and they are: (1) How is China using its military and economic capabilities in the context of YIRTM (York Intelligence Red Team Model) to weaken the U.S. position as the world's sole hegemony? And (2) why is China using its military and economic capabilities in the context of YIRTM to weaken the U.S. position as the world's sole hegemony?

LOGIC MODEL

To forecast a situation that might occur, a logic model was used to analyze the four instruments of national power through the dimensions of diplomacy, information, military, and economics (D.I.M.E.). The D.I.M.E. is a method used by the intelligence community assessing national power of a country. President Trump has brought certain nations to the forefront in his NSS, including the People's Republic of China (PRC) and their recent activities. Since the release of the NSS, it has revealed that China is making economical leaps and using their economic prowess to spread their influence not only in surrounding nations but nations far out into the African continent. Such economic and military capabilities have continued to advance, which is a physical threat to enemies of China. These issues are directly tied in to the D.I.M.E. instruments.

An additional qualitative assessment method used was the York Intelligence Red Team Model (YIRTM). As depicted in Figure 1, those linear relationships among the variables of threats were further investigated. Additionally, this model also provided how the U.S. could best deal with those threats.

The YIRTM depicts the strategic direction of an entity, and the shaped outcome of the entity's actions that are stemmed from cumulated cause-effect on the United States. The leader within a state or the one who heads a non-state actor guides that entity to adversely affect the national security of the United States. At the core, the leadership could employ the D.I.M.E. instruments to implement tactics and techniques with the specific leader designating objectives to directly or indirectly affect the U.S. position.

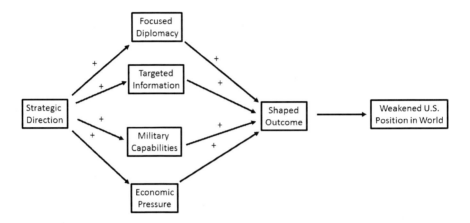

Figure 1. YIRTM.

Diplomacy is the first dimension a country may take. This dimension is most useful when a leader engages others in order to foster favorable conditions. Diplomacy entails not just the application to one specific country but also looks regionally or globally at the effects that decisions will have in surrounding countries and beyond to overtake the advancement of the interests of the United States. An example includes President Xi Jinping's speech at the 19th National Congress of the Communist Party of China (CPC); he applied diplomacy by discussing the socialism and its increasing effect on China's progress, in attempts to fully conform the country to the CPC. The prevalence of the CPC will put more emphasis on the "one country, two systems" principle, promoting China's jurisdiction over Hong Kong, Macao, and Taiwan, in turn, weakening the U.S.' ability to influence those regions economically or diplomatically (Xi 2017).

Information is the second vital dimension in today's world that the leadership of a country can use to influence its people's minds and views. Through targeted messaging and illegally exploiting other countries' sensitive information, a county can advance its own agenda. Leaders of a country can maximize targeted messaging to promote their point of view and impose influence over another country. A state can act like an adversary against another country by passing information through social media to its citizens, whether these messages support or denounce another entity's position. The Chinese government implemented a strict internet censorship by firewalls. Social media such as Google and its products have been driven out of the country. Largely state-controlled news media praise the supremacy of the Chinese Communist Party and President Xi Jinping (Shenyang Municipal Information Office 2018).

The military is another instrumental dimension of power that establishes the defense power for a nation through show of force, combat operations, and peacekeeping forces. A nation's armed forces protect a nation by leveraging its military capabilities, communications, intelligence, and surveillance systems. To ensure that a country is ahead in the capabilities of one's armed forces, a country should maintain a balance of technological advances and pull from the strength of its manpower. China is increasing their military presence in the South China Sea and is allegedly committing harmful cyber-attacks, threatening the position of the U.S. in the world. With their booming economy, China is able to invest millions of Renminbi into new technology and increasing the number of its military personnel. China currently has the highest quantity of active soldiers in the world, amounting to nearly one million more than the United States. In U.S. currency, China has increased their military spending by almost nine times since the early 1990s and they are continuing to push more money into their military capabilities (Khong 2019).

The economic component is the last strategic tool of power used by a country to influence other nations and non-state actors. By leveraging a state's domestic markets, trade policies and financial investments, countries are able to shape the geopolitical landscape to their own designs all without firing a single bullet. Factor in the globalized nature of economics in the 21st century and one begins to understand that countries who strategically utilize their economy as a soft power tool can exert great influence on the world stage to enact the changes they desire.

METHODOLOGY

Data used came from unclassified secondary open sources. To better guarantee data quality, triangulation was employed as data quality control (Remler and Van Ryzin 2010).

According to Creswell (2008), the strength of qualitative techniques is to explore in-depth understanding of the relationships among variables. Through deliberate rigorous research designs, researchers can gain granularity into the meaningful interpretation of data (Creswell 2008). One can find supporting data regarding this section in Annex A.

Contemporary research has underscored the relevance of use of secondary data (Remler & Van Ryzin 2010, 180). Since this data is readily available in the public domain and is inexpensive, researchers and practitioners alike can acquire this kind of data without too many difficulties to leverage the information for the purpose of conducting research (Remler & Van Ryzin 2010, 180). This study utilizes only secondary data with regards to China where this type of data has an advantage in cross-sectional designs.

The specific model used as a balance for data sources was the Federal Qualitative Secondary Data Case Study Triangulation Model, depicted in Figure 2 (Weaver 2015). The model shows three main document components that were used to arrive at results. The first of these includes plans and systems. This component looks at what is readily in existence today and the premise focuses on what tactics, techniques, and procedures (TTPs) that have been used by others thus far against the United States. Plans look to secondary data sources to see what has been identified in the U.S. to protect against a country as well as information on those plans that are in existence and directed at the U.S. and its national security establishment. It is through knowing what is codified that those conducting research can delve into the intent behind how one can leverage the economic and military powers to their advantage. Systems look deeper into procedures and/or capabilities that exist to initiate actions towards the United States. A subcomponent of this is used to assess the outcomes achieved to date and looks at the continuance of vulnerabilities that exist with regards to the infrastructure in the United States. Through this first component of the model one can get a better feel for what is in the realm of the possible by state and non-state actors against the U.S. as well gaining insight into what infrastructure security measures that are being used by the U.S. to protect against existential threats.

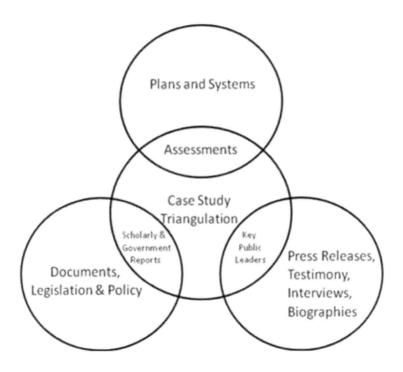

Figure 2. Federal Qualitative Secondary Data Case Study Triangulation Model.

A second component of this model turns to documents, legislation and policy to more succinctly understand the threat and the types of exploitation and attacks that have occurred in this country. It considers other written sources and delves deeper into government reports and peer reviewed publications published over the last five years to better orient in on results. Generally, this component of the Federal Qualitative Secondary Data Case Study Triangulation Model moves beyond sources that lack academic rigor like news reports and turns to more credible sources of information for raw data. More specifically, a multitude of sources were utilized and included such reports generated by the Government Accountability Officer, the Congressional Research Service, the Congressional Budget Office, books on China's economy, as well as peer refereed articles like those published by journals. Many of these sources also contained detailed information on China's military movements and some of their specific equipment. These written sources provide an understanding of current capabilities and threats confronting the U.S. and the subsequent assessment will look at synthesizing these themes.

The final component gravitates around orally generated accounts to further lead to a balance in the triangulation process. This includes subsets like official press releases on exploitation attempts and attacks, testimony (before Congress), public interviews and biographical accounts. Likewise, the process turns to key leader statements and the messaging coming from those both inside the government of the U.S., as well as other prominent figures from potential adversarial states and non-state actors. Sources particularly look to official transcripts of testimony conducted in Congress by economic experts, official press releases by Defense Department personnel and professionals working in the intelligence community, in addition to key interviews of economic experts, defense sector employees, and intelligence careerists.

Validity is a primary concern with all academic research. Accordingly, validity considers two things. Specifically, variable checks were conducted. These included efforts to ensure that the variables measured what they were supposed to measure (Jaeger 1993, 384). Construct validity procedures, according to Jaeger (1993, 80) are subjective, so these researchers used peer reviewed articles to corroborate findings in this study.

Face validity, according to Creswell (2008), considers whether or not something inherently makes sense. Likewise, face validity techniques in this research evaluated the logic model, variable directionality and purpose to ensure that what was presented was not counterintuitive to what one reasonably considers when looking at impacts. As was stated previously in the methodology section of this chapter, the authors used the logic model in order to frame the issue as to how state actor, China, might consider using the instruments of national power against the U.S. to weaken its strategic position on the world and why. Moreover, the Federal Qualitative Secondary Data Case Study Triangulation Model, which has been extensively used in other studies, afforded these researchers the opportunity to ensure a balance of raw data secondary sources to better interpret results.

Emphasis was also afforded to the topic of reliability. The researchers used consistency in their approach to similar projects to contribute to reliability (Creswell 2008, 190). Likewise, Remler and Van Ryzin (2010, 118) espouse the necessity of striving for consistency in measures when looking to achieve reliability when conducting research. Facilitating this was underscored by the consistent application of the D.I.M.E. as instruments of power and the use of the YIRTM and the Federal Qualitative Secondary Data Case Study Triangulation Model to analyze the textual data. Multiple sources were considered to corroborate information.

The intent is to use the models to drill down into the economic and military issues to better understand threats. This will better facilitate answers to the two prevailing research questions presented through this research project (Mattern et. al. 2014, 704). What is better to understand, is the various military and economic activities taking place in the world, who is most likely behind these, why they are occurring, and what might be next from China's perspective.

LIMITATIONS

As is the case with most studies that focus solely on secondary data, research using this type of data is limited in such areas as the variables explored and the temporal period considered. Generally, the scope of this research was limited to a three-year period from 2015 to August of 2018. More weight was assigned to data in the latter years due to the relevance as it pertains to the future and because of the constantly evolving situation in the context of a globalized market. Though the variables in the YIRTM were selected, other influencers exist that could impact on the true value of the variables. Understandably, changes will arise, and findings might not be as relevant in recent past years as more contemporary data otherwise would.

Only intervening relationships were considered. It is possible that other moderators could have an impact on the interpretation of results. These could include the likes of legacy trade agreements, treaties, sophistication of technology, and more. Forthcoming studies might also consider these to build upon the results of this study.

Likewise, as is the case with all qualitative research, it is difficult to generalize beyond the study at hand. The analysis of data and the results focus solely on the actions of China in particular as it applies to specific actors mentioned in the study.

Other weaknesses from secondary data emanate from the implementation of a cross-sectional design. Due to the reliance on secondary data, it is often difficult for one to understand whether bias existed from how the data was originally collected (Cross-Sectional 2012). Challenges can also spring up regarding cross-sectional design when interpreting results in part based on bias issues and the lack of full inclusion of all relevant events (Cross-Sectional 2012). Primary sources were not considered, and these include such techniques as interviews, personal observations, focus groups, and surveys. Though excluded, future studies might consider these research techniques to either reconstruct the study or to complement its findings. Provided that one understands that no research is a complete panacea, results can still be useful. Moreover, as additional information becomes available, results from this project can be used in confirmatory research or in a contributory effort to help expand on efforts looking at China as a major threat in the context of the YIRTM.

Another weakness is due to the lack of available information directly coming from the studied country as Chinese government exercises censorship and tight control of outflowing information. With the internet, information on the website for government stance maybe seen as political propaganda and specifically targeting an audience and therefore the neutrality of the data can and should be questioned. In addition, lack of Chinese language skill may also prevent direct data acquisition.

ANALYSIS

By using the YIRTM and the Federal Qualitative Secondary Data Case Study Triangulation Model, the data collected, shown in Annex A, assisted in the systematic analysis on what China is doing. Specifically actions looked to see what would weaken the United States' dominant role on global stage.

The diplomacy instrument is one that China has been slowly growing into, becoming more adept in its use over time. Although it has been an isolationist country in its more recent history, China has been slowing increasing its spread of influence to the surrounding nations. President Xi Jinping is currently the leader of the Communist Party of China and is using his large base of followers and a strong grip on his government to push his agenda outward. With China's economic capabilities, they have been using funds to bolster their reputation and garner support. Specifically, they have been contributing billions of dollars into African infrastructure and developing ports in the South China Sea to expand influence. This nation has been actively pushing U.S. trade out of the South China Sea and has recently turned away a U.S. warship from entering the Hong Kong port (NSS 2017). The warship was carrying arms for the Taiwanese, but China refuses to acknowledge them as a sovereign nation and considers them to still be a province. The U.S. support of Taiwan is a direct offense against the Chinese, which has been another motivator for President Xi Jinping to undermine U.S. power. The greatest threat through diplomatic means is their interference in South China Sea, limiting the amount of trade ships entering and leaving the area.

China's new foreign policy is being spearheaded by the CPC and entails becoming more "involved" with the affairs of other nations to emerge as a more global power, much like the United States. With President Donald Trump refocusing U.S. affairs and concerns internally, China is looking to fill the gap left behind in the Pacific region (Swaine 2017). With waning U.S. power, the CPC sees a rebalancing of world powers and a turn towards bipolarity instead of unipolarity. Being considered a world power comes with many perks that China wants to use to bolster themselves even higher in the world's hierarchy. These perks include more international influence, sway over smaller countries, and a stronger influencer in international organizations like the United Nations.

The importance of information is important and useful as China uses it in a plethora of ways to achieve dominance over their adversaries. The snatching/procurement of intellectual property is a major way this country is increasing access to information and to expand its economy by compressing research and development (R & D) timelines by acquiring blueprints for key items manufactured by other countries. Along with the isolation of its own people, its state-owned news stations play a major role in spreading its influence in and out of its region.

The procurement of new advances technologically, economically, and militarily not only stem from their own R & D efforts but mainly from the taking of intellectual property of the many governments that have a stake in China's economy. This poses a threat to America where, "Every year, competitors such as China steal U.S. intellectual property valued at hundreds of billions of dollars" (NSS 2018). This method of gaining innovative advances has strengthened China where instead of investing large sums of money into R & D, they are able to minimize timelines to produce goods of comparable quality to what other nations are manufacturing. They can take this property due to the USA amending section 301 in the World Trade Organization which "was amended in 1984 to authorize the president to impose trade sanctions against countries that failed adequately to protect intellectual property rights" (Harper 2018). This leads to the U.S. practicing intellectual protection unlike China where their policy is less strict due to them not following this clause. This system causes harm to the U.S. economic system because some U.S. goods are copied and subsequently manufactured and sold thereby reducing the American economic profit and revenue. Examples include the two-wheel self-balancing scooters (Segways), paint white (titanium white), and wind turbine software.

China's new isolation of its own people and its state provide the perfect climate for information safe keeping. Unlike America and its freedom of flow of information where it is easy to find recent news and what is going on in the country, as well as what the nation's goals are, such as the National Security Strategy, and Join Strategic Plan, China conversely, isn't as forthcoming with its recent government agenda. This leads the U.S. to dig deeper into what China is doing causing them to expend resources. The use of China's state sponsored news is a way where China is able to promote its Communist Party to everyday national and international viewers.

Conventionally, the instrument of power most understood by the defense establishment and those that comprise the National Security Council is the military. Under normal circumstances, the use of this element of power could include show of force exercises, humanitarian relief support, peacekeeping forces, peace enforcement missions and combat operations. However, while Chinese military capabilities are ostensibly used for the goal of security and protection of the homeland, Chinese military development show inclinations to create a military that has parity with what one would consider as a great power.

As outlined in the Annual Report to Congress regarding Chinese military and security developments, "In early 2017, China promulgated a White Paper on China's Policies on Asia Pacific Security Cooperation, placing this strategy in the context of China's development interests. It stresses the need for a People's Liberation Army to be able to conduct expeditionary operations and other activities to defend and secure growing Chinese national interests overseas from 'destabilizing and uncertain factors'" (Office of the Secretary of Defense 2018). To that end, the Chinese military doctrine and strategy focuses on creating a blue water navy with the power projection capabilities to secure China's interests, both in its territorial waters and beyond. The construction and fielding of aircraft carriers is integral to the creation of a navy capable of power projection. The ability to secure air supremacy anywhere around world will afford China serious leverage in global foreign affairs. Consequently, this explains why China's Type 001 *Liaoning* aircraft carrier has been at the forefront of its naval expansion plan. Though the Annual Report to Congress on China concedes that the *Liaoning* is far less capable than a U.S. aircraft carrier, it does note that the training and lessons learned from its maneuvers in the South China Sea will play an essential role in shaping modern Chinese naval doctrine (Office of the Secretary of Defense 2018).

With these goals of power projection and a blue water navy to undermine existing U.S. hegemony in East Asia made clear, the limitations and areas of difficulty for these plans can more easily be discerned. China's breakneck economic growth has necessitated the development of a military capable of defending Chinese interests - interests that are increasingly being developed in places outside of China's borders. Investments in East Africa as well as leased ports along the Indian Ocean are just a few of these strategic interests that China must commit military resources to maintain and defend. Perhaps the most significant roadblock in this path towards power projection is Taiwan, or more specifically, the U.S. guarantee of de facto Taiwanese independence. Though the U.S. has committed itself to a "One China" policy and has recognized the People's Republic of China as the sole legitimate government of China, it still has extensive informal political, economic and military ties with the Republic of China's government on Taiwan. The "One China" policy is China's diplomatic policy since its founding in 1949 which states that there is only one China; if a country recognizes the PRC, then it cannot have formal diplomatic relations with Taiwan which is RC. So, when a country establishes the relationship with China, its formal diplomatic relation with Taiwan would automatically be ended. During the Nixon Administration in 1972, when he and his administration were exploring possible ways to defreeze the relations between the U.S. and PRC, the U.S. then recognized the "One China" policy and officially ended its agreement with Taiwan. However, the U.S. still uses the China-Taiwan dynamic as a leveraging tool against the PRC, specifically in the form of commercial and military guarantees that all but assure Taiwan's continued autonomy. As detailed in the National Security Strategy, "We will maintain our strong ties with Taiwan in accordance with our 'One China' policy, including our commitments under the Taiwan Relations Act to provide for Taiwan's legitimate defense needs and deter coercion" (NSS 2017).

This means that while on paper, Taiwan is part of the greater Peoples Republic of China, Taiwan is a free and independent nation with the full backing of the U.S. and her allies in the region. Not only does Taiwan's strategic position off the coast of China pose a significant buffer to any Chinese naval strategy in the region but rather American military relations with the island threaten the very existence of the PRC, as Taiwan could be used a staging ground for American military operations against China should conflict between the two countries arise. Though the Taiwanese Strait spans just 110 miles, American naval and air supremacy in the region makes any plans for securing the island via a military intervention unlikely under current Chinese military capabilities. With incorporation of Taiwan back into the greater PRC, a staple of Chinese foreign policy, the prioritization of a blue-water navy by the military is China's way of circumventing existing U.S. military advantages in the region. Should Chinese naval development continue, and the People's Liberation Army Navy become a blue-water navy then it could pose a direct challenge to U.S. naval presence in the region. Washington would then have to decide whether to commit further resources to maintain the status quo in East Asia or accept coexistence with the ascendant PLAN, neither option being ideal given the increased risk of hostilities breaking out between the two nations.

As was previously mentioned, China has begun expanding into the South China Sea in the form of investments and the creation of artificial islands. Though these expansions into the South China Sea are ostensibly China's development of this land they claim sovereignty over, the construction and expansion of these islands has been almost entirely militaristic in nature. Within Annex A, one will find evidence that supports China's military capabilities and its plan to gain control of the South China Sea trade via militarized islands and contesting American global naval supremacy. The National Security Strategy outlined these territorial ambitions and their consequences, saying, "China has mounted a rapid military modernization campaign designed to limit U.S. access to the region and provide China a freer hand there. China presents its ambitions as mutually beneficial, but Chinese dominance risks diminishing the sovereignty of many states in the Indo-Pacific" (NSS 2017). The South

China Sea is not only important for U.S. allies in the region, but also for global trade as a whole. The sea and its chokepoint, the Strait of Malacca, account for roughly $3.4 trillion dollars of annual international shipping trade, according to the Congressional Research Office (CFR 2018). The sea is also the main transit point for oil and other natural resources for U.S.' allies like Japan and South Korea. It is for these reasons that the U.S. seeks to maintain stability in the South China Sea and the militarization of this key waterway puts that stability in jeopardy. China's construction of air strips and naval ports on the Spratly Islands as well as their artificial islands gives Beijing a decisive military advantage in the South China Sea as the islands essentially act as unsinkable aircraft carriers. If China were to continue the militarization of the South China Sea, it could dictate the terms of trade leaning more towards its own design and control the economic chokepoint to East Asia. Doing so would not only nullify any existent U.S. military advantages in the region but also weaken U.S. allies like Japan and South Korea, whose supply chains would then be at the mercy of Beijing (NDSC November 2018). While China can't keep the U.S. completely out of the South China Sea, they can seriously hinder efforts. It will only be in the coming decades that China could hope to completely exclude the U.S. (Nye 2019, 73).

Perhaps the most obvious and forthright approach China has taken to undermining the U.S. hegemony in both East Asia and the world has been through their economic maneuvering and posturing. In an attempt to gain an advantage over the U.S., China is investing greatly in developing regions of the world such as the South China Sea and East Africa (NSS 2017). Along with investing and influencing regions, China has shown a continuous pattern of undermining the open economic system of the U.S. to gain an unfair advantage. In President Trump's statement regarding U.S. trade with China, it was determined that China is raising tariffs on $50 billion worth of U.S. exports to keep the U.S. in a perpetually disadvantaged state. China directly violated Section 301 of the Trade Act of 1974 to eliminate commerce barriers yet seems to not care. Its resilience has pushed President Trump to continue to raise tariffs against China until the country adopts fair trade practices (Trump 2018). China's unfair practices are a strategy to overtake the U.S. in the global economy. It has the advantage of a large population to bolster its economic success, but as recent data has shown, China's upward climb is slowing down.

Consequently, China has been raising tariffs on U.S. exports to hurt American businesses. Its use of investments, inducements and penalties in the South China Sea, as well as the modernization of the military in the region, limits the United States' influence in the area. China is using military threats to persuade sovereign states to agree to its agenda to put the U.S. in an unfair position. The campaign is limiting U.S. freedom of movement in the South China Sea region which is endangering the free flow of trade, the sovereignty of surrounding nations, and regional stability (NSS 2017). The Human Rights Watch report on China mentions the country's harsh treatment and the detainment of human rights defenders. Police officers are in the position to torture those that are detained and deny them the right to a lawyer. Xi's drive to spread communism is prevalent in Hong Kong as its courts called for the disqualification of pro-democracy politicians (World Report 2017). China is directly infringing on the sovereignty and stability of surrounding nations, limiting the fight for democracy of those nations.

Beyond the East Asian region, China's economic influence has been felt globally, especially in East Africa where they have invested considerable resources and manpower. It is rapidly expanding on this continent, becoming Africa's largest trade partner in 2009. China's economy presently has a heavy reliance on coal and oil, leading them to use Africa to secure those resources. Although China has a very strong presence on the continent, its exploitation of the resources is not allowing the local economies in Africa to build themselves up (CFR 2017). By investing in this region, China is diminishing the United States' influence in the developing continent by destabilizing the local African economic systems with the influx of Chinese workers and strengthening the Chinese economic structure. This influence in the region will take Africa's local businesses and natural resources away, which could spawn illegal migration and extremism in the region, leading to instability (NSS 2017). Economically, it can be predicted that there is not yet anything to fear from China in the next few years. It is when analysts look 30 or 40 years into the future that the threat of China's dominance becomes a danger. The U.S. needs to keep an eye on the movement of the Chinese economy and their involvement in more foreign nations. There has been the start of a shifting of power towards the East and China will take full advantage of it (Khong 2019, 139).

FINDINGS AND CONCLUSION

China is a threat that has been and will be both extremely unpredictable and seemingly unstoppable for the foreseeable future. The advancement and expansion of their military along with the breakneck speed at which their economic power has grown has allowed them to far outpace most other nations, and they continue to directly challenge the U.S. position as the world's sole hegemony.

When looking at the first research question, these authors analyzed how China is using their military and economic capabilities to undermine the United States' role as the world's sole hegemony within the context of the YIRTM model. By analyzing the means and methods by which China is seeking to challenge America's dominance on the global stage, one can better assess the threats and possible challenges that China will pose in the immediate future. The South China Sea is of significant importance to not only China's military goal of global dominance but also to its economic growth. Beijing has taken considerable steps in creating a permanent and deliberate presence in the sea in an effort to counter the existing U.S. primacy in the region. In short, China is using its economic might in conjunction with its expanding military in an attempt to dictate trade in the South China Sea to its advantage. Given the increasingly globalized nature of today's economy, economic dominance will not only solidify China's chance at becoming the dominant power of East Asia but will also facilitate its direct challenge to the existing United States' global hegemony.

When looking at the second research question and while analyzing the reasons and motives for China's increased interest in becoming the world's sole hegemony, one must look back to the YIRTM and their military advances and economic progress. China's particular goals are that of a nation unwilling to accept a full peaceful coexistence with either the U.S. or her allies. These most recent economic expansions could inhibit the U.S. from accessing the developing areas which may be problematic in times of crisis and puts China in a position of power in those regions, usurping the United States. These efforts in the developing regions are supplemented by the intense ongoing trade war between the two competing powers. The inequitable relationship that Beijing is forcing upon Washington will lead to an imposition of tariffs by both sides, negatively affecting American-based businesses and industries. With the American-based industries weakening, China can step in and fill the manufacturing vacuum left behind. Given the increasing importance of the Indo-Pacific region and the extensive U.S. investments in the area, China need only secure its position as a dominant regional power there through the use of combined military and economic efforts to severely undermine the United States and its position as the world's sole hegemony. As Chinese foreign involvements and its aggressive posturing increase, so does the likelihood of China's ascension to the position of the dominant world power.

Two elements of the YIRTM model that are less prevalent in this research were information and diplomacy. Information is a difficult subject to investigate, with the Chinese government having nearly complete control over what leaves and enters the country on the internet. It can be hypothesized that what little information that is allowed to leave China is propaganda or construed to make China look more powerful. President Xi Jinping and his advisors are very careful about what information is conveyed from the decision makers in Beijing to the Chinese public and the world at large, providing speeches that have little to no real substance. In addition to this utter lack of transparency on the part of the Politburo, there is an intense grip on what the Chinese media is allowed to report and disseminate to the public, with every news organization in the country being under the state's jurisdiction in one form or another. Under the Trump Administration, tensions remain between countries, exacerbated by both sides' unwillingness to back down from their aggressive positions. This means that soft diplomacy is crucial, as to not upset what tentative treaties and ongoing negotiations are in place now.

ANNEX A

How/Why	D.I.M.E	Source	Source Type	Date	Page (if applicable)
An overview on the strengths of China from the viewpoint of the CIA.	D.I.M.E.	The World Factbook	Government Document	2018	N/A
Dr. Yuen Foong Khong looks at what types of power have the greatest chance of instigating change and which ones China has been advancing in. He also investigated the possible power shift form the West to the East.	M.E.	International Affairs	Scientific Journal	January 1, 2019	N/A
By China investing billions into developing economies, the U.S. infrastructure is being threatened.	D.I.M.E	National Security Strategy of the U.S.	Government Document	December 2017	8, 38, 46, 53
China seeks to challenge U.S. economic dominance in Europe and Asia by creating extensive overland and sea infrastructure investments throughout Eurasia.	M.E.	Foreign Affairs of Australia	Government Document	2016	N/A
President Xi Jinping is attempting to make China fully follow the CPC, Communist Party of China, further putting the country under his control. The "China Dream" and their attempts to strengthen their efforts in unifying China.	D.I.	President Xi Jinping	Speech	October 18, 2017	31-36, 54-63
China's economic growth is on the surface more terrifying than the numbers suggest according to Dr. Joseph Nye Jr. but China should still be a major concern militarily and the U.S. should be	M.E.	International Affairs	Scientific Journal	January 1, 2019	N/A

Annex A. (Continued)

How/Why	D.I.M.E	Source	Source Type	Date	Page (if applicable)
concerned for the far out future.					
Region through militarization of the South China Sea, disobeying cyberspace norms by committing cyber-attacks, supporting North Korea, and committing trade and human rights violations.	I.M.E.	Joint Strategic Plan (2018-2022)	Government Document	February 2018	30
China is the third largest export market for the United States. The U.S. is the largest export market to China. U.S. wants to protect Americans from China's unfair economic actions.	E.	Bureau of East Asian and Pacific Affairs	Government Document	August 22, 2018	N/A
China's major political party has been slowly taking over the politics of China, to the point of other political parties fleeing the country to Taiwan.	I.	Opposing Viewpoints Online Collection	Book	Jan. 25, 2017	N/A
China is strengthening its nuclear weapons and space capabilities, as well as its presence in South Asia, Africa, and several other regions.	M.E.	National Defense Authorization Act	Government Document	2018	11
China went against Section 301 of the Trade Act of 1974 by raising tariffs on $50 billion of U.S. exports in order to keep the United States at a disadvantage.	E.	The White House	Press Release	June 18, 2018	N/A

How/Why	D.I.M.E	Source	Source Type	Date	Page (if applicable)
China's increasing influence in Africa strengthens the Chinese economy while destabilizing Africa and decreasing the U.S. influence.	E.	Albert	Government Document	July 12, 2017	N/A
In-depth research on China's foreign affairs and policies in the upcoming years.	D.E.	Swaine	Research Article	October 16, 2017	N/A
United States Vice-President Mike Pence delivers a speech on China's aggressive economic, diplomatic and military posturing against the U.S. in recent years	D.M.E.	Mike Pence	Speech	October 4, 2018	N/A
Commissioned by the United States Armed Services Committee, this report highlights the weaknesses and challenges the U.S. would face if put into conflict scenario with China and/or Russia	D.I.M.E.	National Defense Strategy Commission	Government Document	November 14, 2018	6

Methodologically, the authors found that the Federal Qualitative Secondary Data Case Study Triangulation Model and the York Intelligence Red Team Model (YIRTM) were valuable models to use in order to analyze information on state actors. The Federal Qualitative Secondary Data Case Study Triangulation Model was helpful in beginning stages of research as the researchers investigated press releases, testimonies, and federal documents for reliable sources of information. The YIRTM was helpful in helping answer "how" and "why" questions using four variables predicated on the instruments of national power. Some other findings that one could have used would take into account the culture of the state actor to improve the understanding of what a culture is like. This background information helps illuminate ideas on the role of the average citizen well as the government's impact on the culture to understand if they have significant or little influence. Lastly, China has grown technologically; therefore, it would have been beneficial to look at this as a possible fifth variable and future research might want to consider this one.

In summation, through China's adeptness at using the economic and military instruments is quite effective, China has become a global power that competes against the U.S. by its comprehensive steps towards weakening the U.S. position as the world's sole hegemony. The dangers that a dominant China would pose is a significant threat to U.S. global supremacy, it is understandable why Washington and her allies view China's rising power as the rival for hegemonic status.

REFERENCES

Babones, Salvatore. 2018. Leader for life: Xi Jinping strengthens hold on power as China Communist Party ends term limits. Accessed on December 15, 2018. https://salvatorebabones.com/leader-for-life-xi-jinping-strengthens-hold-on-power-as-china-communist-party-ends-term-limits/.

CIA. 2018. The World Factbook: CHINA. Accessed on December 11, 2018. https://www.cia.gov/library/publications/the-worldfactbook/geos/ch.html

Council on Foreign Relations. 2017, July 12. China in Africa. Accessed on December 15, 2018. https://www.cfr.org/backgrounder/china-africa.

Council on Foreign Affairs. 2017. *Annual Report 2017 Current Affairs Report*. Accessed on December 15, 2018. https://www.cfr.org/sites/default/files/pdf/CFR_Annual_Report_2017_0_0.pdf.

Creswell, John W. 2008. *Research Design; Qualitative, Quantitative, and Mixed Methods Approaches*. Thousand Oaks, CA: SAGE Publications.

Cross-Sectional. 2012. *Cross-Sectional Studies*. Accessed on December 10, 2018 http://www.healthknowledge.org.uk/public-healthtextbook/research-methods/1a-epidemiology/cs-as-is/.

Gale, a Cengage Company. 2016. *China - Opposing Viewpoints Online Collection*. Detroit, MI: Gale. Updated on January 25, 2017. Accessed on December 16th, 2018. http://link.galegroup.com/apps/doc/PC3010117166/OVIC?u=ycp_main&sid=OVIC&xid=7528714b.

Harper, Zachary. 2018. The Old Sheriff and the Vigilante: World Trade Organization Dispute Settlement and Section 301 Investigations into Intellectual Property Disputes. *Mississippi Law Journal*. Accessed on December 15, 2018. https://papers.ssrn.com/sol3/papers.cfm?abstract_id=3109842.

House – Armed Services. 2018, August 13. John S. McCain National Defense Authorization Act for Fiscal Year 2019 (United States, Congress, Armed Services). Congress. Accessed on October 23, 2018. https://www.congress.gov/bill/115th-congress/house-bill/5515/text.

Jaeger, Richard M. 1993. Statistics A Spectator Sport, 2nd Edition. *Sage Publications*. London, U.K.

Khong, Yuen F. 2019. Power as Prestige in World politics. *International Affairs*, 95(1), 119- 142. doi:10.1093/ia/iiy245.

Li, Chunding, Chuantian He, and Chuangwei Lin. 2018. Economic Impacts of the Possible China–US Trade War. *Emerging Markets Finance and Trade*, 54(7): 1557-1577. Accessed on October 26, 2018. https://www.

tandfonline.com/doi/full/10.1080/1540496X.2018.1446131?scroll=top&needAccess=true.

Mattern, Troy, John Felker, Randy Borum and George Bamford. 2014. Operational Levels of Cyber Intelligence. *International Journal of Intelligence and Counterintelligence.* 27(4): 702-719.

Nye, Joseph S. 2019. The Rise and Fall of American Hegemony from Wilson to Trump. *International Affairs, 95*(1), 63-80. doi:10.1093/ia/iiy212.

Office of the Secretary of Defense. 2018. Annual Report to Congress Military and Security Developments Involving the People's Republic of China 2018. 2018. Accessed on December 15, 2018. https://media.defense.gov/2018/Aug/16/2001955282/-1/-1/1/2018-CHINAMILITARY-POWER-REPORT.PDF

O'Rourke, Ronald. 2018. China's Actions in South and East China Seas: Implications for U.S. Interests—Background and Issues for Congress. Congressional Research Service. Accessed on October 23, 2018. https://fas.org/sgp/crs/row/R42784.pdf.

Pence, Mike. 2018, October 4. *Vice President Mike Pence's Remarks on the Administration's Policy Towards China October 4 Event.* Accessed on December 16, 2018. https://www.hudson.org/events/1610-vice-president-mike-pence-s-remarks-on-the-administration-s-policy-towards-china102018.

Remler, Dahlia K. and Gregg G. Van Ryzin. 2010. *Research Methods in Practice: Strategies for Description and Causation.* Thousand Oaks, CA: SAGE Publications.

Swaine, Michael D. 2017. *The 19th Party Congress and Chinese Foreign Policy.* Accessed on December 15, 2018 from http://carnegieendowment.org/2017/10/16/19th-party-congress-and-chinese-foreign-policy-pub-73432.

Shenyang Municipal Information Office. 2018, January 18. *World Report: Rights Trends in China.* Accessed on November 4, 2018. https://www.hrw.org/world-report/2018/country-chapters/china-and-tibet.

The White House. 2015. *National Security Strategy (NSS) 2015.* Accessed on October 20th, 2018. https://obamawhitehouse.archives.gov/sites/default/files/docs/2015_national_security_strategy_2.pdf.

The White House. 2017. *National Security Strategy (NSS) 2017.* Accessed on October 20th, 2018. https://www.whitehouse.gov/wp-content/uploads/2017/12/NSS-Final-12-18-2017-0905.pdf.

Trump, Donald. 2018. *Statement from the President Regarding Trade with China.* Accessed on October 23, 2018.https://www.whitehouse.gov/briefings-statements/statement-president-regarding-trade-china-2/.

U.S. Department of State, U.S. Agency for International Development. 2018, February. Joint Strategic Plan. Accessed on October 20, 2018. https://www.state.gov/documents/organization/277156.pdf.

U.S. Department of State2. 2018, August 22. U.S. Relations with China. Accessed on December 10, 2018. https://www.state.gov/r/pa/ei/bgn/18902.htm.

Wade, Geoff. 2017. *China's 'One Belt, One Road' initiative.* Accessed from https://www.aph.gov.au/About_Parliament/Parliamentary_Departments/Parliamentary_Library/pubs/BriefingBook45p/ChinasRoad.

Weaver, John M. 2015. The Department of Defense and Homeland Security Relationship: Hurricane Katrina through Hurricane Irene. *Journal of Emergency Management.* 12(3) 265-274.

Xi, Jinping. 2017, October 18. Secure a Decisive Victory in Building a Moderately Prosperous Society in All Respects and Strive for the Great Success of Socialism with Chinese Characteristics for a New Era. Address presented at 19th National Congress of the Communist Party of China in China, Beijing. Accessed on October 25th, 2018. http://www.xinhuanet.com/english/download/Xi_Jinping's_report_at_19th_CPC_National_Congress.pdf.

In: Global Intelligence Priorities
Editors: John Michael Weaver et al.
ISBN: 978-1-53615-836-6
© 2019 Nova Science Publishers, Inc.

Chapter 4

POSTMODERN IMPERIALISM: A QUALITATIVE ASSESSMENT OF THE AGGRESSIVE SPREAD OF RUSSIAN INFLUENCE

*Kyra Shoemaker, Mitchell Forrest,
Jennifer Ohashi and Rachele Tombolini*
York College, York, Pennsylvania, US

ABSTRACT

As President Trump entered the White House in January of 2017, he inherited a presidency that faced numerous world issues in the form of foreign and domestic threats. His National Security Strategy (NSS) drafted during his first year as president listed Russia, or the Russian Federation, as a political actor that must be continuously monitored while reducing their threat level to the national security of the United States. Taking an approach of a qualitative methodology, this study investigated those processes Russia has engaged in elevating its position as a world superpower using the four instruments of national power to weaken America's hegemony. Framed by using the logic model, this chapter concludes what, how, and why Russia's actions would weaken the United States' influence by examining the 2014-2018 period.

LITERATURE REVIEW

In the United States' National Security Strategy, the Russian Federation is specifically named as a direct "challenge to [United States] power, influence, and interests, attempting to erode [United States] security and prosperity" (Trump 2017). The Russian Federation is one of only four nations named as threats in the entire sixty-eight paged document alongside China, Iran, and North Korea. Some issues listed in the National Security Strategy are the use of information tools, such as cyber security, establishing spheres of influence near the Russian Federation's borders, weakening the relationship between the United States and its allies, and inciting a Eurasian conflict (Trump 2017). The Russian Federation is not the only topic covered in the National Security Strategy; the document also outlines areas of concern and plans to "protect the American people, the homeland, and the American way of life," "promote American prosperity," "preserve peace through strength," and "advance American influence" (Trump 2017).

Similar to the United States, the Russian Federation releases a National Security Strategy, which is the single most important government document revealing Russia's national security priorities and strategies. On December 31, 2015, Russia published The Russian Federation's National Security Strategy as a replacement for Russian Federation Presidential Edict 537 titled, "On the Russian Federation's National Security Strategy Through 2020," published back on May 12, 2009 (Russian Federation 2015). This document focuses on the economic, spiritual, cultural, military, and political health of the Russian Federation, providing a window into how Russia sees itself on the world stage, and how they intend to react to any actions taken by western countries in East European and North Asian nations. As a roadmap, this document guides Russia's domestic affairs and international relations. All actions taken by any Russian government organization has to emanate from the ideas held within its security strategy.

In the global energy sector, Russia has been active through the export of their energy reserves to negotiate favorable trade agreements with Belarus and Ukraine as mentioned in an article published in Energy Economics. Seventy-two percent (72%) of the world's natural gas deposits were located in the former Soviet Union and the Middle East. This study had been conducted in response to the realization that energy demands had been projected to rise by 200% between the years 1990 and 2035, starting a search for "cleaner" sources of energy than the traditional coal and oil (Nagayama & Horita 2014). In the study conducted by Nagayama and Horita (2014), they attempted to discover exactly how much a new pipeline would affect trade relations between the Russian Federation, Belarus, Ukraine, and Western Europe specifically Germany and Italy. The political strategic idea of the new pipeline was to bypass Belarus and Ukraine to lessen their bargaining power over the natural gas trade in Europe and allow the Russian Federation to deal more directly with the rest of Europe. From this study, it was discovered that the implementation of the new Nord Stream pipeline through the Baltic sea, bypassing Ukraine and Belarus, the amount of natural gas to reach Western Europe would increase by 12.94% while Belarus decreased by 3.8% and Ukraine decreased by 13.97% (Nagayama & Horita 2014). This pipeline is currently in progress, but it has effected, and will affect multiple trade agreements between the Russian Federation and the rest of Europe. This new pipeline is not the only tool the Russian Federation is using against its neighboring states. As stated in the Journal of Eurasian Studies, the Russian Federation is creating "price scissors" where they raise the price of natural gas for all consumers, but raise the prices even more for their perceived enemies (Newnham 2011). For example, the Russian Federation raised the price of natural gas for Belarus to $100 per thousand cubic meters (tcm), but Belarus cannot easily combat this or their price could be more than doubled to a price similar to what Georgia is paying (Newnham 2011). Energy dominance has become so critical to Russia's economic strategy that the government has invested in ice breaking carrier vessels which allow ships to navigate the Arctic Waterway in the dead of winter, as mentioned in the Wilson Quarterly (Brigham, 2017). The significance of this deep-winter construction project is that it shows how the Russian Federation is throwing its weight behind the energy market and showing that they will do just about anything to make it work.

Another means for Russia to enhance its economic standing in the world is through direct foreign investment in other nations. In an article in *Studies on Russian Economic Development*, Russia looks to invest money in development projects in direly poor countries of Africa and Asia (Kuznetsov 2016). The Institute of World Economy and International Relations (IMEMO) 2017 Forecast is a document that looks at most of the countries and regions of the world then compares their policies to see how effective they are and how they interact with other world powers. This paper was also useful in the analysis of Russian economic policy. It contained information about the BRICS (Brazil, Russia, India, China, and South Africa), an agreement among the countries to float money to one another in an attempt to influence world economies and power by passing money among countries which were deemed investment risks and were searching for any way to grow their economies (Dynkin, Baranovsky, Kobrinskaya, Machavariani, Afontsev, Kuznetsov, Shvydko, Utkin, Malysheva, Mikheev, Lukonin, Fedorovsky, Frumkin, Zhuraveva, Kuznetsov, Voda, Toganova, Devyakov & Shyshkina 2017). This document's importance is its comprehensive look at similar policies and economics from around the world, allowing these analysts a point from which to start their research.

The final way the Russian government seeks to expand their soft power economically is through investment in high-end real estate in the major markets in the United States, as mentioned in the International Journal of Housing Policy. In 2016, the Russian Federation's direct foreign investment was about $336 billion, with 20% of that being real estate, making the Russian Federation the second largest foreign direct investment economy (Budenbender & Golubchikov 2017). According to an article in *Environment and Planning*, Russia is able to use real estate as vehicle to maintain financial "liquidity" or portability, while avoiding real estate transfer fees and the payment of taxes in the United States by use of offshore monetary transfers to hide assets. When studied, non-residents found that they owned around 89 thousand real estate properties in New York City, with a rough fair market value of $80 billion, and around $2.5 million of residential purchases are made through shell companies (Fernandez, Hofman, & Aalbers 2016).

At the end of 2017, the Russian Federation released a ten-year plan depicting how the military plans to grow. This plan delineates the uses for 19 trillion rubles from 2018 to 2027 (PONARS 2017). The Russian Federation plans to have 14 total submarines, six Delta IV-class and eight Borei-class ballistic missile submarines (PONARS 2017). There are also plans in motion to develop a long-range cruise missile predicted to be able to deliver a nuclear payload up to 4,500 kilometers away (PONARS 2017). With the ground forces, there is a focus on research and development for a new Uragan and Tornado-S multiple launch rocket system. As for the air forces, there are plans for the acquisition of 10-12 new fighter jets of varying styles each year through 2027 (PONARS 2017).

Located at the conclusion of the literature review section is the collection of United States State Department press releases. Roughly, a dozen press releases derived from the United States' State Department provided these authors with an idea as to how the United States government officials view Russia's actions as harmful. Their disregard for human rights protections established by the North Atlantic Treaty Organization (NATO), is exemplified by their continued imprisonment of Ukrainian filmmaker Oleg Sentsov (United States State Department1 2018). In addition, the use of the United States' State Department publications is a near first-hand look at what has been occurring between the Russian Federation and the United States. As evidenced by a U.S. Department of Homeland Security press release, this details the U.S. Intelligence Community's new partnership with third parties, such as the Multi-State Information Sharing and Analysis Center to assess and combat the threat of Russia's cyber influence (U.S. Department of Homeland Security 2018). In research that is dominated by secondary data, it is essential to employ sources that come from as close to the original source as possible.

Using the information contained within this section, along with the research questions and logic model explained in later sections, these authors will explain the Russian Federation's attempt to become a word power once again.

RESEARCH QUESTIONS

Based on the literature review, the following research questions focus on the past five years, examine how the Russian Federation has been strengthening their military, economy, and political foothold as a state actor, and at the same time weaken the United States' hegemonic power. The two questions are:

Q1: What has Russia done to usurp the United States' standing as a world power? And why?

Q2: How would Russia be a threat to the United States' standing as a world power?

LOGIC MODEL

The framework used during this analysis is based on the four instruments that are indicative of national power. The four instruments of national power are diplomacy, information, military, and economic (known as D.I.M.E.). Russia's national power is the result of Russia's effective use of these instruments not only on its political positioning but to diminish the authority of competing state actors. In addition, as a means of providing an answer to the previously stated research questions for this chapter, these authors applied these instruments of national power vis-à-vis the York Intelligence Red Team Model (YIRTM) (See Figure 1). This logic model functions by referencing a single state or non-state entity and how, through the substantiation of the four instruments mentioned above, to reach the desired outcome.

Figure 1 begins with a given strategic direction of the actor that seeks to undermine or inhibit the well-being of another country. The authority of said actor often decides this strategic direction whether they act as a central government or as a prevailing ruling figure. When used for this qualitative assessment of Russia, the governing body that dictates the strategic direction is comprised of both the Russian Federation and its leader, Vladimir Putin. The leading entity will often construct a plan or system in which they shall exercise the different instruments of national power thus allowing one to examine the methods by which they plan to achieve their strategic goal.

The first of the D.I.M.E. instruments seen in Figure 1 pertains to focused diplomacy. Diplomacy, in its purest form, occurs when members and representatives of state or non-state actors converge to discuss how each respective actor can come to an agreement that results in the betterment of each state's situation. Among the four instruments of power that a nation can use, diplomacy is often viewed as the most convenient since, in most scenarios, political actors stand to lose far less concerning resources or military power should diplomacy negotiations result in no change to their current situation. One can see this instrument in Russian Foreign Minister Sergei Lavrov's extended phone conversation with United States Secretary of State Mike Pompeo and operates as an example of their utilization of diplomacy as both Russia and the United States would prefer that their relationship improve in the coming years through future dialogue and negotiations (United States Department of State 2 2018).

Information, while far more difficult to measure in a physical capacity when compared to the other instruments of power, this one can be seen as the most impactful and influential of the components in this logic mode (at the least cost). Targeted information acts as a crucial tool for any nation to respond to domestic and foreign issues. The baseline for any analysis of a national entity that may have malicious intentions is formed through discerning precisely what information the opposing force may currently possess and learning how they may use said information to inflict harm, and to what end their efforts may be attempting to reach. When referencing the information that Russia has equipped in the form of an instrument of national power one can refer to their National Security Strategy to provide insight into how Russia's information in the modern world influences what their plans may entail (Russian Federation 2015).

The instrument that is the most expensive and most perceivable component to the instruments of national power are military capabilities. While the application of military might is often viewed as an alternative to diplomacy if negotiations fail, the YIRTM logic model places military power as if it is used in tandem with the other factors in D.I.M.E.; one such military action observed by the Russian Federation includes its continuous possession and imposition of chemical weapons to discourage political actors from taking military action against them (United States Department of State 3 2018). Military capabilities of countries that are the subject of qualitative research can give researchers an idea as to how they may exercise that power and, concerning the Russian Federation, will be used to maintain a grip on their authority over foreign territories.

The final component of D.I.M.E. is economic pressure. The authority and prosperity of a state or non-state actor is measured through the factors that contribute to their overall economic status that may include looking at such issues as a nation's Gross Domestic Product (GDP) or the unemployment rate of the citizens of that country. In the case of Russia, their economic pressures from 2014 to the present can look at the impact of trade sanctions placed on them and what measures they are taking to acclimate to them. One such example showing their efforts towards economic resurgence are their interactions in the growth of the natural gas trade in Belarus (Energy Economics 2014).

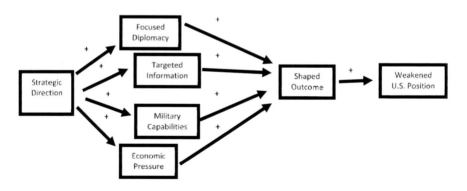

Figure 1. YIRTM.

As the factors of D.I.M.E. are dissected and applied, they will inevitably converge to formulate a single outcome, if it is the expected then the planned outcome is subject to scrutiny. The purpose of the use of the York

Intelligence Red Team Model in this analysis is to show how the four instruments of national power have been working collectively towards a single desired goal of reducing the role of the United States as a leading world power. This is done while simultaneously improving Russia's role in the ever-evolving politics of the modern world. Should Russia's use of these instruments continue to strengthen and evolve, the national security of the United States could be in danger as America's power is called into question.

METHODOLOGY

The methodology used in this research is a qualitative one looking at Russia as a case study. The Federal Qualitative Secondary Data Case Study Triangulation Model was used to organize the data collected. One of the most challenging parts of conducting a qualitative research is to avoid bias as much as possible. One way to avoid or reduce bias is to include sources that ensure diversity in the types of information collected for analysis. Data collected for use in this chapter came solely from open-source secondary information points that are available to the public regardless of security clearance or intended use.

The techniques of a qualitative assessment and analysis were used as a means of discerning Russia's threats to national security as well as their aspirations, as stated in their 2015 National Security Strategy (Russian Federation 2015). This study's specific focus was on Russia and Putin's exercises that jeopardize the security of the United States and its allies utilizing analytical models such as the York Intelligence Red Team Model (YIRTM, Figure 1) and the Federal Qualitative Secondary Data Case Study Triangulation Model, as seen in Figure 2, to arrive at balanced and accurate results.

As described in Chapter 6 of Creswell's (2006) Designing and Conducting Mixed Methods Research, qualitative research functions most efficiently when the author or inquirer purposefully selects data sources that pertain to the needed information for the topic of the chapter. These authors used this process, often referred to as "purposeful sampling" to create conditions that will lead to quality results (Creswell 2006). Qualitative researchers are also prone to identifying smaller but more in-depth sources for use in their research rather than sources that stem from a broader range that might otherwise lead to greater generalizability like studies that use quantitative research techniques. As evidenced by the data subsequently used in this research, the methods used by these researchers were centered on official government documents as they include but are not limited to the parts that comprise the Federal Qualitative Secondary Data Case Study Triangulation Model. This model can be broken down into three sections; press releases, legislation and government documents, and the plans and systems employed by any number of organizations (see Figure 2).

The information that is often gathered through the qualitative assessments is not restrictive in its use or who is capable of obtaining the information. All information sources collected for the analysis originated from unclassified sources recorded and documented previously by officials in American and Russian government agencies, and scholars from multiple disciplines. Accordingly, the triangulation model seen below a multitude of secondary data helped provide relevant information for these writers' qualitative assessment.

Of the three core components seen in Figure 2, press releases, testimonies, and government documents were the most readily available sources. Of the total of 17 data sources (see Annex A), roughly a dozen press releases and congressional testimonies from the United States Department of State and the Russian government provided necessary data that supports the central argument to help ascertain results and answers to the research questions. These releases provide an American perspective on issues such as Russia's 2018 Crimea Declaration and their potential use of maliciously motivated imposition of chemical weapons following sanctions placed on Russia (United States Department of State 4 2018). These press releases also reference questionable political actions committed by Russia on a smaller scale. One such example is the continuous unlawful imprisonment of Oleg Sentsov, a filmmaker from Ukraine that occurred in August of 2018. Most striking about this source is that Sentsov has openly opposed Russia's annexation of Crimea as a territory; his imprisonment is likely acting as a method of silencing critics of Putin's political opponents (United States Department of State 1 2018). Also, testimonies such as the Department of Homeland Security's (DHS) response to concerns on election security provide official statements and perspectives on issues that serve as potential detriments to the United States (United States Department of Homeland Security 2018). When it comes to releases by the Russian government, the analysis benefits by seeing the other side of the United States' information. With the Russian side, one can see that that they view those actions as ones aligned with self-defense, and entirely rational in nature and therefore necessary. This component of the model in Figure 2 is beneficial to a researcher in a way that is unique when compared to the separate components that comprise it, yet contributes the perspective of key public figures to add to the model's reliability and has an oral feel to it when conducting qualitative analysis.

The triangulation model also includes a component consisting of documents, legislation, and policy that served as another base for the data necessary for this research. This component's contribution to the triangulation model comes in the form of scholarly and government reports that can help a researcher gain insight into an idea of a state's intentions in addition to the threats that they perceive around them that may potentially harm the country. For example, Director of National Intelligence Daniel Coats provided his official worldwide threat assessment in the form of a government report to provide information as to how Russia can pose a cyber and political threat to the United States (Coats 2018). With the knowledge that this component of the triangulation model seen above may contain assessments of threats, it stands that documents, legislation, and policy share similarities with the third and final aspect of the model: plans and systems.

Plans and systems provide a basis for further analysis in this research and most effectively helped these authors in obtaining sources of knowledge of the current and near-future goals of the United States and Russia through their National Security Strategies; both were published within the past five years. As stated in the NSS for the United States, as of 2017, the office of the Executive Branch views Russia as a challenge to the influence and power of America and also illuminates the perspective that Putin is determined to "make economies less free and fair" while expanding Russia's military influence (Trump 2017). The Russian NSS allows for analysts to have a better understanding of Russia's long-term goals in the realm of security, stability, and foreign policy (Russian Federation 2015).

The purpose of using the Federal Qualitative Secondary Data Case Study Triangulation Model as one of the critical components for this research is to gather official, reputable, and heterogeneous sources that reflect Russia's intentions as a state actor through these past five years. When employing this model one can use it to visually understand data sources thus allowing researchers to see if there is an aspect of research that they are missing, and then address the issue, or acknowledge whether or not their information is partially flawed. The use of this model in combination with utilizing the York Intelligence Red Team Model allowed these researchers to answer the research questions that served as the foundation for this research into Russia's actions.

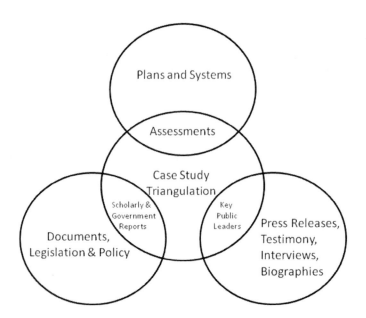

Figure 2. Federal Qualitative Secondary Data Case Study Triangulation Model.

LIMITATIONS

As is typical with analysis of secondary sources, this research is subject to limitations in the variables that were explored and the period in which the information was initially gathered. In regards to the research into Russia's potential threats to the national security of the United States, these limitations include a limited scope of variables to analyze as Russia's potentially nefarious activities throughout the recent years have remained relatively narrow in their variety. The information sources referenced in this research are restricted only to Russian actions and occurrences spanning the years from 2014 to 2018 to ensure all data gathered encompassed events that are both recent and ongoing. Moreover, the secondary sources used in this chapter's research process are required to originate from reputable sources that include official government reports, testimonies, and press releases; because they are potentially biased information outlets, news media would not provide credible and usable data for this project and were therefore excluded. In addition, a vast majority of these official documents originate from the more recent years of Donald Trump's presidency as Putin has been most active with his political and military maneuvers during the period running from 2017 and into 2018.

An additional drawback to consider for this research, and qualitative analysis as a whole, that regardless of the research methodology, none is a panacea, or 100% reliable. This data has been collected and analyzed by peering into the potential motivations and future actions of Russia, more specifically its president, and is subject to human error on both sides of the assessment.

The inevitability that this data is subject to change must also be taken into account. Since the relevance of this research has been restricted to the past five years, future developments with any state and non-state actor can render previously acquired information and analysis as less valid in the years following the research.

ANALYSIS

This section first provides the implementation of the YIRTM on the information gathered with the use of the Federal Qualitative Secondary Data Case Study Triangulation Model to determine what Russia is doing to weaken the United States. Then, a geographic analysis of nation state Russia is followed.

As shown in Annex A, the frequency of coding by the D.I.M.E. is "E" with ten, "I" for eight, "D" for eight, and "M" for five. Although tied at second place, diplomacy as the first instrument of national power, is significant; when it is used in conjunction with the economic instrument – the highest ranking, especially concerning the natural gas trades occurring with Belarus, Ukraine, and the Russian Federation it shows even more potency. While the Russian Federation is overtly using the economic power, it is also implementing diplomacy to exert dominance over another country to acquire more wealth, land, and physical power (Nagajama & Horita 2014). Another diplomatic move the Russian Federation has made close to their home is playing a hand in increasing commerce in the Caspian Sea area (Ministry of Transport of the Russian Government 2018). The theme here is that the Russian Federation uses diplomacy and economics almost in the same stroke. However, there are sometimes when diplomacy does not include economics. One such moment was the phone call that occurred between the Russian Foreign Minister and the United States Department of State's Secretary which laid the foundations for future talks between the nations (United States Department of State 2 2018).

The Russian Federation also employs the information arm of national power. Specifically, it uses the internet, to spread false and misleading information about political candidates in both the United States and Western Europe, often giving the advantage to far-right candidates who are more likely to make policies favorable to Russia, such as was seen regarding the Donald Trump of the United States and Marine Le Pen in France. The Department of Homeland Security can directly prove that Russia launched malicious cyber operations against the United States' voting infrastructure during the 2016 Presidential Elections as was testified by Kevin Mandia, the

CEO of FireEye (Mandia 2017). During Operation Hydra, the Russian government-sponsored teams of cyber experts that hacked into not only electoral databases, but also government agencies, banks, hospitals, and retails outlets (European 2016). Cyber actors connected to Russian intelligence stole the identities from millions of Americans. In 2016, the United States District Court in Washington, DC placed several key members of President Putin's administration under indictment on multiple counts of aggravated identity theft and conspiracy to commit offenses against the United States (Mueller 2018).

The third instrument of national power, military, is another tool that the Russian Federation readily uses. The Russian Federation's most recent armament program, released at the end of 2017, is a ten-year plan depicting how the military is predicted to grow. The plan reports on a total cost of 19 trillion rubles spanning from 2018 to 2027, though there is still debate over the specifics regarding which military branch gets what percentage of the budget (PONARS 2017). However, the goals for the military branches are mostly clear and depict an obvious growth in its military thereby increasing Russia's hard power. For the navy, the Russian Federation plans to have 14 total submarines, including six Delta IV-class and eight Borei-class ballistic missile submarines in their nuclear triad (PONARS 2017). This increase in nuclear development also follows along with a new long-range cruise missile, the Kh-101, predicted to be capable of delivering a nuclear payload to a target up to 4,500 kilometers away (PONARS 2017). As for the ground forces, there is a focus on developing their artillery-based capabilities, markedly with the research and development of new Uragan and Tornado-S multiple launch rocket systems. When it comes to the air forces, the Russian Federation anticipates acquiring 10-12 new fighter jets of different styles each year through 2027 (PONARS 2017). This extensive plan for military procurement leads to the conclusion that the Russian Federation is radically increasing the capability of its armed forces. When this idea is paired with the rest of the D.I.M.E., it appears as if the Russian Federation clearly will have the ability to transition into offensive operations at some point in the future.

In order to usurp the United States' standing on the world stage, Russia has sought to establish itself as a major power by entering into diplomatic, military, economic relationships outside of the Western sphere of influence and by promoting Russian identity around the world. Russians have secured its interests by diplomatic and economic alliances with other emerging nations, such as the following: Brazil, India, China, South Africa via the BRICS and the Shanghai Cooperation Organization (SCO) to provide third world nations with streams of funding for development projects in Africa, and Southeast Asia that would otherwise be unable to secure funding through the International Monetary Fund (IMF) and the World Bank (WB) because the countries are deemed "high risk" due to being hotbeds of terrorism, politically unstable (Sudan), politically corrupt, and direly impoverished (Vietnam) (Dynkin et al. 2017). Russia has also made a substantial direct foreign investment in the Latin American nation of Brazil, in an area of the world that is heavily influenced by the United States, making the United States government nervous over its proximity to regional allies (Dykin et al. 2017). Russia has also strengthened its alliances with the states that share the Caspian Sea (Iran, Azerbaijan, Kazakhstan, and Turkmenistan) by building a robust global transportation hub to encourage international trade within the area (Russian Federation 2018).

Russia seeks to weaken western alliances through near total dominance of the energy market in Western Europe. Russia provides nearly all of the natural gas to both Eastern and Western Europe via a pipeline that runs through Ukraine (Newnham 2014). Europe's dependence on Russia's oil and natural gas is not lost on President Putin, as he uses access to energy as a powerful negotiating tool. Russia uses this access strategically especially concerning the nations of Belarus and Ukraine. Any attempt to sanction Russia over its annexation of Crimea ends in the other nation losing its access to Russian energy (Nagayama et al. 2014). Russia has had the extraordinary good fortune to have vast oil and natural gas reserves in the Russian Arctic territory, that Russia now has the technological capability to retrieve (Brigham 2017). Accordingly, Russia has developed a nuclear-powered carrier ship that breaks the Arctic ice during the coldest part of the year, when temperatures can dip to well below -20 Fahrenheit, making the

Arctic Waterway (aka, the Northern Sea Route) passable all year long (Brigham 2017). The ability to pass through the Northern Sea Route has been an economic boon to Russia, as its state-owned energy company Gazprom has been able to ship liquefied natural gas from the Arctic to Western Europe even in the dead of winter, with the bonus of the newly navigable waterway serving as an alternate trade route with China. With Russia's energy sector booming, it has to have a place to put its money; that is where high-end real estate comes into play.

For many years high end real estate in desirable markets such as New York City, has served as a type of "safety deposit box" for nations and extremely wealthy individuals seeking to exploit banking secrecy laws created in the wake of 9/11 and after the implementation of the Patriot Act that scrutinized all foreign investors (Fernandez. et al. 2016). The Bank Secrecy Act made it possible for the Russian government to hide the true ownership of real estate through multiple Limited Liability Corporations (LLCs). The reason for the purchase of real estate is because of its relative ease. Real estate transactions have minimal fees or banking oversight, and real estate purchases are a good way to maintain the "liquidity" (easily recouped) of financial investment (Fernandez et al. 2016). The problem arises when the property is sold, and the proceeds from the sales are then transferred to an offshore account in a location without any taxation (Fernandez. et al. 2016). The practice by foreign investors (especially Russians) buying property as a tax shelter has become highly problematic because it drives up housing prices to such an extent that it makes entire areas unaffordable to the people who live there turning entire neighborhoods into "ghost estates" (Fernandez et al. 2016).

Taking these four instruments of national power into account and following the YIRTM to the desired shaped outcome leads this analysis down the path to the Russian Federation's goal of a weakened United States. The Russian Federation is using diplomacy to encroach geographically to get as close to the United States as possible and strong-arm countries into trade agreements that benefit the Russian Federation and diminish the power of the United States. Information is being used to spread misinformation and influence the reactions of people in other countries to obtain the desired election outcomes. The military is being built up to be stronger than ever, partly to keep stride with the United States and possibly to be able to act overtly when the time is right (PONARS 2017). Lastly, the Russian Federation is employing economic measures to gather wealth quickly and in doing so is also weakening the United States by disallowing the collection of taxes (Fernandez et al. 2016).

Russia uses its position on the United Nations Security Council to veto any sanctions concerning the annexation of Crimea and as an energy supplier to dominate Western Europe. Russia seeks to use every instrument of national power (D.I.M.E) to weaken the United States and its western alliances. The following subsection explains how Russia takes advantage of its geography continuing its engagement strengthening its national power.

Geographic Analysis of Russia

Russia, formally known as the Russian Federation, occupies the northern Asian landmass and borders the Arctic Ocean to the north and the Pacific Ocean on the east and it is the largest country in the world with a total area of 17,098,242 square kilometers, which is approximately 1.8 times to that of the United States. Russia stretches from east to west dimensionally across eleven time zones as it straddles both the Europe and Asia regions. Such vastness has brought Russia blessings and challenges. Russia's geographic centroid is located at the coordinates of 61.5240°N, 105.3188°E indicating its northerly geographic location. Moscow, the capital of Russia, and is the largest city of European Russia. It is ranked as the 11th megacity in the world with 12.41 million people.

Being the world's largest country, Russia has one of the world's longest national borders on land making it difficult to defend. In a counter-clockwise order, these adjacent neighbors are the rich and tranquil Finland and Norway to the northwest, Poland, Belarus, Ukraine and the three small Baltic republics - Estonia, Latvia and Lithuania on the west, the turbulent Caucasian republics of Azerbaijan, Georgia, and Kazakhstan, China, Mongolia, and the well armed North Korea in the south. Sharing such an extensive land border with many neighboring countries makes its international relations complicated from time to time.

Russia also has extensive coastlines; however, its higher latitudinal location prohibits these coastlines from remaining open for all year-long navigation and thereby sees lesser transportation in trade and economic activities during certain times of the year. A total distance of 37,653 kilometers of coastline right on the Arctic Ocean waters is closed by ice for approximately six months in the year. With recent global warming, shorter freezing months during the year on these Russian's Arctic coasts have somewhat reversed this original geographic limitation. Border water features including the Baltic Sea and the Black Sea located at relatively lower latitudes thus are of super importance for Russia's connectivity. For example, St. Petersburg on the Baltic Sea has been strategically located here. To the east of the country, the Okhotsk Sea of the Pacific Ocean in the east separates its eastern Siberia coast with Japan (CIA 2018). The Kuril Islands on the southeast remain as a disputed area between the two countries.

Due to Russia's latitudinal location, the main climate characteristics is continental. According to the Köppen climate classification system, Russia's climate is characterized by a warm summer continental climate. In this type of climate region, the annual temperature range fluctuates wide and fast as land's low specific heat capacity. On nearly two thirds of the territory, the snow remains on the ground for about 200 days a year, and for at least 240 nights the thermometer drops below freezing. The lowest temperatures of the northern hemisphere were recorded in the northeastern Siberia. Regionally, variable prevailing winds further exacerbate the pattern of temperature fluctuation. In the summer months, the western winds prevail in the Russian western European part; the northern and eastern winds prevail along the Arctic coasts and in central Siberia; on the Pacific coasts, the winds blow from southeast, and can see the creation of monsoons. Vegetation regions in Russia reflect its several main climatic zones. From south to north, climate regions shift from subtropical steppes to the northern humid continental Russia and to the subarctic in Siberia to tundra in the polar north. From west to east, Russia sees decreasing precipitation from mild and wet to cold and dry.

Given its size, Russia's topography is diverse, complex, and interspersed with mountains, plateaus, and plains. The most prominent mountain range is the Ural Mountains. Many people use the Ural Mountain as a natural divide between Europe and Asia. It extends 2,500 kilometers in length and only 160 kilometers in width at most. Due to its old geological history, the mountain itself has been eroded down quite bit. The highest peak - Mount Narodnaja stands at 1,895 meters above sea level. In the southwestern peripheral Russia, the Caucasus is the highest mountain chain in the country. Down to the west, the highest mountain is Mount Elbrus at an elevation of 5,642 meters. An altitude of more than 4,000 meters is also reached in the mountain ranges on the border with Kazakhstan, China and Mongolia (Beluccha at 4,506 meters in Altaj) and the Eastern Siberia, especially in Kamcatka (Kljuchevskaja Sopka at 4,750 meters). Four large plains consist of Russia's lower landscape and include: (1) the Russian plain, which is part the Northern European Plain, covers a large area from the Baltic Sea to the Ural Mountains with a minimum elevation of 200-300 meters; (2) the Caspian basin, a depression between the Black Sea, the lower course of the Volga and the Caspian Sea is below sea level; (3) continuing eastward, one would find the lowlands of Western Siberia; and (4) finally Eastern Siberia that is more variable and rugged in elevation (World Atlas 2018).

Russia's surface water resources are descent, given the existence of many rivers that reach considerable lengths on the landscape. The most well-known river in Russia has to be the Volga River, "the Mother of Russia." It flows through 3,694 kilometers connecting Moscow to the Caspian Sea. With numerous tributaries in the Volga drainage basin, the estuary is not only heavily populated by humans but also plants and animal communities such as pelicans, flamingos, and lotuses. Russia's other important cities are also found on the western side of the country, with a proximity to its European neighbors (CIA, 2018). Known as the "Galapagos of Russia," the Lake Baikal is an ancient mountain lake in Russia's eastern Siberia region. It is the largest unfrozen surface freshwater feature accounting for nearly 20% of the world's freshwater. With respect to river systems, the Lena River is the longest and has the largest catchment basin flows northward and drains into the Arctic Ocean. Other large Siberian rivers are the Irtys, Yenisei and

Ob rivers flowing in same direction. Down to the southern part of the country, Russia has the Ural, the Don, the Pechora, the Kama and the Oka. During the Soviets period, the government used the copious river water for hydroelectric power production. Today, Russia is the second country in the world for its massive hydropower production (IHA 2017). Siberia and the eastern part of country remains with an enormous hydropower potential that is awaiting to be exploited.

Russia is an energy superpower just as it is diverse. In fact, together with hydropower, the country possesses the largest stock of natural gas in the world, the eighth regarding crude oil and the second for coal. Russia is the first in the world for natural gas production and export, together with Saudi Arabia (CIA 2018). Russia has been the first country to develop nuclear energy for civilian purposes and constructed the first nuclear plant in the world. Most of Russia's nuclear power plants and reactors are in European Russia, with one in Kaliningrad. Russia has been able to exploit its gigantic geography and natural resources through a net of oil and gas pipelines that supplies Europe, China and Central Asia. Russia provides 70% of energy product to Europe and it is becoming the first energy exporter to China, beating the Kingdom of Saudi Arabia (U.S. Energy Information Administration 2017). Russia also possesses the largest reserves of mineral resources in the world. About one third of the world's deposits of metallic minerals and fossil carbon are found in Russian territory. The richest coal deposits are in Siberia and in eastern Russia. The main oil fields are found in western Siberia and the Volga-Ural region. The natural gas deposits of the Siberian Arctic coast, the region of the North Caucasus and the Autonomous Republic of Komi are also important.

The agricultural sector of Russia is rather small due to its higher latitudinal location and only constitutes 4.7% of the GDP (CIA 2018). The main agricultural areas of the country are those included in the so-called "fertile triangle," between the Baltic Sea and the Black Sea, which is the west of the Ural Mountains as it is the eastern part of the world's largest plain – the North European Plain. Other areas that are suitable for farming include the southwest edge of Siberia and the Far East region. The main agricultural products are wheat, barley, milk, eggs, sunflowers, and potatoes, of which Russia is the largest producer in the world Russian industry, particularly aerospace sector outweigh all other sectors as most state's investment is spent in this field. In planning the industrialization, the Soviet government devoted attention to the geographic distribution of the vast industrial complexes, initially concentrating manufacturing establishments in the districts of Moscow and St. Petersburg, and by pursuing steel and the heavy industry sectors.

Russia is a multi-national state. It has more than 190 ethnicities and each with its unique language and culture. A share of 77.7% of the population is ethnic Russians who are mainly settle in the heartland of Russia. A couple of largest national minorities include Tatar minorities (3.7%) and Ukrainian (1.4%). Other notable minorities include Chechens, Mordvini, Chuvaks, and Baschiri (CIA 2018). Such ethnic diversity presents a challenge for a unified cultural identity and easily create frictions between majority Russians and minorities.

The fall of the Soviet Union in 1991 resulted in Russia's independence and loss of sovereignty over territories in Central Asia and Eastern Europe. Despite the dissolution of the Soviet Union, Russia maintained its geographical magnitude, being, as mentioned above, the first country by area in the world. Ratmanov Island is only a few kilometers away from the Alaskan Diomede islands. In this regard, Russian territory extends for a part, in a nearly endless circle, to the Western Hemisphere. The Russian latitude stretches from the northern peaks of the land of Franz Joseph to the border between Dagestan and Azerbaijan.

Despite of its vastness, Russia's recent history has remained relatively in place regardless of constant territorial ambitions given its restricted geographical location. Since the 1990s, the country has invaded other territories reclaiming their sovereignty. For example, from Afghanistan in Central Asia to the bloody conflict for the control of Chechnya in Northern Caucasus; it was involved in the Georgian wars in the Southern Caucasus, and the most recent invasion of Ukraine for the annexation of Crimea to Russia. These aggressive postures are further manifested by Vladimir Putin's recent actions in Syria who has been fighting along with Assad's government. Lack of accessibility to Europe through the Mediterranean for commercial and security purposes has seen the installation of the government and its need to expand territorially in strategic locations which would enable Russia's commercial interests, energy sector, and military freedom of movement. Taking a look at the examples Crimea and Syria, Russia had geographic strategic objectives in both scenarios. Crimea, besides having a large Russian population to leverage on, is the key country to Putin's Eurasia project. That is to create a connected economy between Asia and Eastern Europe. In addition, Ukraine has Russian pipelines connected to Europe. As for Syria, Russia saw an opportunity to expand its tentacles to the Mediterranean Sea, protecting its only naval base in the region.

As discussed above, Russia's large size endows it with abundant natural resources. However, its rather cornered geographic location has been an obstacle prohibiting Russia from realizing the true potential of a connection to the outside of the world. Moreover, being a multination state, Russia must maintain internal stability among its cultural diversity. Last but not the least, Russia's government must address its borders with peaceful means. On January 17, 2018, Russian secret service (FBS) published a document entitled "Fundamentals of the State Border Policy of the Russian Federation" in which President Putin implemented new laws regarding Russian borders (FSB 2018). The new border policies aim to guarantee the right to sovereignty and exclusive rights of maritime areas under Russian jurisdiction, political and social stability, with attention to citizens living in border areas, conservation of natural resources and environmental security, as well as maintaining good neighborly relations with contiguous countries (part I and II). Some preventive measures will be put in place with the aim of defending the safety of citizens residing in the border areas are: avoiding border incidents (including armed conflicts), neutralizing border religious and ethnic conflicts, maintaining the current border administrative regime, preventing separatist actions in border areas, as well as smuggling, illegal immigration and epidemics. The bill explains that Russia fears not only territorial claims by a number of foreign states, but also attempts at terrorist and extremist acts, which would hit the inhabitants of the border areas in the first place and puts at risk the safety of the entire national territory.

FINDINGS AND CONCLUSION

It is no secret that the Russian Federation holds animosity towards the United States. Understanding the threat against the United States required analysis of measures taken by both competing political actors to uphold their positions of world authority. The analysis of the National Security Strategies for both the United States and Russian Federation granted these authors this perspective needed for this assessment. The geographical analysis further contextualizes Russia's location and implications.

To diminish the authority of the United States, the Russian Federation has taken measures ranging from simple economic trade agreements to directly meddling in elections of their opposition of which were discussed in congressional testimonies given by the Department of Homeland Security (United States Department of Homeland Security 2018). The DHS provided its written testimony before a Senate Select Committee for Intelligence to assess how Russia's malicious cyber operations were used during recent American elections could serve as a hindrance on the future of American election infrastructure. The issue of election security eventually became dire enough for the DHS' National Protection and Programs Directorate (NPPD) to become involved in the investigation into the extent of Russia's involvement. The testimony continued, stating that the NPPD was forced to work collectively with government and election officials to discern whether or not future elections were at risk of cyber-attacks.

For a state actor as large and influential as the Russian Federation, it was essential for these researchers to use a qualitative assessment of their tactics and motivations behind their policies. This forms the basis behind the first research question referenced throughout the analysis section on why Russia may be motivated to if not overtaking the United States' world authority to at least limit its power and influence. The NSS for the Russian Federation exemplifies their intentions for both socio-economic growth and for strengthening Russia against a "backdrop of new threats" (Russian Federation 2015). These new challenges are further explained in the NSS, taking the form of the United States and its allies as they argue that Russia's independent domestic and foreign policies have garnered a negative response and a sense that Russia threatens their power. Going further, Russia cites NATO as another critical form of endangerment to the Federation's national security by declaring that the organization has violated norms of international law. In reality, Russia's disdain for the NATO and the United Nations stems from the economic and military sanctions placed on them for their annexation of Crimea. The United States and its allies in NATO and the United Nations (UN) have a long-standing history of opposing the extremist policies of Putin, and this has remained the case in the past five years that have been covered throughout this assessment. As such, the reasoning as to why Russia would seek to usurp the hegemonic position of the United States, and therefore threaten its national security, would be to reclaim its superpower status and have a stronger opposition against the international laws and proceedings drafted by NATO and the United Nations.

The second question examined the secondary data to discuss how Russia poses a threat to the national power and security of the United States by using the YIRTM and Triangulation models. By utilizing D.I.M.E., these authors were able to decipher the potential instruments of national power that Russia may employ to regain its grip in the East and how these four instruments work in tandem to result in a single outcome of a weakened United States. The use of the Federal Qualitative Secondary Data Case Study Triangulation Model allowed these researchers an opportunity to provide credible secondary data sources to support the notion that Russia is working to undermine the United States.

It was through this process of analyzing the instruments of national power that the way that the Russian Federation was utilizing them that the idea of Postmodern Imperialism formed. Traditional imperialism is the exertion of control over another country either territorially, or through economic or political means (Imperialism 2018). Postmodernism is the return to traditional ideas, but with a dramatic modern reprisal (Postmodern 2018). Postmodernist Imperialism makes use of diplomatic, information, military, and economic actions to weaken other states' position in the world, and then either take over that state or step in once that state is too weakened to maintain its grip to power. So, why would Russia seek to usurp the United

States' standing as a world power? The Russian Federation is doing this to spread and exert their control throughout the world. How is the Russia Federation a threat to the United States' standing as a world power? The Russia Federation is using a postmodernist version of imperialism, the D.I.M.E. in order to do so.

These conclusions were derived from the use of the targeted research found through the application of the Federal Qualitative Secondary Data Case Study Triangulation Model. That data was then applied to the YIRTM in an attempt to analyze the Russian Federation's actions towards the United States. However, this analysis should not be taken as a cap off to the Russian Federation threat. Since information is ever changing and growing, these authors recommend that more research be conducted with a focus on data found after this piece's publication. One should also consider the inherent difficulties in restricting their research to secondary sources when examining a time span limited to roughly five years.

Additionally, these authors recommend that more information should be collected within the plans and systems section of the Federal Qualitative Secondary Data Case Study Triangulation Model, particularly if one has open access to accurate intelligence gathered on the Russian Federation's capabilities, plans, and systems. Another improvement that should be acted upon regarding future research is to focus more on collected intelligence than on open source information. When limiting one's research solely to secondary data sources, those conducting the research have to look for bias that might lead someone down the wrong path to arrive at incorrect conclusions, which the Russian Federation wants the United States to think. Lastly, another improvement could add on to the YIRTM. While this model is suitable for starting the analysis, it can be very broad and open to interpretation. One potential improvement to it would be to create sub-categories in the D.I.M.E. and could, for example afford consideration to subsections for propaganda, cybersecurity, and past actions under the information instrument. In the end, all information is fluid and changes with time, when another analysis of the threats from the Russian Federation is conducted it should consider this information but must focus more on the most recent intelligence gathered.

ANNEX A

How/Why	D.I.M.E.	Source	Source Type	Date	Page (if applicable)
Russia is using the Northern Sea Route to export oil and as an alternative trade route with China.	E	Brigham	Scholarly Journal	Summer 2017	1-3
Russia is using direct investment in Asia and Africa to expand domestic corporate interests and create additional spheres of influence	E	Kuznetsov	Scholarly Journal	April 16	79-86
Russia uses strategic interactions in the International trade of natural gas with Belarus and Ukraine to exert dominance	D, E	Nagayama et al.	Scholarly Journal	Nov 11	89-96
Russia uses its BRICS and SCO in Latin America to steer political development away from Western alliances.	D, E	Dynkin et al.	Scholarly Journal	Jan 17	85-121
Russia uses energy exports to gain favorable political advantage from Western and Eastern European neighbors and punish those who do not comply.	D, E	Newnham	Scholarly Journal	July 11	134-143
Russia is being rivaled by Iran in possible energy exports to the European Union	D, E	Tichy et al.	Scholarly Journal	2016	110-124
Russia uses real estate markets as a means of soft power	I, E	Budenbender et al.	Scholarly Journal	2017	75-96
Russia uses real estate markets to hide liquid assets	E	Fernandez et al.	Scholarly Journal	2016	2443-2461
Prepared Statement of Kevin Mandia, CEO of FireEye, addresses Russia meddling in elections	I	Mandia	Testimony	2017	1-7

Annex A. (Continued)

How/Why	D.I.M.E.	Source	Source Type	Date	Page (if applicable)
The United States of America places under indictment key members Putin's administration	D, I	Mueller	Testimony	2018	1-28
Addresses the intelligence capabilities of Russia.	I, M	European	Policy Briefing	2016	3-9
Military Acquisitions such as fighter jets, submarines, and multiple launch rocket systems.	M	PONARS	Plans	2017	N/A
Acquisition of Tu-95MS bombers, Kh-101 long range cruise missiles, T-90 and T-14 Armata tanks, Admiral Gorshkov-class frigates, and more.	M	PONARS	Weapons Systems	2017	N/A
The Russian Federation's National Security Strategy declares what countries are viewed as most dangerous to their economic and cultural health	D, I, M, E	Russian Federation	Plan	2015	N/A
Vladimir Putin approved Russia's State Armament Program to state their military reorganization goals for the next ten years	M, I	PONARS	Plan	2017	N/A
Russia agrees to develop a transport hub in the Caspian Sea to encourage international commerce	D, I, E	Ministry of Transport of the Russian Government	Government Publication	2018	N/A
Russian Foreign Minister Sergey Lavrov calls Secretary Pompeo to lay foundation for future negotiations	D, I	United States Department of State 2	Press Release	2018	N/A

REFERENCES

Ashley, Robert. (2018). *Worldwide Threat Assessment*, (pp. 11-16, Rep.). Defense Intelligence Agency. Government Report. http://www.dia.mil/News/Speeches-and-Testimonies/ArticleView/Article/1457815/statement-for-the-record-worldwide-threat-assessment/.

Brigham, Lawson. W. (2017). The Arctic Waterway to Russia's Economic Future. *The Wilson Quarterly*, (pp. 1-5). https://www.wilsonquarterly.com/quarterly/into-the-arctic/the-artic-waterway-to-russiasn-economic-future [accessed on October 5, 2018].

Budenbender, Mirjam. & Oleg, Golubchikov. (2017). The geopolitics of real estate: Assembling soft power via property markets. *International Journal of Housing Policy*, *17*(1), (pp. 75-96). http://dx.doi.org/10.1080/14616718.2016.1248646 [accessed on October 20, 2018].

Buneman, Peter., Heiko, Müller. & Chris, Rusbridge. (2018). Curating the CIA World Factbook. *International Journal of Digital Curation*, *4*(3), 29-43. doi:10.2218/ ijdc.v4i3.126.

Central Intelligence Agency. (2018, October 17). The World Factbook: Russia. https://www.cia.gov/library/publications/the-world-factbook/geos/rs.html. [accessed on October 18, 2018].

Coats, Daniel. (2018). *Worldwide Threat Assessment of the U.S. Intelligence Community*, (pp. 5-7, 11, 23-25, Rep.). Director of National Intelligence. Government Report. February 13, 2018.

Creswell, John W. (2006). Chapter 6: Collecting Data in Mixed Methods Research. *In Designing and Conducting Mixed Methods Research*, (pp. 110-127). Los Angeles, MD: Sage. https://www.sagepub.com/sites/default/files/upm-binaries/10983_Chapter_6.pdf. [accessed on October 18, 2018].

Drobizheva, Leokadia., Rose, Gottemoeller., Catherine, Kelleher. & Lee, Walker. (2015). Ethnic Conflict in the Post-Soviet World: Case Studies and Analysis: Case Studies and Analysis. Routledge., p. 209.

Dynkin, A., Baranovsky, V., Kobrinskaya, I., Machavariani, G., Afontsev, S., Kuznetsov, A., Shvydko, V., Utkin, S., Malysheva, D., Mikheev, S., Lukonin, S., Fedorovsky, A., Frumkin, B., Zhuraveva, V., Kuznetsov,

V., Voda, K., Toganova, N., Devyakov, A. & Shyshkina, O. (2017). "Russia and the world: 2017 IMEMO forecast." *New Perspectives: Interdisciplinary Journal of Central & East European Politics and International Relations*, 25, no. 1, 85-121. url: https://www.ceeol.com/search/article-detail?id=546901.

European Council on Foreign Relations. Putin's hydra: Inside Russia's intelligence services. by Mark Galeotti. Policy Breif 169. London, UK: European Council on Forgein Relations, 2016. https://www.ecfr.eu/page/-/ECFR_169_-PUTINSHYDRAINSIDE_THE_RUSSIAN_INTELLIGENCE_SERVICES_1513.pdf.

Fernandez, Rodrigo., Hofman, Annelore. & Aalbers Manuel, B. (2016). "London and New York as a safe deposit box for the transnational wealth elite." *Environment and Planning A: Economy and Space*, 48, no. 12, 2443-2461. doi: doi.org/10.1177/ 0308518X16659479.

FSB (ФСБ). (2018, January 17). RUSSIA: I servizi segreti mettono al sicuro i confini di stato. Prevenire è meglio che curare [Secret services secure state borders. Prevention is better than cure]. http://www.eastjournal.net/archives/88014 [accessed on December 5, 2018].

Goble, Paul. & Azerbaijan Diplomatic Academy. (2015, January 27). Expert: Looming ethnic conflicts in Russia will be 'more devastating' than in Europe. Retrieved from http://euromaidanpress.com/2015/01/19/expert-looming-ethnic-conflicts-in-russia-will-be-more-devastating-than-in-europe/.

James, Patrick. & David, Goetze. eds. (2001). Evolutionary theory and ethnic conflict. Greenwood Publishing Group. P.169.

Mandia, Kevin. (2017). Prepared Statement of Kevin Mandia, CEO of FireEye, Inc. before the United States Senate Select Committee on Intelligence, 1-7.

Ministry of Transport of the Russian Federation. (2018, August 2). Approval of the draft Agreement on Cooperation in Transport in the Caspian Sea. The Russian Government. Retrieved from http://government.ru/en/docs/33505/.

Mueller, Robert. S. III. (2018.) United States of America v. Defendants (pp. 1-28) (United States, U.S. Department of Justice, U.S. District Court for the District of Columbia). Washington D.C.: U.S. District Court for the District of Columbia. https://www.justice.gov/file/1080281/download [accessed on October 23, 2018].

Nagayama, Daisuke. & Horita, Masahide. (2014). "A network game analysis of strategic interactions in the international trade of Russian natural gas through Ukraine and Belarus." *Energy Economics*, *43*, no. 1, 89-101. doi: https://doi.org/10.1016/ j.eneco.2014.02.010.

Newnham, Randall. (2011). Oil, Carrots, and Sticks: Russia's Energy Resources as a Foreign Policy Tool. *Journal of Eurasian Studies*, 2 (2), (pp. 1-5). http://link. galegroup.com/apps/doc/EJ3010232257 [accessed on October 20, 2018].

Office of the Director of National Intelligence. *Assessing Russian Activities and Intentions in Recent U.S. Elections*, (pp. 1-12, Rep.). (2017). Intelligence Community Assessment. January 6, 2017.

PONARS Eurasia. Russia's Military Modernization Plans: 2018-2027. by Dmitry Gorenburg. Policy Memo No. 495. Washington, D.C.: Institute for European, Russian and Eurasian Studies, 2017, http://www.ponars eurasia.org/memo/russias-military-modernization-plans-2018-2027 (accessesed September 16, 2018).

Russian Federation 1. (2015). The Russian Federation's National Security Strategy (Russia, Russian Federation, Office of the President). Moscow: Russian Federation. http://www.ieee.es/Galerias/fichero/OtrasPublicaci ones/Internacional/2016/Russian-National-Security-Strategy31Dec20 15.pdf.

Russian Federation 2. (2018, September 25). Government Decisions. http:// government.ru/en/docs/ [accessed on October 2, 2018].

Tichy, L. & Odintsov, N. (2016). "Can Iran Reduce EU Dependence on Russian Gas?" *Middle East Policy Council*, *23*, no. 1,110-124. url: https://www.mepc.org/journal/can-iran-reduce-eu-dependence-russian-gas.

Trump, Donald J. (2017). *National Security Strategy of the United States of America*, (pp. 2-9).

(United States of America, Executive Branch, Office of the President of the United States). Washington D.C.: The White House.

United States Department of Homeland Security. (2018, March 21). Written Testimony of DHS for a Senate Select Committee on Intelligence hearing titled *"Election Security"*, 1-7.

United States Department of State 1. (2018, August 21). Russia's Continued Unlawful Imprisonment of Ukrainian Filmmaker Oleg Sentsov [Press release]. https://www.state.gov/r/pa/prs/ps/2018/08/285266.htm [accessed September 19, 2018].

United States Department of State 2. (2018, August 10). Secretary Pompeo's Call with Russian Foreign Minister Sergey Lavrov [Press release]. https://www.state.gov/r/pa/prs/ps/2018/08/285084.htm [accessed September 16, 2018].

United States Department of State 3. (2018, August 8). Imposition of Chemical and Biological Weapons Control and Warfare Elimination Act Sanctions on Russia [Press release]. Retrieved September 20, 2018, from https://www.state.gov/r/pa/prs/ps/ 2018/08/285043.htm.

United States Department of State 4. (2018, July 25). Crimea Declaration [Press release]. https://www.state.gov/secretary/remarks/2018/07/28 4508.htm [accessed on September 20, 2018].

U.S. Energy Information Administration (EIA). (2017, November 14). Independent Statistics and Analysis. https://www.eia.gov/todayin energy/detail.php?id=33732.

Vilnius. (n.d.). (2015). *Assessment of Threats to National Security*, (pp. 9-21, Rep.) (D. Eidintas, Ed.). Military Cartography Centre of the Lithuanian Armed Forces. Government Report.

Vilnius. (n.d.). (2018). *National Threat Assessment*, (pp. 1-49, Rep.) State Security Department of the Republic of Lithuania. Government Report.

In: Global Intelligence Priorities ISBN: 978-1-53615-836-6
Editors: John Michael Weaver et al. © 2019 Nova Science Publishers, Inc.

Chapter 5

A QUALITATIVE ASSESSMENT OF IRAN: MIDDLE EASTERN THREATS, NUCLEAR AMBITION, STATE SPONSORED TERRORISM, AND MORE

Stephanie M. Savage and Michael Richardson
York College, York, Pennsylvania, US

ABSTRACT

Complex bilateral relations exist between the U.S. and Iran. With the Trump administration, the relations between the two are even more tumultuous. This chapter explores and analyzes how Iran through the use of the instruments of national power in the context of the York Intelligence Red Team Model (YIRTM) could potentially degrade the security of the United States as a world hegemony. It concludes that the U.S. continues to monitor Iran as it stands as a significant Middle Eastern power house and is a destabilizing force within the region. Through comprehensive examinations of Iran's activities after the U.S. withdrawal from the Joint Comprehensive Plan of Action (JCPOA), patterns and processes of state sponsored terrorism were identified, historic and current diplomatic turmoil with the United States was acknowledged, and Iran's strengthening cyber capabilities were revealed. The chapter also explores Iran's illicit financial activity to bolster terrorism, human rights abuses, environmental exploitation and even cyber and naval threats. It suggests that Iran will continue to be a destabilizing force throughout the Middle East as well as a national security threat to the United States because of its ever-growing terrorist capability from state sponsorship, a strengthening offensive and defensive cyber military, proliferated aggression through both governmental and religious ideologies, and potential nuclear capabilities and its ambitions in the future.

LITERATURE REVIEW

Iran is currently led by President Hassan Rouhani who works closely with the Supreme Leader of Iran, Ali Khamenei, and operates a theocracy that is fueled by the Islamic ideology (United States Central Intelligence Agency 2018). In the National Security Strategy (NSS) of 2017, President Trump states concerns over Iran's state sponsorship of terror organizations, and the possibility that the country may return to uranium enrichment in order to develop nuclear weapons (Weaver 2018).

After President Trump withdrew from the JCPOA, the NSS states that the U.S. must "lean on the United Nations (U.N.) and the International Atomic Energy Agency (IAEA) to keep pressure on Iran to compel it to move away from terror support and from going back to pursuing a nuclear weapons' development program" (Trump 2017). Additionally, the National Defense Authorization Act of fiscal year 2019 shares this concern by stating that "America's military is facing challenges on multiple fronts… the nuclear ambitions of Iran; and the imperative to keep up the pressure on the Islamic State of Iraq and Syria (ISIS), al Qaeda, and other terrorist groups" (United States Department of Defense 2019). Ultimately, Trump yearns for a Middle East that is not hostile towards the U.S. but also contributes to the global energy market (Trump 2017).

Furthermore, as a broad national security strategy document, the NSS ranks priority risks such as Iran's strengthening cyber threats, their financial banking sector, public safety and health, and energy (Trump 2017). With this, it does not mean other threats are not in existence. Other related themes co-opt local security forces, and conduct insidious operations in support of Iran throughout the Middle East (United States Department of State 2018).

Iran holds one of the most active and up and coming cyber programs, next to China (United States Department of State 2016). Cyber warfare provides Iran with auxiliary means to assert its influence and intimidate others with operations that could be perilous to the U.S. and its allies and could be difficult to effectively counter. These techniques include the following: hacking social media accounts, spear-phishing attacks for personal data, deploying spyware for sensitive missions, and the acquisition of operational data on critical infrastructure. Iran is also responsible for initiating global cyber espionage operations that target specific individuals, government entities, and critical infrastructure in more than sixteen countries. These critical infrastructures include oil and gas companies, defense contractors, major airlines and transportation networks, educational institutions, and health care providers (Eisenstadt 2016).

Cyber warfare allows Iran an ability to repeatedly harass and attack other countries and organizations with little-to-no risk because Iran acts with impunity on the world stage. These types of operations can successfully be used during peacetime, because espionage and cyber-attacks would not completely justify a military response or be seen as an overt act of war. Cyber actions raise questions on whether the event is a planned cyber operation authorized from the regime or a "rogue" actor. Iran is heavily investing in soft warfare (non-physical actions) capabilities in order to strengthen their cyber capabilities and place themselves as even more of a national security threat. One can reasonably conclude that it is not acceptable to allow Iran to strike at adversaries and project its power globally and instantaneously through cyber capabilities and allowing it the ability to sustain power in differing ways (Eisenstadt 2016).

The attention that the JCPOA has demanded of the world has done such a spectacular job of concealing the national threat that Iran could easily continue to develop through its nuclear program, support and funding of terrorism, and also fostering of human rights abuses (United States Government Accountability Office 2013). As the world turned its attention toward the JCPOA, Iran continued to conduct human rights violations, support terrorism and proxy military organizations in the region, as well as across the globe, and it developed stronger offensive cyber capabilities (United States Department of State 2016). Iran's cyber threat is becoming increasingly more significant as the U.S. focuses more time and attention on deterring the state from weaponizing in the years ahead. The cyber capability of Iran is growing exponentially and is a current issue that can infiltrate the U.S. cyber zone in order to degrade both military and civilian operations. After mastering cyber defense, the Islamic Republic has transitioned to cyber offensive tactics, similar to those conducted by China. Previously, Iran had focused all efforts on censoring the internet and social media as well as monitoring what its population can see and what they can say in order to identify early warning signs of a revolution (Kagan 2015). Within the last few years, the regime has transitioned to pursue offensive cyber capabilities, producing a massive threat and including them in the new era of cyber warfare.

Frederick Kagan (2015), the director of the Critical Threats Project for the American Enterprise Institute assessed that cyber capabilities of Iran are already skilled enough to breach power plant systems, electrical grid control systems, hospital control and record systems, and university record systems. Not only is Iran working on accessing America's electrical grids and other energy control systems, which promotes the threat of power outages, they can also steal civilian information and hack into medical files leading to a significant Health Insurance Portability and Accountability Act of 1996 (HIPAA) violation. It is fair to say that Iran's cyber capabilities are similar to early Chinese cyber capabilities. Terrorism in Iran and those who pledge allegiance to terrorism around the world will thrive on information obtained from cyber hacking and will only strengthen attacks on innocent people. Kagan (2015) also states that the Islamic Republic has already seized and destroyed sensitive data through malicious activity and will only continue this behavior to strengthen their own capability while simultaneously degrading the United States. Ultimately, cyber-attacks have grown rapidly since 2014 and Iran will continue to exploit information and technology (IT) infrastructures in America, Canada, and Europe in order to terrorize the West.

Even if all the politically agitating and threatening behavior conducted by the Islamic Republic were ignored, Iran is truly a camouflaged national security threat mainly because they are the world's largest sponsor of global terrorism (Margin Scope 2017). Another thought is that, Iran has been acting with impunity which has catalyzed terroristic events such as attacks on embassies, heightened cyber-hacking, and the use of improvised explosive devices (IEDs) in warfare. Iran continues to act with aggression because historically, no real consequence has been implemented, which aggrandizes their number one technique, terrorism (United States Department of Defense 2019). The top security concern is the way in which terrorists fight with no regard for international humanitarian laws and how they illegally obtain funds. These tactics pose an extreme threat because they offer advantages and shortcuts that opposing forces have to consider and work around. Ultimately, Iran is a national threat due to the pure fact that they support global terrorism with absolutely no regard for human life (United States Government Accountability Office 2013).

In a country beleaguered with terrorism, it is a horrifying thought that Iran could weaponize a nuclear device in the next couple of decades. The Islamic Republic has tried and failed to fully convince the world that their yearning for nuclear technology is for peaceful purposes. Michael Rubin, a resident scholar at the American Enterprise Institute states that withdrawing from the JCPOA might compress the amount of time in which Iran will weaponized a nuclear device (Margin Scope 2017).

RESEARCH QUESTIONS

The literature review outlined Iran's aggressive acts in past nuclear weaponization and cyber-attacks against the U.S. national security, described the impacts of those aggressions, and laid out possible solutions. Largely framed by using a D.I.M.E. (diplomacy, information, military and economic instruments of power) logic model, this chapter askes two questions investigating the Iranian threat: The D.I.M.E. logic model is a theoretical framework that provides broad categories of assessing of national power.

> Q1: How has Iran used the instruments of national power in the context of the York Intelligence Red Team Model, otherwise referred to as the YIRTM (Figure 1) to weaken the position of the United States as the world's sole hegemony?
> Q2: Why has Iran used the four instruments of the YIRTM to weaken the position of the United States as the world's sole hegemony?

LOGIC MODEL

To help make sense of what can occur, the authors used a logic model predicated on the four instruments of national power (JP 1-02 2010, 112). More specifically, it looks to diplomacy, information, military, and economic means in order to extend pressure on other countries and non-state actors. Historically, these instruments have been used throughout the high-level staff and faculty at war colleges to foster an appreciation for making use of all available resources when trying to shape world outcomes. Particular to this study focused the use of these instruments in order to "turn the concept on its head" to visualize how potential belligerents could use these against the United States as a way to weaken the country's national security.

THE YIRTM LOGIC MODEL

To attempt to demonstrate how Iran could weaken the national security of the United States, a logic model was used to analyze the present activities, goals, and actions of Iran predicated on the four instruments of national power. In Figure 1, the model will present the instruments of national power and the efforts by Iran to counter the U.S. pushback of Iranian Regime influence throughout the Middle East.

Iran has been known to be developing weapons of mass destruction, serving as a destabilizer within the Middle East, a state sponsor of terror activities, a supporter of extremist organizations, and deploying proxy militant forces in the region in recent years. Accordingly, Iran is known to be a national security threat to nations globally through cyber warfare and been involved with major human rights violations within its own country. In reference to Figure 1, one can visualize how the YIRTM creates a shaped outcome of how Iran could potentially weaken the United States position as the world's sole superpower.

Figure 1 is a model of the direction provided by Iranian President Hassan Rouhani, and Supreme Leader Ali Khamenei to shape the advancement of its nation favorably while perpetually dwindling United States efforts to remain as the world's superpower. The model will be used to explain the "what," "where," "who," "when," "how," and "why."

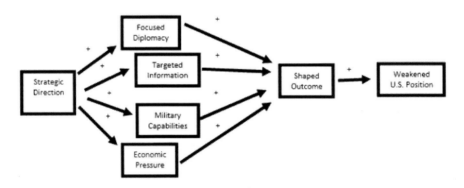

Figure 1. York Intelligence Red Team Model (YIRTM).

Focused diplomacy is the first national instrument of power. This instrument entails leaders engaging with other leaders moving towards conditions favorable to their cause. Diplomacy looks even further than just one specific country; it also examines the regional and global effects that decisions will have in neighboring countries and beyond to hinder the development of the United States as a continuing hegemony. For example, Iran has used the global market, through the use of the United States, European allies of the United States, and the United Nations to open trade, while liberating itself from sanctions that existed prior to the JCPOA's implementation. However, Iran has no formal diplomatic relations with the United States since 1980.

Information is an infinite resource from which power is drawn, allowing large amounts of information to be disseminated toward certain government's agendas and could influence national, regional, and global decisions. As shown in Figure 1 above, targeted information is the directive to promote one's values while using information to form the desired story while also besmirching the messages of another state or non-state actor. Tehran continues to use cyber propaganda and textual attacks to support Iranian state agenda. In doing so, the specifically shaped outcome is that the United State and its allies are perceived as the enemy in the Middle East (Clapper et al. 2017) and instantaneous negative projection globally (Eisenstadt 2016). Today, with many advancements in technology, cyber operations are relatively inexpensive when compared to the other instruments of national power.

The military is another instrument a state actor could use to exercise and project national power. Militarily, Iran is ranked 35th globally for defense spending and expended as little as 2.69 percent of its Gross Domestic Product (GDP) in 2015 (Unites States, Central Intelligence Agency 2018). Knowing this disadvantage, Iran regularly searches for strategies expansion and forwarding of its military defense. The most acclaimed military unit, the Quds Force, is part of the Islamic Revolutionary Guard Corps (IRGC), which trains and equips proxies sympathetic to Iranian interests. In addition, Iran lends its supports to its allied militias and insurgent groups across the Middle East (Central Intelligence Agency 2018).

As another instrument of national power, economic pressure can be used to foster unfavorable conditions directly against an enemy nation. A state or non-state actor can exert influence by leveraging a favorable outcome to achieve its cause. The United States has adversely enacted financial sanctions which restrict Iran's access to the U.S. financial system (United States Government Accountability Office 2013). Conversely, the Iranian economy relies heavily on revenue from its oil and gas industry. The United States has tried to limit Iran's ability to explore for, extract, refine, or transport its petroleum resources" to curtail Iran's national economic development (United States Government Accountability Office 2013).

METHODOLOGY

As previously stated, the main objective of this research was to analyze and evaluate the Iranian threat to the U.S. national security in terms of how and why Iran is a national threat to the United States. In order to conduct concrete and unbiased analysis, large amounts of unclassified secondary data from a variety of sources were collected, evaluated, and incorporated. Throughout this research, the authors relied heavily on a qualitative approach specifically using the two models, the York Intelligence Red Team Model (YIRTM) in Figure 1 above, and the Federal Qualitative Secondary Data Case Study Triangulation Model, as depicted below in Figure 2. This is because of the nature of the research questions that call for an in-depth research approach. The research conducted for this study relied extensively on using qualitative techniques which allowed the authors to better understand how and why certain things have happened through the use of triangulation. As shown below, a number of data types were used such as scholarly articles and government reports, quotes from key public leaders, documentaries, and plans and systems.

A qualitative research approach can be as rigorous as any empirical research approach if the data quality can be ensured. According to Creswell (2018), by using qualitative techniques, the authors were able to observe and analyze any possible information gaps during the research phase. The authors were able to take advantage of these benefits by looking for gaps, creating links, and to ultimately answer the research questions (Creswell 2018). For example, specific timelines and historical accounts were included. Journal articles written by independent scholars were also being brought in to discover precise pieces of information the authors needed to answer research questions. Using secondary data made the cost of this research more feasible. Public access to secondary data improves research endeavors and allows more information to be collected under strict timelines (Remler & Van Ryzin 2010, 180).

Threaded use of the Federal Qualitative Secondary Data Case Study Triangulation Model, depicted below, helped to balance data inclusion. The model is composed of three sectors which elaborate on what types of sources that can be utilized. The first stage focuses on plans and systems in which the authors of this chapter deeply dissected the JCPOA to gain a better understanding in what this meant to Iran. Analysis was primarily conducted through the model's second component: documents, legislation and policy, documentaries, and scholarly and government reports to better analyze how and why Iran is a national security threat to the United States. Research focused heavily on how Iran plans to degrade the U.S. and what the motive is behind these actions. By assuming the role as a red team, this allowed the authors to better understand the objectives of Iran and how it could counteract potential threats.

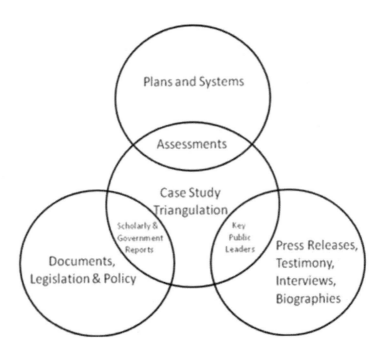

Figure 2. Federal Qualitative Secondary Data Case Study Triangulation Model.

The next sector explored legislation and policy alongside documents which include scholarly and government reports to minimize biases. The government documents represent each state's official position and the freedom of utilizing peer reviewed scholarly articles within a five-year period to ensure only timely and essential data were available for this analysis.

Lastly, the third sector of this model focuses on sources such as interviews, testimonies, press releases, and even biographies because they are important individual accounts in their public official roles. The central concern and even challenge for this literary work was conducting thorough and reliable research. Ultimately, the overarching method used to conduct appropriate research was through the use of the Federal Qualitative Secondary Data Triangulation Model.

LIMITATIONS

A qualitative research approach is not perfect and has several notable limitations. To begin, this research was conducted solely using secondary data, such as scholarly articles, books, and other academic sources that are meant to minimize bias and skewed data. Researchers need to be mindful about potential human errors when collecting and encoding data. Not being able to use primary data to answer research questions directly could potentially lead to incomplete findings.

The temporal period of this chapter builds off of data over a five-year span. The five-year period of data used within this research cuts off past historical information about the rise of the theocracy in Iran and the rising tensions between Iran and the United States. On the other hand, since only secondary data sources were used, news articles were also excluded due to exemplified biases. Ultimately, forming complete analysis with the selective information found on this topic presented a major challenge. Primary sources, which would provide direct accounts such as interviews, autobiographies, interviews, blogs, and photographs, were not utilized in this research due to time and cost constraints.

When addressing a certain question or topic, it took an extensive amount of time to sort through information, academic articles, and scholarly sources. Due to new findings and not enough coverage of these nascent political and business events, it was difficult at times to use the variables associated with the YIRTM. If primary data sources were used to compliment all types of sources listed in the Federal Qualitative Secondary Data Case Study Triangulation Model depicted earlier, then results might even be more complete.

ANALYSIS

Iran is an emerging national security threat to the U.S., but such threat is often overlooked (Newman 2019). There have been a substantial number of American deaths due to terrorist activities that are sponsored by Iran, and their proclivity towards pursing advanced missile systems and the potential for seeking weapons of mass destruction has continued to further exacerbate such threat. Iran state-sponsored terrorist organizations relentlessly torment the Middle East by spreading a forceful Islamic Revolution that destabilizes regional peace (Mohammadi 2018). This compounded with Iran's support of terrorism through illicit financial activity, human rights abuse, environmental exploitation, threats to cyberspace, and its conventional navy in maritime settings are often reported by international news media as the state chooses to participate in obvious and malign destructive activities upon the global stage (Mohammadi 2018).

A brief geographic analysis was used to contextualize Iran's location and its general geographical makeup. Iran is located in the Southwest Asia region, with the Caspian Sea to the north, and the Persian Gulf, Strait of Hormuz, and Gulf of Oman to the south. Iran also holds a land bridge for southern Asia, between the Caspian Sea and the Persian Gulf (Stratfor 2011).

Iran is the 17th largest country in the world, measuring to 1,684,000 square kilometers, making it the second largest in the Middle East, just behind Saudi Arabia with a combined landmass of 2,149,690 square kilometers (United States Central Intelligence Agency 2018). Its western part is defined by mountainous terrain while the internal country is flat, and the east fringe exhibits higher elevation, but not as high as those western coastal mountains. Iran's population of over 70 million citizens primarily are hosted in the upland mountains due to the almost impassable salt-mud flats, which historically have caused a major geographical problem for the economy of Iran (Stratfor 2011).

Iran has been ranked as the 28th largest economy in the world, it possesses the third largest oil reserve on the planet and is the fourth largest oil producer in the world. The lack of development of industry within Iran is attributable to the costs of transportation. Oil continues to be Iran's most critical economic pillar, but is the only resource keeping Iran afloat. Iran holds one of the world's largest offshore crude oil terminals and possesses the most important sea terminal in the Middle East (Stratfor 2011).

The diplomatic turmoil dates back to the development of an anti-American government after the fall of the Shah in the late 1970s (Mohammadi 2018). In 1977, President Jimmy Carter stated that "Iran, because of the great leadership of the Shah, is an island of stability in one of the more troubled areas of the world" (Margin Scope 2017). The Shah was working closely with the United States' Central Intelligence Agency (CIA), who gave complete support through the provision of continuous income streams. The Shah, also known as, Mohammad Reza Pahlavi, was overthrown by an Islamic fundamentalist. After another overthrow, the CIA withdrew its support from Iran, in which the regime built its government on an anti-American sentiment out of animosity. By having a singular enemy, Hassan Rouhani, the current president of Iran, is able to galvanize his population to loathe America and American culture.

Through diplomacy, Iran continues to develop and acquire weapons of mass destruction, in spite of U.S. interference and sanctions (United States Department of State 2018, 23). As mentioned in the National Security Strategy, Iran used economic gains from the diplomatic deal of the JCPOA to further destabilize the region, aid in the development of its ballistic missiles, and support terrorist groups in the region. Also illustrated in Annex A, of the four instruments, diplomacy had the highest frequency measuring in at 14. Annex A frequency ranking also shows the military instrument is another strong tool Iran used with a frequency of 14. Iran supported terrorist and extremist organizations through a combination of training, equipment and financial aid provided to Hezbollah, Hamas, the Taliban, and al-Qaeda (United States Department of State 2018, 26). Iran has also been using militant non-Iranian fighters to act as a proxy force by extending Iran's influence and conducting lethal operation under Tehran.

Moreover, Iran's diplomacy with Yemen has created a civil war extending its influence outside of the region of the Middle East. Houthi rebels occupied the city of Hodeidah, Yemen's main port that has a strategic location of importing and exporting goods. Stopping the humanitarian aid that is being directed to millions of Yemenis and preventing them from receiving critical help after four years of civil war has created even more harm. U.S. involvement through material contributions led to possibly one of the worst humanitarian disasters of the century. Saudi airstrikes carried out through American targeting and refueling support, have killed as many as 5,000 civilians, seen the displacement of millions, and millions more were affected by starvation, and thousands have died as a result of one of the worst cholera outbreaks in history (Thrall 2018). Yemen has also become an issue for the U.S. due to this nation being the last refuge of al-Qaeda in the Arabian Peninsula (AQAP), which is known to be the most active arm of al-Qaeda at present (Thrall 2018). Throughout all these conflicts, Iran is able to frustrate American interest in Yemen and the Middle East (Thrall 2018). Through Iranian diplomacy with other Middle Eastern countries, the U.S has been attempting to thwart Iran in exerting its influence further. The U.S. will stay committed to its goals of counterterrorism and counterinsurgency within the Middle East. This resulted in the U.S. spreading its forces far and wide, and now sees itself involved in proxy wars within the region (Ayoob 2018).

The United States' economy has been disrupted by Tehran through funding and sanctions relief from the global market which has ultimately allowed multiple terrorist networks like al-Qaeda, Hamas, Hezbollah, and the Taliban to continue freely with support stemming from Iran (Trump 2017, 49). Such extraterritorial influence allows Iran to be the world's biggest sponsor of global terrorism as well as a major national security threat to the United States (Trump 2017, 49). The actions that terrorists and other religious or political extremists take, with no regard to international laws, and how they illegally obtain funds have made it difficult for the U.S. to take direct and immediate military and economic action. As previously stated, these tactics pose an extreme threat because they offer advantages and shortcuts that the United States, an entity which operates under the Geneva Convention, have to consider and work around.

Iran has been able to effectively secure its interests defensively through economic means. Iran holds the third largest oil reserves in the world and oil, being Iran's most critical resources, has become a bargaining chip for negotiations on the global market. The possible disruption of the world's oil supply is not a gamble worth jeopardizing. Furthermore, Iran is capable of maintaining a position to counter national security to limit American freedom of movement due to the Khuzestan region, which is the most physically vulnerable part of Iran, where the oil reserves are located. This has caused various reports of clashes and seizures of British military personnel and raised U.S. attention and intervention. Iran is also capable of instigating ethnic and religious tensions in Iraq and Afghanistan to undermine the American position, and to further divert the attention to defensive goals, rather than offensive ones directed towards Iran (Stratfor 2011).

Iran is a very unique country in which it can have a low-cost, low-risk-to-power projection through the use of its covert abilities. Iran could move towards the development of nuclear weapons, providing it with deterrence from outside attacks longitudinally, and affording it a bargaining chip for negotiations with much larger countries in the short term. The Iranian nuclear program is safe from attacks for now because the consequences of such an event would lead to the loss of oil from the Persian Gulf. Iran could thereby attempt to disrupt the flow of oil from the Persian Gulf. The possible disruption of the world's oil supply is a significant issue (Stratfor 2011).

Through the strategic direction of information, Iran's cyber army has been able to impose its own values upon its citizens and the world, projecting its power regionally and instantaneously throughout the globe. Cyber warfare allows Iran to repeatedly harass and attack countries and organizations with rarely any consequences. Iran has also been found complicit in global cyber spying operations that focused on particular individuals, government entities, and critical infrastructure in more than 16 countries (Eisenstadt 2016, July).

"Tehran continues to leverage cyber espionage, propaganda, and attacks to support its security priorities, influence events, and perceptions—including those directed against the United States' allies in the Middle East. Iran has also used its cyber capabilities directly against the United States, as in distributed denial of service attacks in targeting the American financial sector in 2012-13." (Clapper et al. 2017). Likewise, Iran is able to use the uncertainty surrounding the country as a mechanism. The world isn't fully certain of its pursuit of covert offensive nuclear capabilities. Additionally, Iran has crafted an image of ideological extremism and instability, forcing countries to use extreme caution in dealing with this country (Stratfor 2011). To conclude, Iran's past five-year activities exhibit a modified D.I.M.E. model - the D.M.E.I to its state's agenda running it's internal and foreign affairs. Conversely, the cumulative impact of the Iranian government has shown that it is able to successfully take advantage of the diplomacy, military and economic instruments.

The United States' former Secretary of Defense James Mattis has described Iran as "the single most enduring threat to stability and peace in the Middle East" (Mattis, n.d.). America hoped rolling back Iranian influence in the region would lead to the restoration of order to the Middle East. With that in mind, the United States is being weakened by the active use of Iranian tactics, techniques, and procedures and its involvement in the affairs of the Middle East (Nasr 2018).

Conclusion

Historically from the point of view of the U.S., Iran has been viewed as a destabilizing force within the Middle East, but through the use of the YIRTM and The Federal Qualitative Secondary Data Case Study Triangulation Model, Iran has been strengthened to an emerging as a more formidable actor in this region. Specifically, Iran has an ever-growing terrorist capability due to state sponsorship, a strengthening offensive and defensive cyber military, proliferated aggression through both governmental and religious ideologies, and potentially will pursue nuclear capabilities in the future. Although other countries seek to engage Iran as a trading partner to boost their economies and diplomatic relations, the overall situation has not been improved. It is no secret that Iran remains a potent purveyor of terrorism. Its continuing activities in developing its nuclear arms within the next few decades will enable the state to continue to fund terrorism. Such continuation would most likely cause an irreversible and heightened threat to becoming a nuclear weaponized state in the Middle East, further affecting the region by fostering greater instability. Due to the fact that terrorists are funded by Iran, they are able to conduct more attacks on Americans abroad, threaten security, obtain sensitive information about critical infrastructure, transportation, banking, and hospital systems in United States, ultimately affecting the safety of the general population.

Recently, Iranian aggression has only grown against the U.S. interests after President Trump withdrew from the JCPOA which is outlined in the NSS, the National Defense Authorization Act, the National Defense Strategy, and other strategic national policies. It is most likely that Iran will resume its work on its nuclear program if sanctions aren't eased which could seriously threaten the security of the United States and its partners if it one day develops a nuclear weapon (United States Department of State 2018). Also mentioned in the dissection of the 2017 National Security Strategy, President Trump has vividly expressed his "concerns that Iran might renege on its agreement to halt uranium enrichment" (Weaver 2018). These types of weapons in the hands of important agent actors, such as the Iranian government, are the very existential threat that the U.S. could see come to fruition. This threat has been noted and the "DoD will be involved in implementing a missile defense system and will be called to pursue transnational terror threats at their source" (Trump 2017). Additionally, the Department of Defense (DoD) will focus on deterring Iran's heightened cyber capabilities which target sensitive information in the United States.

The recent behavior of the Iranians has set the stage for turmoil between the two countries.

To conclude, as the first research question asks how Iran plans to weaken the position of the United States as the world's sole hegemony by using the instruments of national power: diplomacy, information, military, and economics, a comprehensive analysis of data found in Annex A helps provide answers. The answers are Iran's recent plans to strengthen its "cyber Army" and to continue to fund terrorism as these means would open the door to Iran potentially jumpstarting and funding a nuclear weapon's program. Through cyber capabilities, Iran can attack civilians, hospitals, transportation, major infrastructures, political elections, and even the economy. This keeps Americans unsafe and highly exposed to the vulnerabilities. Other Iranian tactics that could degrade the United States include the use of cyber tactics, techniques, and procedures exploiting weaknesses in software and through open borders. State-sponsored terrorism can be spread quickly through social media, funding, and propaganda as more and more attacks are documented every year in which the instigators pledge their allegiance to a terrorist group and reveal their political and ideological plots.

The second research question seeks answers as to why Iran plans to use the four instruments of the YIRTM to weaken the position of the United States as the world's sole hegemony. As shown in Annex A through the frequency ranking, Iran used both diplomatic and military efforts to exert significant pressure to weaken the United States. Essentially, with more countries that want to trade with Iran through the easement of sanctions, there is increased likelihood that Iran's economy will grow and thereby increase the financial capabilities available to its government to pursue means that could enhance its own national security. One reason Iran plans to degrade the U.S. is often overlooked and dates back to the fall of the Shah as mentioned previously. Religion and ideology of the Middle East is also a significant factor in why Iran, through the use of their growing terrorist community plans to attack and weaken the Unite States and its interests throughout the region and the world.

ANNEX A

How/Why	D.I.M.E	Source	Source Type	Date	Page (if applicable)
The strongest branch of al-Qaeda, a group that the U.S. has been targeting for years, is taking refuge in Yemen, presenting a conflict of interest to the U.S. military forces.	D.M.E	Ayoob, M	Scholarly Journal	2018	N/A
President Hassan Rouhani works closely with the former supreme leader of Iran, Ayatollah Ruhollah Khomeini who both operate off of a theocracy fueled by the Islamic ideology, which supports dangerous terrorist organizations.	D.E	CIA World Factbook	Government Publication	2018	N/A
Iran continues to use cyber capabilities to disrupt the U.S. and its allies to further influence events in favor of Iran.	I.M	Clapper, J. R., Lettre, M., & Rogers, A. S.	Assessment	2017	N/A
Iran is sponsoring terrorism, abusing human rights, and continuing to develop their nuclear program.	D.M.E	United States Government Accountability Office	Assessment	2016	N/A
Iran is responsible for global cyber espionage aimed at government entities and critical infrastructure of the United States and its allies.	I.M	Eisenstadt	Assessment	2016	1-20
Iran has historically censored internet availability and social media in order to identify early warning signs of a revolution. Cyber capabilities continue to strengthen, in which Iran has seized and destroyed U.S. sensitive data.	D.I.	Kagan	Online Interview/ Documentary	2015	N/A
Iran is the largest sponsor of terrorism and yearns to weaponize in the next decade.	M.E	Margin Scope	Online Interview/ Documentary	2017	N/A
Iran uses forward defense advancing its military presence in the region and currently supports militants and insurgents through financial means.	D.M.E	Nasr, N.	Book	2018	108-118
Iran threatens the U.S. economically because they hold the largest oil supply and offshore crude oil terminals. Iran is built on rigorous terrain including	M.E	Stratfor	Online Publication	2011	N/A

Annex A. (Continued)

How/Why	D.I.M.E	Source	Source Type	Date	Page (if applicable)
impassable salt-mud flats which presents severely restricted terrain for the U.S. military					
Failure to comply with the JCPOA specifically through the violation the Treaty on the Non-Proliferation of Nuclear Weapons. Iran is also known for being a state sponsor of terrorism.	D.E	The White House Publication	Scholarly Report	2018	N/A
President Trump ends U.S. participation in the JCPOA, re-imposing sanctions and causing tension between Iran and the United States.	D.E	The White House Publication	Scholarly Report	2018	N/A
Houthi Fighters are fueling the civil war within Yemen, blocking Yemen's main port. This has caused one of the worst humanitarian disasters of the century.	D.M.E	Thrall, A. T.	Government Document	2018	N/A
In the National Security Strategy, President Trump states that he is concerned Iran will continue to enrich uranium in order to bolster the nuclear program and sponsor terrorism, to which, President Trump replaced the previous released sanctions.	D.I.M.E	Trump, D. J	Plan	2017	7-14, 48-50.
Joint Strategic Plan FY 2018-2022 covers Iran's continuing development of their nuclear program, and how the U.S. will protect the nation from any existential threats from weapons of mass destruction.	D.I.M.E	U.S. Department of State and U.S. Agency for International Development	Government Document - Joint Strategic Plan FY 2018-2022	2018	23-27
The Dissection of the 2017 National Security Strategy expresses concerns that Iran will continue to gather uranium enrichment deposits and fund state sponsored terrorism.	D.M.E	Weaver, J. M.	Scholarly Article	2017	283-284

How/Why	D.I.M.E	Source	Source Type	Date	Page (if applicable)
Diplomacy concerns between the U.S. and Iran has led to further aggression and nuclear ambition after President Trump withdrew from the JCPOA. The homeland is no longer a sanctuary, it is a target for terrorism.	D.M	National Defense Strategy	Government Document	2018	1-11
America faces challenges regarding the nuclear ambitions of Iran, and the imperative to keep up the pressure on ISIS, al Qaeda, and other terrorist groups.	D.M.	National Defense Authorization Act	Government Document	FY 2019	1-17
Explains the four instrument of national power within the YIRTM.	D.I.M.E	Department of Defense Dictionary of Military and Associated Terms	Government Publication	2010	112
Saudi Arabia's publicized approval of President Trump's withdrawal from the JCPOA due to Iran's ambiguous positions and nuclear ambitions	D.I.	The Middle East Media Research Institute	Special Dispatch Report	2018	N/A
The onset of security concerns from Saudi Arabia and other regional states by the faulty enforcement of the JCPOA	D.I.	Center for Strategic & International Studies	Scholarly Project	2016	11

It is clear that the U.S. stance is well represented by President Trump who wants to see an Iran that is not hostile to its neighbors, especially Saudi Arabia, and for it to move away from sponsoring terrorism. Through the use of the YIRTM and The Federal Qualitative Secondary Data Case Study and as outlined in Annex A, it is evident that Iran will continue to serve as a serious threat to the U.S. and international peace for the foreseeable future.

REFERENCES

Ayoob, Mohammed. 2018. "How America Could Get Pulled into a War in Yemen." *The National Interest*. Accessed September 10, 2018.

Clapper, James R., Marcel Lettre, and Michael S. Rogers. *Foreign Cyber Threats to the United States*. Department of Defense. Svobodneslovo. January 5, 2017. Accessed September 12, 2018. https://www.svobodneslovo.com/akl/Clapper-Lettre-Rogers_01-05-16.pdf.

Cordesman, Anthony H. *Saudi Arabia and the United States: Common Interests and Continuing Sources of Tension*. Report. Center for Strategic and International Studies. March 10, 2016. Accessed January 15, 2019. http://csis-prod.s3.amazonaws.com/s3fspublic/legacy_files/files/publication/160310_cordesman_saudi_arabia.pdf.

Creswell, John W. 2008. *Research Design; Qualitative, Quantitative, and Mixed Methods Approaches*. Thousand Oaks, CA: SAGE Publications.

Eisenstadt, Michael. 2016, July. *Iran's Lengthening Cyber Shadow*. Washington, DC: The Washington Institute for Near East Policy.

JP 1-02. 2010. Department of Defense Dictionary of Military and Associated Terms. Joint Publication 1-02. November 8, 2010.

Kagan, Frederick W. 2015. *Iran's Growing Cyber Security Threat*. Accessed September 20, 2018. http://www.aei.org/publication/one-pager-irans-cyber-arms-race/.

Margin Scope. 2017. *Menace in Disguise - A Documentary Film about the Danger of Iran*. Accessed September 15, 2018. https://www.youtube.com/watch?v=nx7Urs8ABRU.

Mattis, James. (n.d.). *Summary of the 2018 National Security Strategy of the United States of America: Sharpening the American Military's Competitive Edge.* Accessed September 20, 2018. (pp. 3-11).

Memri. 2018. *"Saudi Arabia, UAE, Bahrain, Egypt Welcome President Trump's Withdrawal From JCPOA."* The Middle East Media Research Institute. Accessed January 12, 2018. https://www.memri.org/reports/saudi-arabia-uae-bahrain-egypt-welcome-president-trumps-withdrawal-jcpoa.

Mohammadi, Elaheh. 2018. Review: Behrooz Ghamart – Tahrizi, Foucault in Iran: Islamic Revolution after the Enlightenment. *International Sociology.* Accessed September 15, 2018. https://journals.sagepub.com/doi/full/10.1177/0268580918757117a.

Nasr, Vali. 2018. Iran Among the Ruins. *Foreign Affairs.* Accessed October 1, 2018. https://heinonline.org/HOL/Page?collection=journals&handle=hein.journals/fora97&id=335&men_tab=srchresults.

Newman, Lily Hay. 2019, January 29. "The Threat That the U.S. Can't Ignore: Itself." WIRED. Accessed January 31, 2019. https://www.wired.com/story/worldwide-threats-briefing-donald-trump-china-northkorea/.

Remler, Dahliak. & Gregg G Van Ryzin. 2010. *"Research Methods in Practice: Strategies for Description and Causation."* Thousand Oaks, CA: SAGE Publications.

Stratfor. 2011. *"The Geopolitics of Iran: Holding the Center of a Mountain Fortress."* Stratfor Enterprises. Accessed September 11, 2018. https://worldview.stratfor.com/article/geopolitics-iran-holding-center-mountain-fortress.

Thrall, Trevor, A. 2018. *"Time for Diplomacy, Not War, in Yemen."* Washington DC: CATO Institute. Accessed September 12, 2018. https://www.cato.org/blog/time-diplomacy-not-war-yemen.

Tillerson, Rex W and Mark Green. 2018. "Joint Strategic Plan FY 2018-2022." Washington DC: Department of State. Accessed September 10, 2018. https://www.state.gov/documents/organization/277156.pdf.

Trump, Donald J. 2017. *National Security Strategy of the United States of America* (NSS). Washington, DC: The White House.

Trump, Donald J. 2018. *"President Donald J. Trump is Ending United States Participation in an Unacceptable Iran Deal."* Washington DC: The White House. Accessed October 2, 2018. https://www.whitehouse.gov/briefings-statements/president-donald-j-trump-ending-united-states-participation-unacceptable-iran-deal/.

United States, Central Intelligence Agency. 2018. *"The World Factbook: Iran."* Central Intelligence Agency. Accessed September 12, 2018. https://www.cia.gov/library/publications/resources/the-world-factbook/geos/ir.html.

United States, Department of Defense. 2019. *"National Defense Authorization Act - Reform and Rebuild: The Next Steps."* House Armed Services Committee Communications. Accessed on September 13, 2018.

United States Department of State. 2016. *"State Sponsors of Terrorism"* Washington DC: Bureau of Counter Terrorism and Countering Violent Extremism. Accessed September 20, 2018. https://www.state.gov/j/ct/rls/crt/2016/272235.htm.

United States Government, The White House. 2018. *"Ceasing U.S. Participation in the JCPOA and Taking Additional Action to Counter Iran's Malign Influence and Deny Iran All Paths to a Nuclear Weapon."* Washington DC: The White House. Accessed September 13, 2018. https://www.whitehouse.gov/presidential-actions/ceasing-u-s-participation-jcpoa-taking-additional-action-counter-irans-malign-influence-deny-iran-paths-nuclear-weapon/.

Weaver, John M. 2018. *"Dissecting the 2017 National Security Strategy: Implications for Senior Administrators (the Devil in the Details)."* Global Policy. Accessed October 12, 2018. https://onlinelibrary.wiley.com/doi/full/10.1111/1758-5899.12542.

Young, Chuck. 2016. *"Iran Nuclear Agreement: The International Atomic Energy Agency's Authorities, Resources, and Challenges."* Washington DC: United States Government Accountability Office. Accessed January 12, 2018. https://www.gao.gov/assets/680/677783.pdf.

In: Global Intelligence Priorities ISBN: 978-1-53615-836-6
Editors: John Michael Weaver et al. © 2019 Nova Science Publishers, Inc.

Chapter 6

EAST ASIA'S FORMIDABLE FOE: NORTH KOREA

Joseph D. Hurd, Joseph Soreco and Gunnar Nemeth
York College, York, Pennsylvania, US

ABSTRACT

The debate on North Korea is one of most divisive foreign policy issues for the United States. In the latest National Security Strategy (NSS), Trump and his administration identify that one major threat comes from the Democratic People's Republic of Korea (DPRK) and their possession of nuclear weapon and cyber capabilities which is the focus of this study. Employing a qualitative research approach, this chapter takes in-depth investigation using the four instruments of national power and investigate how North Korea in particular has utilized these instruments and is threatening the United States. The chapter also assesses what the current North Korea's activities mean to future regional peace. It concludes that much of North Korea's strategy in the region has been decisively defensive due to its governmental mission and economic structure, putting the country in a situation without many options to gain greater influence in the region and nearly no contribution to the world economy. The nuclear proliferation in North Korea has opened a new door for the country to negotiate a more and better position of power. North Korea has been and further plans to utilize their nuclear capabilities in the context of D.I.M.E to weaken the United States as the world's hegemony. Additionally, the chapter finds that nuclear proliferation has also greatly boosted their military power in the region and is a direct threat to the United States and her influence in the region. North Korea also has been using information technology on platforms such as twitter to hopefully gain more support from the world stage.

LITERATURE REVIEW

The debate on North Korea is one of most divisive foreign policy issues for the United States. In December of 2017, President Donald Trump released his first National Security Strategy. The document, which is over 50 pages in length, provides guidelines for the United States government. As one of the most important unclassified documents, it amplifies America's new priorities and emphasis for the current administration. As stated in the document, the top priorities for this administration list the following: protecting the American people, the homeland, and the American way of life, promoting American prosperity, preserving peace through strength, and advancing American influence in a regional context (NSS 2017). North Korea remains as one of most complex issues. This chapter focuses on each of these four priorities that will be subsequently be evaluated by using the D.I.M.E through the York Intelligence Red Team Model (YIRTM) and the Federal Secondary Data Case Study Triangulation Model to characterize North Korea's activities to assess its threat to the United States. It is argued that the current North Korean regime should be viewed as the most formidable foe not only in East Asia region but also globally because of this aggressive state actor's behaviors in military and diplomatic dimensions, along with frequent use in information and economic aspects; the North Korean threat must be taken more seriously with some innovative approaches.

North Korea has launched numerous cyber-attacks that have affected 150 nations proving how capable North Korea is in the cyber realm (Trump 2017). The National Security Strategy offers ways to combat these threats and to keep Americans safe. Some of these strategies include political, economic and military means. One main component of the National Security Strategy talks about defenses against weapons of mass destruction. These counter offensive measures include enhanced missile defenses, detecting and disrupting weapons of mass destruction (WMD), enhancing counter-proliferation measures and to target terrorists pursuing WMDs. Another way to combat these threats is through diplomacy. The a summit meeting between Donald Trump and Kim Jong-un has been seen as moderately effective in reducing tensions between the two countries and accordingly, Trump hopes to lessen the number of nuclear weapons that the DPRK possesses (White House 2018). Chairman Royce (House Foreign Affairs Committee Chairman) said that the willingness of Kim to talk, shows that this nation will be able to slowly but surely be able to apply more pressure through diplomacy (Royce 2018).

The National Defense Strategy also underscores the North Korean threat to the American people (Mattis 2018). The National Defense Strategy labels this country as a rogue actor that seeks to guarantee regime survival and increase leverage by seeking a mixture of nuclear, biological, chemical, conventional and unconventional weapons and a growing ballistic missile program to gain coercive influence over South Korea, Japan, and the United States. In the National Defense Strategy, one sees that in some cases North Korea intends to proliferate these capabilities to malign actors to include the likes of Iran (Mattis 2018). The National Defense Strategy expressly underscores the importance to defend the homeland and remain the preeminent power in the world. They will achieve these goals with specific defenses to all threats posed by the rogue regime of the DPRK.

When looking at the Joint Strategic Plan FY 2018-2022 (JSP 2018), the State Department acknowledges the rising power of North Korea and their developing nuclear program. Under its strategic goals, the State Department aims to continue its protection of America's security at home and abroad (JSP 2018, 23), particularly in strategic goal 1.1; the document espouses the need to counter the proliferation of weapons of mass destruction (WMD). In the case of the North Korean state, the State Department understands the country's recent development of an intercontinental ballistic missile

(ICBM), and with the DPRK's regime specifically stating its objective of striking the United States and posing a clear threat to international security (JSP 2018, 24).

Yet, the United States recognizes the threat posed by North Korea's unlawful nuclear missile program not only to the United States, but its allies throughout the international stage. Realizing this threat, this then thrusts the United States to vehemently pursue denuclearization as the first step (Nauret 2018). The State Department has requested sanctions in the past to be put forth upon the North Korean state as well as for all countries to cut their ties (economic, financial, and diplomatic) with the country in recent times (JSP 2018, 24). After recent WMD tests performed by the DPRK, these authors have seen executive orders being brought to attention in effort to control what this actor is doing. One of the latest tests has been in 2017 where North Korea conducted a ballistic missile test. The president labeled this as reckless and something that this country needs to act upon (White House 2017). This is complementary to what the Department of State is wishing to do with its sanctions that they have brought forth to the United Nations in recent years.

In addition to the rising threat of North Korea as a nuclear-armed nation, this department comprehends the People's Republic of China's continued support for North Korea and inhibiting the United States from going forward with stronger sanctions when addressing North Korea's illegal proliferation of missile technology and nuclear tests (JSP 2018). The State Department plans to engage with China on its influence in the region particularly on the topic of North Korea and address the rising threat of this nation as it tries to minimize the compromise on solutions to the developing threat in the region and international stage (JSP 2018, 30).

Congress is also aware of the rising threat of a nuclear-armed North Korea as it addresses the recent diplomatic breakthrough between the United States and North Korea, while it still works with the Department of Defense (DOD) on developing authorization and appropriations acts dealing with the rising threat of Kim Jong-un's regime as addressed in the National Defense Authorization Act (NDAA) for the Fiscal year of 2019 (Congress 2018, 16). Likewise, the U.S. Government Accountability Office also recognizes the rising threat presented by North Korea. There have been several successful weapons' tests over the past few years that have put the U.S. at a higher state of readiness, specifically on the Korean Peninsula (GAO 2016). Congress has restated the importance that the United States stands behind its treaty obligations and extended nuclear deterrence commitments, as well as maintaining that U.S. forces should remain on the Korean Peninsula with a strong and enduring presence (Congress 2018, 16). Moreover, Congress prohibits the DOD from reducing the number of armed forces within South Korea below the 22,000 thresholds unless in the interest of U.S. national security while also appropriately consulting U.S. regional allies, specifically South Korea and Japan (Congress 2018, 16).

While remaining on the topic of South Korea, Chairman Royce recently commented on her talks with the Minister of Foreign Affairs from the Republic of Korea. She said that while continuing talks with North Korea, it is imperative to continue with the application of pressure on this nation which serves as evidence that sanctions are working (Chairman Royce 2018). The DOD in coordination with other agencies is to report on the status of North Korean WMDs including nuclear, chemical, and biological. In the case of whether an agreement between the United States and the DPRK should come to fruition, DOD in coordination with other agencies should provide updates and assessments for any verified dismantled, destroyed, or rendered permanently unusable WMDs to Congress (Congress 2018, 16). Congress assures the continuance of strengthening the United States' military capabilities in the region to ensure U.S. forces are ready to defend themselves and American allies in any scenario on the Korean Peninsula (Congress 2018, 16). Congress also affirms its support for the President's budget request for the Army's precision strike missile program to serve as a deterrence to missile strikes from North Korea (Congress 2018, 16).

RESEARCH QUESTIONS

This study looks at the effects of several variables, most notably diplomacy, information, military and economic (D.I.M.E.), and the potential of these having a direct effect on the United States. To be more specific, the authors looked at the following research questions to consider plausibly what could happen from an adversarial perspective if North Korea continues developing its cyber, nuclear (and other WMDs), and conventional military capabilities.

> Q1: How is North Korea using its developing cyber, WMDs and other military capabilities in the context of the YIRTM to weaken the position of the United States as the world's sole hegemony?
>
> Q2: Why is North Korea using its developing cyber, WMDs, and military capabilities in the context of the YIRTM to weaken the position of the United States as the world's sole hegemony?

Logic Model

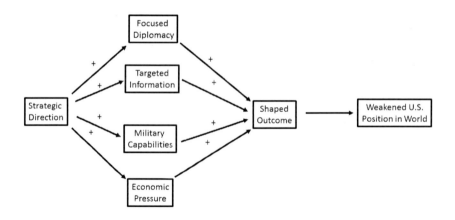

Figure 1. YIRTM.

To help obtain a better understanding of what has occurred, a logic model based on the four instruments of national power which include diplomacy, information, military, and economic means (for D.I.M.E.) were used. In using this model, how North Korea could extend pressure to other countries and non-state actors most notably efforts directed against the United States thereby weakening the U.S. power and influence. The National

Security Act of 1947 has all but one (information) as ways to extend influence on behalf of the United States (Brantly 2016). In the past, the world has seen how these instruments can be used by staff and students at war colleges to make use of all available resources when trying to shape outcomes all over the world. In this study, the researchers used the four instruments to see how potential threats to the U.S. could weaken the country's national security.

The York Intelligence Red Team Model (YIRTM) found in Figure 1 was used by the authors to analyze those current activities and events. The layout of the figure shows a flow process from causes to the shaped outcome. The chief merits of the model include the identification of the key actor that are explicitly centered on influencing the national security of this nation. It begins with the bearing and direction of that leader from a state or non-state actor accentuating "who," "what," "where," "when," and "why." With the course and direction of this leader, one can view the four instruments as a manner by which to underline tactics, techniques and procedures (TTPs) to help achieve that leader's goals and objectives. To be more specific, in this study these authors looked at what can be done by North Korea through either nuclear or cyber-attacks to weaken the position of the United States in the world.

Diplomacy is the first instrument to which the authors afforded consideration. This explicit instrument includes leaders that hope to work with others to shape conditions that accompany their plans or initiatives. It should not look at only one application to one nation, instead it should take a view on how these choices influence the region or globe with an end goal to keep the U.S. from asserting its interests on one's nation. It could be viewed as significantly more affordable with respect to transient expenses by making connections that proceed with one's situation to support them. When looking at North Korea, Donald Trump and Kim Jong-un as of mid-2018 met at a summit meeting. At this session, Kim Jong-un guaranteed a denuclearization of his nation. Before, the North Korean leader and his predecessors have neglected to keep guarantees like these.

Information is power and assembling the accurate data and utilizing it viably can have worldwide impacts. North Korea is a hermit kingdom, a reclusive state, with a controlled society where data is a highly controlled so very little information is known about it external to the country. The United States being unable to know the majority of what occurs from within this nation puts other nations off guard.

The instrument that is probably most understood by the National Security Council is that of the military. This instrument can be employed in numerous ways and includes such things as peacekeeping, military engagements, and more. They have been trying to enhance their ICBM capacities and has even segued into rockets with a shorter range than ICBMs. In spite of the fact that these tests do not present an imminent danger at present time, the way that they are testing them demonstrates that North Korea is still investing in these systems regardless of the financial hardship endured by the country.

Economic efforts can also have an impact on helping a nation achieve its goals. Countries can apply the influence using this instrument with the advantage of a considerable measure of money on others to change their behavior to fall more in accordance with what that nation's targets are. There have been a few reports that North Korea has been shipping supplies to Syria that can be utilized in conjunction with chemical weapons thereby enhancing its access to hard currency (Nauret 2018).

METHODOLOGY

The information used for this qualitative assessment was gathered from secondary open source (unclassified) data. Qualitative techniques are useful when triangulating one to other data sources because they can provide amplification on how and why things have occurred (Remler & Van Ryzin 2010). Specifically, this study looked at nuclear proliferation and what has been done by the North Korean Regime through the use of the YIRTM to better triangulate in on results.

Creswell (2008) states a benefits and limitations of provision of enumeration on qualitative techniques. In particular, he underscores the quality in utilizing this methodology to support the end goal and to investigate connections among factors in the journey to answer the research questions (Creswell 2008). Contemporary research has underscored the practicality of secondary data (Remler & Van Ryzin 2010, 180). Since this data often requires moderate effort and low cost, experts and analysts alike in the humanities' field have seen this data as useful to conduct research (Remler & Van Ryzin 2010, 180). This examination makes use of auxiliary data where the data has a favorable position in cross-sectional structures.

With respect to data quality, the authors chose the Federal Qualitative Secondary Data Case Study Triangulation Model portrayed in Figure 2 (Weaver 2015). Hereafter it is referred to as the Federal Model. The Federal Model is comprised of a Venn diagram that looks to achieve balance in secondary data use. The first of these incorporates plans and systems. This segment looks to what is at present in and the preface centers around what TTPs have been utilized by North Korea in contemporary times that are directed towards the United States. Plans look to secondary data sources to acquire information on what has been recognized by the United States when turning to the topics of WMDs, especially ICBMs (and North Korea's nuclear ambitions). Systems look to methods or capabilities in use by the regime to enhance its nuclear deliverable capabilities and other concerns like cyber and its conventional military. Through this first segment of the model, one can see signs of improvement to feel for what can happen by the Kim Jong-un regime against the United States.

The second part of this model segues to documents, legislation, and policy to comprehend the dangers and current pursuits of North Korea. It affords consideration to mostly written works and bores into government reports, books, peer-reviewed publications and the like, primarily published in the course of the last five years to discover outcomes. For the most part, this segment of the Federal Qualitative Secondary Data Case Study Triangulation Model moves beyond news reports and gravitates to sources that are less susceptible to bias. This component of the model hopes to provide amplification on current capacities and the dangers presented by North Korea.

The last part centers around predominately oral accounts to leverage these types of data sources to triangulate in on results. This incorporates such data from official press releases, interviews, testimony and key leader statements to help ascertain what is occurring.

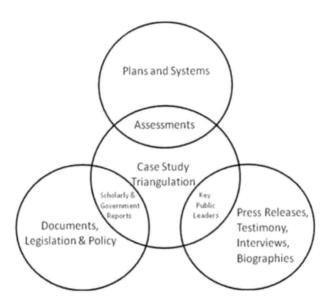

Figure 2. Federal Qualitative Secondary Data Case Study Triangulation Model.

Validity is an essential concern with all academic research. This piece strived for legitimacy by looking at two perspectives. In particular, content validity was reached by looking at the viability of data sources used and checking to ensure data was not biased (Jaeger 1993, 384).

Face validity (Creswell 2008) looks at the surface level to see if the way the study is undertaken inherently makes sense. This study looked at variable use, their directionality, and past model application and use to ensure that all made sense.

Emphasis likewise turned to the topic of reliability. The authors utilized consistency when running comparative undertakings to help ensure that reliability was achieved (Creswell 2008 190). In like manner, Remler and Van Ryzin (2010, 118) embrace the need of consistency in measures when hoping to accomplish reliability when directing exploration.

LIMITATIONS

By and large, the extent of this examination was restricted to a two-year time frame from 2017 and through 2018. More weight was apportioned to information in the latter years because of the importance associated with what would likely take place in the near future. Despite the fact that this study limits itself to the variables found in the YIRTM, there are other factors that could have bearing on the problem.

Likewise, only intervening relationships were considered. It is conceivable that different factors like moderating variables could affect results. These could include issues like legacy trade agreements, treaties, the advancement of technology, some of which were excluded from this study.

In a like manner, similar to the case with all qualitative research, it is hard to generalize beyond this study. This study focused solely on North Korea and the results should not be interpreted as being relevant to other nation states.

Primary sources were not considered, and these incorporate such methods as observations, interviews, and surveys. Future examinations into North Korea could use primary data to confirm or refute parts of this study.

ANALYSIS

This section first provides a geographic analysis and then the D.I.M.E. analysis by applying the YIRTM. Annex A contains all secondarily publicly available data for the D.I.M.E. analysis.

Commonly known as North Korea, the country is located on the northern part of the Korean Peninsula. The Korean Peninsula is a mountainous region that is influenced in summer by warm, monsoonal weather, whereas the winter season brings cool to cold, drier weather. Natural forests remain in small protected areas that are in the high elevations of northern North Korea. Lowland and valley vegetation have long since been altered, replaced by human inhabitation and cultivation. Elevations that exceed 2,000 meters are characterized by alpine vegetation and bare ground, and most of the valleys have been used for agriculture. Lands that exceed 400 meters have poor cultivation potential due to elevation climate relationships, slope angle, and soil conditions (Palka 2002). The most popular crops in North Korea are rice and maize, with a small concentration of winter grains and soybeans (Tatsumi 2017).

The country's absolute location is 40.00° N and 127.00° E. North Korea sits at the base of the Korean Peninsula and shares its borders with China to the northwest, Russia to the northeast, and the Republic of Korea to the south. North Korea is bordered by two bodies of water, the Sea of Japan (East Sea) to the east and the Yellow Sea to the west. Pyongyang is the capital and largest city in the country; it is located towards the southwest, near the western coast of the Korean Peninsula. There are four main river systems that run through the North Korean countryside. In the north, there is the Yalu River and the Tumen rivers, in the west lays the Taedong and Ch'ongch'on rivers. The rivers are mostly short, 790 km, 521 km, 439 km, and 217 km respectively. The Tumen river is the only main waterway in North Korea that flows eastward. North Korea does not have many notable lakes or other waterways.

To the north, North Korea shares two borders with the Russian Federation, now referred to as Russia, and the People's Republic of China, now referred to as China. North Korea shares a larger border with China (1,352 km) compared to Russia (18 km). The Chinese border starts along the western coast with the Amnok or Yalu River. The Russian border follows the Tumen River inland starting on the east coast. China has been a strong ally to North Korea in the past and remains to exert heavy influence on the culture, politics, and economy.

North Korea is a humid continental climate according to the Koppen Climate Classification System, with a hot summer and a cold winter. During the summer months (June - August) the temperature fluctuates between 28.9°C and 7.0°C. The winter months (December - February) can range from 2.4°C and -10.7°C. Most of the rainfall occurs during the summer months, borne by monsoon winds determined by the landmass of Central Asia. This abundant water supply during the warm growing season allows for intensive agricultural practices, mostly rice because it is suited for the growing season (Columbia University 2009). The southwestern region is the most well-suited for agriculture. Typhoons can affect the peninsula in May through October during typhoon season.

North Korea's terrain is mostly made up of mountains and hillsides; about 80% of the landmass is considered mountains or uplands. These steep slopes allow for hydroelectric dams to be constructed along the rivers that flow down the mountainside. On August 26, 1940, one day after Sup'ung Dam on the northern Korea border began transmitting electricity to neighboring Manchukuo. Yalu River Hydropower Company officials and colonial bureaucrats called the dam an "eternal pyramid," the "project of the century," and a victory for "Scientific Japan." They noted that it domestically produced 100,000 kilowatt generators and 220 kilovolt transmission lines were the world's most powerful, and that the project would form the basis for "constructing East Asia" (Moore 2013). The tallest peak is Paektu-san on the volcanic Baekdu Mountain, it is located on the northern border shared with China, and the highest point is 2,744 meters above sea level. The mountain ranges that dominate much of North Korea's landscape are a result of the convergence of the Eurasian and Philippine Plates. However, it is not located along an active tectonic boundary; therefore, it is a generally stable landmass with no active volcanoes and rare earthquake shocks (Palka 2002). It is not exposed to many natural disasters since it is not on an active tectonic plate boundary; there is minimal flooding during the rainy season, and wildfires occur very rarely.

The other 20% of the landmass is considered small plains and grasslands, with only 17% available for agricultural use (Palka 2002). Most of the plains are found in the southwestern region where the capital is found. The lack of flat, developable grasslands has put North Korea at a disadvantage. North Korea is a land of steep mountains with narrow valleys that promote a sense of isolation and fragmented land travel and communication. Consequently, North Korea has not been favored with a bounty of level, arable land and the production of food is a pervasive problem driven in part by the rugged terrain. Furthermore, the narrow coastal plain, and lack of quality, deep-water port facilities are additional consequences of its location (Palka 2002). North Korea is not physically able to develop large cities because of the lack of flat land to construct them, with the western valleys having the greatest potential for development.

Not only does North Korea have a limited area for agricultural use, the country has faced an incredible drought. In 2017, the Food and Agriculture Organization of the United Nations wrote a report on the dangers of a prolonged dry season in the summer of 2017. "A severe dry spell from April to June has acutely constrained planting activities for the 2017 main season and adversely affected yield potential of the early planted crops. Rainfall volumes from April to June in key-producing areas were well below the long term average and lower than the rainfall levels of the corresponding period in 2001, when cereal production in the country decreased to the unprecedented level of around two million tons, causing a sharp increase of food insecurity levels. Although some rains in the first decade of July over most of the growing areas provided some relief, they were likely to be too late to allow normal planting and development of the crops" (United Nations 2017). According to Government data and Food and Agriculture Organization (FAO) satellite analysis, around 30% of early crops have been lost due to the dry spell that has struck the country. These crops constitute 10% of the overall harvest (ReliefWeb 2017).

The mountainous geography may prohibit agricultural development and large cities host a plethora of minerals under the surface. There are vast mineral reserves, including iron, gold, magnesite, zinc, copper, limestone, molybdenum, graphite, and more (Mollman 2017). There are also lots of rare earth elements; these are minerals used in the production of computers, cell phones, and other high-tech electronics. North Korea holds the great bulk of the total known mineral deposits on the Korean Peninsula. It is estimated that some 200 of the minerals found have economic values (Yoon 2011). North Korea's reserves of tungsten, molybdenite, black lead, barite, and fluorite, for example, place North Korea among the world's top 10 countries in terms of reserves. The area has not only vast mineral resources, but also abundant energy resources such as coal and uranium, which play major roles in supplying power and industrial materials.

As mentioned before, the excess of mountains and lack of flat grasslands makes North Korea less than accessible than most other nations. Cities in the western part of North Korea have the largest potential for development and industrialization, so most of these cities are connected by road and rails. Three of North Korea's top ten cities by population, Nampo, Songnim, and Sariwon, all are less than sixty kilometers away from Pyongyang, which is in the western portion of the country. All of these cities are on comparatively flat ground and have either road or rail connectivity to Pyongyang. Furthermore, Nampo and Songnim both have direct access to Pyongyang via the Taedong River (Palka 2002). Nampo is a fast-growing port city on North Korea's west coast; it is extremely important to Pyongyang and the rest of North Korea because of the strategic location and proximity to the capital. Nampo is not without problems though; its growth is stifled by the congested river port city's inner area, inability to maintain sufficient accessibility, the West Sea Barrage (Nampo Dam), and by rapid urban growth (Jo and Ducruet 2006).

The Republic of Korea, commonly known as South Korea shares the Korean Peninsula with North Korea. South Korea occupies the southern half of the peninsula and shares its only land border with North Korea. The shared border lies on 38.00° N, referred to as the 38th Parallel, and is an international demilitarized zone that was created by North Korea, South Korea, and the United Nations in 1953 to serve as a buffer region after the Korean War. The Korean Demilitarized Zone (DMZ) divided the peninsula roughly in half, and it is still one of the most heavily fortified borders in the world.

The DMZ is a defining feature of the Korean Peninsula and North Korea itself, and to know it, one needs to understand a little historical background on the subject. The Korean War is an important event in Korean history, with global implications that still influence decisions today. The Korean Peninsula has a long history of being occupied by local empires and dynasties, one of which was the Imperial Japanese rule from 1910-1945. Towards the end of World War II, the allied nations convinced the Soviet Union to join the fight in the Pacific against Japan, and the Soviets occupied northern Korea by August 1945. When Japan surrendered to the allied powers, the United States and the Soviet Union were tasked with dividing the occupied territory. Eventually, these two nations' ideologies drifted apart, and thus began the Cold War.

The Korean War is considered to be a proxy war between the global superpowers, as North Korea was occupied by the Soviet Union, and South Korea by the United States; the two nations were born at odds. Backed by Mao Zedong's newly formed communist government and forces, Stalin gave permission to Kim Il-sung to invade South Korea. A few weeks after the invasion and almost total destruction of South Korea's forces, the United Nations condemned the actions and the United States sent troops to support what remained of South Korea. It is estimated that 2.5 million civilians were killed or wounded with hundreds of thousands of troops killed or injured in battle. The result of the three-year conflict was a military stalemate, the signing of the Korean Armistice Agreement, and the creation of the Korean Demilitarized Zone.

As of 2006, North Korea telegraphed to the world the significance of its development but nascent nuclear technology; in doing so, it demonstrated to the world its latest ballistic missile test and eventually announced its first nuclear test to the world (CIA 2018). Since the early 1980s, North Korea has aggressively pursued a nuclear program and developed increasingly more capable ballistic missiles for both indigenous use and export. The more sophisticated these missiles are, the more important test equipment has grown in validating their design and verifying performance and reliability (CIA 2018). Since the missile and nuclear weapons' test in 2006, several subsequent exercises have occurred under the current North Korean regime (GAO-15-485 2015, 4). Following the successful missile test, a plethora of sanctions have been imposed by the United States and the United Nations on North Korea.

Referring back to the YIRTM one of the four main instruments of power that can lead to a shaped outcome of a weakened U.S. position is that of diplomacy. North Korea has been an isolated hermit kingdom since its founding, under its current national ideology of self-reliance, known as "Juche" (CIA 2018). Recently the world has seen that they are striding away from this practice with the recent summit meeting between Kim Jong-un and

Donald Trump. At this summit meeting there were talks of North Korea beginning to show that it would move towards denuclearization (White House 2018). Having a denuclearized state is the first and foremost goal for the U.S. in regard to North Korea (Nauret 2018). In the eyes of the United States this was seen as a significant success and a moment to celebrate; for Kim Jong-un, this was a time for him to exploit an opportunity to increase his diplomatic standing. Arguably, the North Korean leader used the optics of this event to garner more attention for himself and his country. That stated, historically North Korea has made many promises before and broken most of them in the past which has given the U.S. pause for concern (Royce 2018). This statement by Chairman Royce shows that North Korea is not a nation that the United States can trust based on historical accounts. Moreover, the United States has continued to implement sanctions and direct its rhetoric towards North Korea, but with the United States and North Korea becoming friendlier in the first six months of 2018 and some of these actions or sanctions may begin to lift causing North Korea to seize on this opportunity (NDAA 2018).

China has supported North Korea since its inception. In 1950 when Mao Zedong's Communist Party took military and political control of China, they provided military support to its communist neighbors in Korea to advance their interests. China is North Korea's closest ally, the largest provider of food, fuel, and industrial machinery for this nation, and arguably is the country most able to wield influence in Pyongyang (U.S. Congressional Research Service 2010). China's food and energy aid to North Korea achieves several objectives; it not only helps to stabilize the erratic regime but furthers China's economic influence over North Korea and might help to encourage North Korea to reform and strengthen its own economy (U.S. Congressional Research Service 2010). This kind of aid also increases China's leverage by raising the costs of misbehavior while simultaneously suggesting that rewards are possible for good behavior. China means everything to North Korea; it is safe to assume that without China, North Korea would not be nearly as successful as they are today. As the JSP (2018) states, China itself is a very strong nation with an extremely powerful military and ever rising economy. With these two nations talking and becoming friendly with one another, it can create a concerning alliance that puts the U.S. behind in a diplomatic sense as well as in other ways.

Information is seemingly today's power instrument of choice. As shown in Annex A, "I" achieved a frequency tie number which is 14. North Korea is an isolated hermit kingdom which means not much gets into or out of the nation. Recently, the world has seen Kim Jong-un meet with Donald Trump while simultaneously North Korea also remains in a staunch ally with the PRC (White House 2018). This meeting also served as an opportunity to help Kim gain better insight on where the United States stands with its position regarding current economic sanctions. By talking with the U.S. president, this will allow Kim Jong-un to better gauge expectations to see just how far the North Korean Leader will have to go in order to see an easement of sanctions. That stated, the world has seen that North Korea historically has not been able to adeptly acquire information as directly as it has over the last year and through an enhanced bilateral relationship, this could continue to benefit Kim Jong-un's regime.

That stated, the world has seen times where the DPRK engages in cyber-attacks making use of the information instrument of power from the YIRTM. One specific occurrence gravitated around a ransomware attack also known as the WannaCry. This attack struck more than 150 nations, locking up digital documents, databases and other files where those responsible demanded a ransom for their release (Associated Press 2017). North Korea has also tried to exert its influence over places such as Japan, and South Korea (NDS 2018). These abilities and actions give North Korea the power to weaken the United States as the sole hegemony of the world.

North Korea's greatest strength lies in the military instrument of power. Annex A ranks "M" with a frequency of 16. Likewise, North Korea has a vast array of weapons that make it one of the most powerful and largest militaries in the world. Along with its nuclear capabilities, the DPRK's weapons include an eclectic mix of biological, chemical, unconventional and conventional military systems (NDS 2018). They also possess short, medium, intermediate, intercontinental and submarine launched missile capabilities (Albert 2018). U.S. intelligence assesses that North Korea has between 30 and 60 nuclear bombs (Albert 2018). Moreover, there is a missile whose nomenclature is the Hwasong-15, that if fired from a fixed platform can reach anywhere on the U.S. mainland (Albert 2018). North Korea also ranks fourth in the world in terms of absolute numbers with a military comprised of 1.1 million personnel (Albert 2018). Combined, these military capabilities afford North Korea the capacity to kill millions of Americans and allies in the region and at home (NSS 2017). The fact that North Korea is able to reach anywhere on the mainland of the U.S. with their missiles possess a major threat to the United States. Though North Korea is weaker with regards to the other three instruments found in the YIRTM, it has shown a proclivity to leverage its military capabilities to its advantage. Not only do they possess these capabilities, but they are willing to export their weapons to other countries. More specifically, North Korea has sold chemical weapon capabilities to Syria (DOS 2018).

Due to dedicated isolation, North Korea faces chronic economic problems, as shown with a frequency of 14 in Annex A. The industrial capacity is nearly beyond repair as a result of years of underinvestment, shortages of spare parts, and poor maintenance. Large-scale military spending and development of its ballistic missile and nuclear program severely draws off resources needed for investment and civilian consumption (JSP 2018). Industrial and power outputs have stagnated for years at a fraction of pre-1990 levels. Frequent weather-related crop failures aggravated chronic food shortages has been caused by ongoing systemic problems, including a lack of arable land, collective farming practices, poor soil quality, insufficient fertilization, and persistent shortages of tractors and fuel (CIA 2018).

The regime abides by a policy calling for the simultaneous development of its nuclear weapons program and its economy (CIA 2018). Accordingly, North Korea has been using its nuclear program to gain strategic defensive advantages due to its ever failing economy and increased sanctions from the rest of the world. As a result, the Department of State urges all other nations to cut diplomatic, financial, economic, and military ties with North Korea (JSP 2018). This in turn causes North Korea to shift to other outlets in order to support its military, economic and diplomatic initiatives. They do this by acquiring nuclear technology that the DPRK can showcase in order to gain attention from the international community. North Korea can also negotiate from a position of power to denuclearize with the intent of requesting the cessation of crippling sanctions and negotiate for increased aid to jump-start its economy to enhance the standard of living for their country. North Korea weakens the United States' influence over the region as it gains leverage to operate in a way that it chooses within the region rather than having to follow traditional norms of behavior. To not only have nuclear weapons but through its use of cyber, investment in other WMDs, and its conventional military also to threaten their use to negotiate terms that could lead to the removal of sanctions and increase investment into their economy, and this affords North Korea a distinct advantage within the region and certainly decreases United States' influence in this part of Asia.

FINDINGS AND CONCLUSION

Much of North Korea's strategy in the region has been decisively defensive due to its governmental mission and economic structure, putting the country in a situation without many options to gain greater influence in the region and nearly no contribution to the global economy. The nuclear proliferation in North Korea has opened a new door for the country to negotiate a better position with more power. It is understood that North Korea has been using their nuclear capabilities to gain attention from the world to attempt to open peace talks ostensibly to remove sanctions that are crippling the economy. It is without question that North Korea will use their nuclear capabilities as a final defensive measure if they felt the threat of a regime overthrow was imminent. The United States and the United Nations must continue economic pressure to gain North Korean compliance. It is critically important that other nations, specifically China whose influx of trade accounts for 86.3% of their imports, comply with sanctions to prevent further North Korean development and creation of a nuclear arsenal (CIA 2018). The elimination of resources to North Korea, the dismantling of nuclear plants, and the subsequent removal of nuclear arms and material would greatly diminish the nuclear program and ensure the United States' influence in the region remains strong.

North Korea's using of its nuclear program in the context of the YIRTM demonstrates its aggressive behavior to weaken the position of the U.S. as the world's sole hegemony. Diplomatically, the DPRK has been reaching out towards the United States and her allies for engagement talks and to foster a normalization of relations on the surface. The leader of North Korea, Kim Jong-un, has had multiple peace talks with other representatives throughout the world, including President Trump. Historically, this is one of the first times North Korea has met and spoken with United States bilaterally regarding potential peace negotiations. The peace talks would directly involve North Korea's nuclear program and open up the U.S. to potentially lift sanctions and/or send more aid to help the country, with the exchange of North Korea dismantling its nuclear weapons program. It is speculative that North Korea would forgo existing nuclear weapons by putting North Korea in a better position within the region.

Building off of the diplomacy used by North Korea, the current regime has also been using information and technology in regard to weakening the United States. There are a numerous incidents of tweets exchanged back and forth between North Korean leader Kim Jong-un and President Trump. Mostly these gravitate around the topic of North Korea's nuclear development; there was mostly backlash at President Trump as the United States politically was in a state of political division following the past presidential election. This looked better for the North Korean regime on the world stage, as it more demonized the United States in the conflict rather than North Korea.

Militarily, North Korea gained a significant stance within the region regarding their nuclear capabilities. Since North Korea has a formidable conventional missile capability to strike allies in the area and parts of the United States, the regime can use their weapons to wield power. Because no side wants a nuclear strike to happen, North Korea can use their nuclear capabilities with the intent of a potential strike if the other sides does not negotiate and if it finds a way to deliver a nuclear weapon by missile or rocket. Moreover, as is the case with any military conflict within the area regarding North Korea, the regime can use their nuclear capabilities to gain more influence within the region. This puts North Korea in a better position as now the United States will have not much of a choice but to withdraw their pressure in the region when dealing with North Korea.

Economically there is not much North Korea can do, except negotiate for monetary support in exchange for the dismantlement of the nuclear program, but overall this would not hurt the United States on the economic stage as the United States' economy is just too strong. North Korea at present lacks sufficient resources that it could export to generate money and is encumbered by crippling sanctions that affect its ability to trade internationally.

The situation in North Korea should be handled diplomatically as any military engagement could provoke the North Korean regime to launch its ICBMs against allies regionally in general and globally at the United States more specifically causing a protracted crisis that could result in catastrophic loss of life. The United States, as well as the rest of the world, must stand united to ensure such sanctions will remain unless the number of nuclear weapons North Korea holds drops significantly or better – are completely removed. However, it would be most important to understand the history of the current North Korean regime in the context of past promises and lack of integrity towards honoring them. The United States and the United Nations must push for further involvement and responsibility in the effort of decreasing the number of nuclear weapons that North Korea holds.

Along with handling the situation in the region diplomatically, it is also important for the United States to strengthen its military capabilities in the region so that the North Korean regime cannot push their military boundaries any further. The Defense Department recognizes that after decades of conflict, budget uncertainty, and the potential for a retraction of defense budgets that could degrade the military readiness of the United States that it has many challenges (GAO-16-841 2016). Rebuilding the military capabilities and readiness in the region is of great importance for the United States to show how its power is used as the remaining sole hegemony of the world. The more the United States allows a decreased military presence in the region, the more the current North Korean regime could leverage its military capabilities thereby strengthening its resolve. It would also be in the best interest for the United States as well as her allies to further install anti-ballistic missile capabilities and air defense initiatives among themselves though these still wouldn't work effectively against a conventional artillery strike. With the United States having a multitude of allies in the region, liabilities arise as the United States cannot just worry about defending itself but must also make careful diplomatic and military decisions to ensure an attack on her allies is non-existent.

When turning to research question 1, these authors found that North Korea is using a combination of cyber (information), a nuclear & ballistic missile program, the continued possession of other WMDs, and a significant military in terms of size (military) to exert influence in the region and globally. To a lesser extent, it is using diplomacy in order to leverage relations to get what it wants.

In answering research question 2, this research has shown that Kim Jong-un is using the diplomacy, information, and military instruments of power from the YIRTM to hold onto power and to gain greater credibility and notoriety on the world stage. The DPRK has shown great resilience for almost seven decades and shows no sign of waning anytime soon.

When going back to the YIRTM and Federal Qualitative Secondary Data Case Study Triangulation Model, these authors found that these models were useful. Both helped guide the research to arrive at conclusions. Ultimately, careful and decisive planning is going to be needed for the United States to handle the current situation in the region. The United States must demonstrate resolve and be strong in its diplomacy, sanctions, and military to ensure her influence and current status as the world's sole hegemony is not hindered in the region. However, the United States must also remain smart while dealing with the situation as the problem extends far beyond just an issue between North Korea and the United States; the allies of the United States (and their needs and desires) in the region should also be taken into consideration as well. The United States' allies in the region go hand in hand with U.S. diplomacy, information, military, and economic actions, as its allies' safety and security in the region are also important considerations and influence of power within this part of Asia.

ANNEX A

How/Why	D. I. M. E.	Source	Source Type	Date	Page (if applicable)
North Korea developed an unlawful intercontinental ballistic missile (ICBM) with the stated objective of striking the United States.	D, I, M, E	Join Strategic Plan FY 2018-2022	Government Document	2018	24
Department of State urges all other nations to cut diplomatic, financial, economic, military ties with North Korea. The United States continues to lead efforts in putting sanctions against North Korea.	D, I, M, E	Joint Strategic Plan FY 2018-2022	Government Document	2018	24
China continues to support North Korea. The United States will engage with China to address differences on North Korea. The U.S. reinforces existing regional allies such as Japan, South Korea, and Australia.	D, I, M, E	Joint Strategic Plan FY 2018-2022	Government Document	2018	30
NDAA addresses actions and reinforces its standards for dealing with North Korea following the past diplomatic summit between The United States and North Korea	D, I, M, E	National Defense Authorization Act	Government Document	2018	16
President Trump and Chairman Kim Jong-un meet at the historical summit to discuss diplomatic negotiations of the denuclearization of North Korea at United States-North Korea summit in Singapore.	D, M, E	White House	Press Statements	Jun-18	N/A
North Korea's second test launch of their newly developed ICBM is a danger to the world.	D, M, E	White House	Presidential Statement from White House	Jul-17	N/A
Secretary Pompeo met with Chairman Kim Jong-un prior to Singapore summit between the United States and North Korea.	D	State Department	Press Release.	May-18	N/A

How/Why	D. I. M. E.	Source	Source Type	Date	Page (if applicable)
Chairman Royce makes a statement regarding North Korea and denuclearization.	D, M, E	Foreign Affairs Committee	Official Statement	May-18	N/A
Chairman Royce's statement on meeting with South Korean Foreign Minister.	D, I, M,E	Foreign Affairs Committee	Official Statement	Mar-18	N/A
Chairman Royce's statement on North Korea's desire to talk following U.S. sanctions.	D, I, M, E	Foreign Affairs Committee	Official Statement	Mar-18	N/A
Chairman Royce's comments on President Trump's visit to Asia amid the growing North Korean nuclear threat.	D, I, M, E	Foreign Affairs Committee	Press Release	Nov-17	N/A
GAO research between the years 2006 - 2015 regarding each missile and nuclear test by North Korea and each U.N. or U.S. sanction, as well as each U.S. Executive Order that follows.	D, I, E	GAO-15-485	Case Study	2015	P. 2, 4, 5, 6, 8, 9, 10, 11, 12, 13, 16, 19, 28, 29, 34, 35, 36, 37
Heather Nauret discusses some of the sanctions being put on North Korea by the U.S. as well as what is hopeful for what North Korea plans to do with their nuclear weapons which is denuclearization	D, I, M	U.S. Department of State	Department Press Briefing	Sep-18	N/A
Heather Nauret mentions that North Korea is selling chemical weapon capabilities to Syria	M, E	U.S. Department of State	Department Press Briefing	Feb-18	N/A
Donald Trump states that North Korea seeks the capability to kill millions of Americans with nuclear weapons	I, M	National Security Strategy	Government Document	Dec-17	7

Annex A. (Continued)

How/Why	D. I. M. E.	Source	Source Type	Date	Page (if applicable)
Donald Trump speaks about the weapons capabilities that North Korea has including cyber, ballistics and nuclear, he then talks about all actions that he wants to put forth to eliminate threats involving this country	D, I, M, E	National Security Strategy	Government Document	Dec-17	46
Secretary Mattis discusses the military power of North Korea as they look to gain coercive influence over South Korea, Japan, and the United States	D, I, M	National Defense Strategy	Government Document	2018	3-Feb
The Trump Administration blames North Korea for a ransom ware attack known as the WannaCry ransom ware attack that affected over 150 nations	I, E	Associated Press	Press Release	Dec-17	N/A
Secretary Mattis discusses ways in which the United States can deter any type of nuclear, cyber and missile threats posed to the United States	D, I, M	National Defense Strategy	Government Document	2018	6

REFERENCES

Albert, E. 2018, June 6. "*What Are North Korea's Military Capabilities?*" Retrieved from Council on Foreign Relations. Accessed October 25, 2018. https://www.cfr.org/backgrounder/north-koreas-militarycapabilities.

Brantley, Aaron F. 2016. "Cyber Actions by State Actors: Motivation and Utility." *International Journal of Intelligence and Counterintelligence*. 27(3): 465-484.

Central Intelligence Agency (CIA). 2018, October 17. "*The World Factbook: Korea, North.*" Accessed September 25, 2018. https://www.cia.gov/library/publications/the-worldfactbook/geos/kn.html.

Chairman Royce Statement on Meeting with South Korean Foreign Minister. (n.d.). Accessed September 23, 2018. https://foreignaffairs.house.gov/press-release/chairman-royce-statement-meeting-south-korean-foreign-minister/.

Chairman Royce Statement on North Korea. (n.d.). Accessed September 23, 2018. https://foreignaffairs.house.gov/press-release/chairman-roycestatement-north-korea-2/.

Columbia University. 2009. "*The Geography of East Asia.*" Retrieved from http://afe.easia.columbia.edu/main_pop/kpct/kp_geo.htm.

Creswell, John W. 2008. *Research Design; Qualitative, Quantitative, and Mixed Methods Approaches*. Thousand Oaks, CA: SAGE Publications.

Cross-Sectional. 2012. "*Cross-Sectional Studies.*" Accessed October 17, 2012. http://www.healthknowledge.org.uk/public-healthtextbook/research-methods/1a-epidemiology/cs-as-is/cross-sectional-studies.

Department of State. 2018. "*Travel to Japan and North Korea, May 8-9, 2018.*" Accessed on September 23, 2018. https://www.state.gov/secretary/travel/2018/t7/index.htm.

Jaeger, Richard M. 1993. *Statistics a Spectator Sport* (2nd Edition). Sage Publications London, United Kingdom.

Jo, Jin-Cheol, and César Ducruet. 2006. "Maritime Trade and Port Evolution in a Socialist Developing Country: Nampo, gateway of North Korea."

The Korea Spatial Planning Review 51 (1), pp.3-24. https://halshs.archives-ouvertes.fr/halshs-00459066/document.

JSP. 2018. *Joint Strategic Plan FY 2018-2022*. Accessed December 16, 2018. https://www.state.gov/documents/organization/277156.

Mattis, James. (n.d.). *National Defense Strategy*. Accessed December 17, 2018. http://nssarchive.us/national-defense-strategy-2018/.

Mollman, Steve. 2017, June 16. "*North Korea is Sitting on Trillions of Dollars of Untapped Wealth, and Its Neighbors Want in.*" https://qz.com/1004330/north-korea-is-sitting-on-trillions-of-dollars-on-untapped-wealth-and-its-neighbors-want-a-piece-of-it/.

Moore, Aaron S. 2013, February. "*The Yalu River Era of Developing Asia*": Japanese Expertise, Colonial Power, and the Construction of Sup'ung Dam. https://www.jstor.org/stable/23357509.

Nanto, Dick K., & Mark Manyin. 2010, December 28. "*China-North Korea Relations.*" https://s3.amazonaws.com/academia.edu.documents/33488577/ChinaNorth_Korea_Relations.pdf?AWSAccessKeyId=AKIAIWOWYYGZ2Y53UL3A&Expires=1541724818&Signature=5mNbNiaoAZIKa7JJ6RLVlBnIbnY=&response-content-disposition=inline;filename=China-North_Korea_Relations.pdf.

Nauert1, Heather. 2018, February 27. Department Press Briefing. Accessed October 24, 2018. https://www.state.gov/r/pa/prs/dpb/2018/02/278913.htm.

Nauert2, Heather. 2018, September 20. Department Press Briefing. Accessed October 25, 2018. https://www.state.gov/r/pa/prs/dpb/2018/09/286096.htm.

Palka, E., Galgano, F. 2002, December. "*North Korea: A Geographic Overview.*" https://psugeo.org/Publications/NorthKorea.pdf.

Randall Ireson. 2013, December 18. "*The State of North Korea Farming: New Information from the UN Crop Assessment Report.*" https://www.38north.org/2013/12/rireson121813/.

ReliefWeb. 2017, June. "*DPR Korea: Drought.*" https://reliefweb.int/disaster/dr-2017-000087-prk.

Remler, D.K. & Van Ryzin, G.G. 2010. *Research Methods in Practice: Strategies for Description and Causation*. Thousand Oaks, CA: SAGE Publishing.

Trump, Donald1. 2017, July 28. "*Statement from the President on North Korea's Second ICBM Launch.*" https://www.whitehouse.gov/ briefings-statements/statement-president-north-koreas-second-icbm-launch/.

Trump, Donald. 2017, December. *National Security Strategy*. Accessed on September 20, 2018. https://www.whitehouse.gov/wpcontent/uploads/ 2017/12/NSS-Final-12-18-2017-0905.pdf.

United States, U.S. Department of State. 2018. *Joint Strategic Plan FY 2018 - 2022*. U.S. Accessed on September 20, 2018. https://www.state.go v/documents/organization/277156.pdf.

United States, Congress. 2018. *John S. McCain National Defense Authorization Act FY-2019*. https://www.govinfo.gov/content/pkg/ CRPT-115hrpt874/pdf/CRPT-115hrpt 874. pdf.

United Nations, Food and Agricultural Organization. 2017, July 20. "*Global Information and Early Warning System on Food and Agricultural (GIEWS), Special Alert, No. 340, Country: The Democratic People's Korea, Prolonged Dry Weather Threatens the 2017 Main Season Food Crop Production.*" Accessed September 20, 2018. https://reliefweb.i nt/sites/reliefweb.int/files/resources/a-i7544e.pdf.

U.S. Government Accountability Office1. 2015, May 13. "*North Korea Sanctions: United States Has Increased Flexibility to Impose Sanctions, but United Nations Is Impeded by a Lack of Member State Reports.*" Accessed on November 3, 2018. https://www.gao.gov/products/GAO-15-485.

U.S. Government Accountability Office2. 2016, September 07. "*Military Readiness: DOD's Readiness Rebuilding Efforts May Be at Risk without a Comprehensive Plan.*" Accessed on November 20, 2018. https://www.gao.gov/products/GAO-16-841.

Weaver, John M. 2015. "The Department of Defense and Homeland Security Relationship: Hurricane. Katrina through Hurricane Irene." *Journal of Emergency Management*. 12(3) 265-274.

White House. 2018, June 13. "*Historic Summit with North Korea is a Tremendous Moment for the World.*" Accessed September 20, 2018. https://www.whitehouse.gov/briefings-statements/historic-summit-north-korea-tremendous-moment-world/.

Yoon, Edward. 2011, January 6. "*Status and Future of the North Korean Minerals Sector.*" Accessed on November 20, 2081. http://nautilus.org/wp-content/uploads/2011/12/DPRK-Minerals-Sector-YOON.pdf.

In: Global Intelligence Priorities ISBN: 978-1-53615-836-6
Editors: John Michael Weaver et al. © 2019 Nova Science Publishers, Inc.

Chapter 7

SORTING OUT THE SYRIAN CONFLICT; IMPACTS ON UNITED STATES NATIONAL SECURITY: A QUALITATIVE ASSESSMENT

James Simmons, Austin Cullember and Brendan McDonough
York College, York, Pennsylvania, US

ABSTRACT

"Terrorists and criminals thrive where governments are weak, corruption is rampant, and faith in government institutions is low" (NSS 2017, 49). The conflict in Syria arose after the Arab Spring. Bashar al-Assad, the leader of the Syrian regime, began using military force in order to hold onto control of the country. Consequently, more people rebelled, and Syria was thrust into a civil war. The Regime has been accused of using chemical weapons on his own people. This alerted the United Nations (UN) and global powers to these inhumane acts. Subsequently, the UN responded with various diplomatic acts including UN Resolution 2254. At the same time, terror organizations, specifically the Islamic State of Iraq and Syria (ISIS) and Hezbollah, began finding footholds in Syria. This led to the involvement of the United States (U.S.) in this country, fighting against the extremist groups and the Assad regime. While these groups are the face of the Syrian conflict, international actors such as Iran and Russia enable them to survive against the forces of peace. This study uses qualitative research to interpret trends and findings of official press releases, government documents, and plans in place for Syria to make sense of the situation. The fight in Syria is not only enabled through military tools and tactics, but also through diplomacy and other instruments on the global battlefield.

LITERATURE REVIEW

The United States' ultimate guide to national security is the National Security Strategy (NSS) which is approved by each president during their term. In December 2017, President Trump and his administration released its 2017 NSS that covers a variety of issues concerning the United States' national security and welfare for the country. The NSS serves as a guiding framework to all departments of the United States' government including the Department of Defense (DOD) and the Department of State (DOS), who from this document create their own specific strategies.

The Syrian conflict is mentioned in several sections of the NSS. It is first mentioned in the section: Defense Against Weapons of Mass Destruction (WMD). "The Syrian regime's use of chemical weapons against its own citizens undermines international norms against these heinous weapons, which may encourage more actors to pursue and use them. ISIS has used chemical weapons in Iraq and Syria" (NSS 2017, 8). The United States does not want chemical weapons falling into the wrong hands because that can quickly become a major threat to national security due to concerns over terrorism, and as amplified by the NSS, "[jihadist] have used battlefields as test beds of terror and have exported tools and tactics to their followers. Many of these jihadist terrorists are likely to return to their home countries, from which they can continue to plot and launch attacks on the United States and our allies" (NSS 2017, 10-11). Jihadists are using the Syrian conflict as a catalyst to test tactics and expand their weaponry. While there is not a feasible defense against the multitude of threats that face the United States' homeland, America as well as its partners and allies, must stay on the offensive against these violent non-state actors that target the United States and its allies (NSS 2017, 10).

Jihadist terrorists and foreign criminal organizations are the primary transnational threats that America faces. These actors pose similar challenges to this country's national security although their objectives differ (NSS 2017, 10). Some prominent challenges are that they rely on encrypted communication and the dark web to evade detection as they plot, recruit, finance, and execute their operations (NSS 2017, 10). Another challenge that one observes in actors such as ISIS is that these groups thrive under conditions of state weakness and prey on the vulnerable as they accelerate the breakdown of rules to create havens from which to plan and launch attacks on the United States as well as its allies and partners (NSS 2017, 10). Jihadist terrorist organizations are engaged in a long war with the nation because they are fanatics who advance a totalitarian vision for a global Islamist caliphate that justifies murder and slavery, promotes repression, and seeks to undermine the American way of life (NSS 2017, 10). Both preceding presidents have defined ISIS and al-Qaeda as threats to this nation's national security, even after the territorial defeat of these groups in Syria and Iraq; the threat from jihadist terrorists will continue to persist (NSS 2017, 10).

The United Nations Security Council (UNSC) unanimously adopted Resolution 2254, in 2015 to resolve the Syria conflict. The Resolution 2254 is a plan to create peace in Syria, with a planned-out process and timeline for this. The resolution mentions a ceasefire, and possibly United Nations (UN) led negotiations between the Assad regime and its opposition. Different world leaders chimed in with varying components to the conflict that need intervention, and how they could be fixed. For example, the Russian Minister for Foreign Affairs of the Russian Federation called upon all parties not to engage in rhetoric but rather, to be guided by the need to combat terrorism and find a political settlement of the conflict (UNSC 7588th meeting). Russia claimed that their only goal in Syria was to promote peace through the resolution by fighting back against only the extremist groups.

Assad began his education in Damascus, studying medicine at the University of Damascus, and then shortly served as an army doctor before moving to London to continue his studies in ophthalmology. He was in London less than two years before he was brought back to Syria by the death of his older brother, Basil, who died in a car accident. This began Assad's grooming to be the next leader of Syria. He denies that he was forced to be the next head of state, but many find this unbelievable. He was sent to military academies, and quickly rose through the ranks of the Syrian Army, gaining important roles in the government, such as overseeing Syria's relationship with Lebanon. In 2000, Hafiz al-Assad passed away, and Assad was nominated by the Baath party for president; he ran unopposed. Assad officially began his presidency on July 12, 2000 (Lesch 2005).

Other actors involved in Syria are using the conflict as a military and diplomatic vantage point against the United States, shown by statements made by the Russian UN Ambassador Zakharova along with the support provided by Russia and Iran to Assad. Several conflicting press releases from Russia and the U.S., disputes in the United Nations Security Council over Syria, and general distrust between the United States and Russia, as shown in Zakharova's press release about chemical weapons' locations in Syria, demonstrate the fight for control between the two international powers involved. Russia condemns the United States for interfering in the conflict, attempting to paint the U.S. as a villain (Zakharova1 2018). The use of the Syrian conflict by states, like Russia and Iran, to weaken the U.S. is clearly demonstrated through various press releases and tactics on the battlegrounds. As events in Syria unfolded, Russia used their diplomatic position in the UN and in the Middle East region to protect the Assad Regime, as represented in Annex A, where press releases from Zakharova express a hostile attitude towards the United States (Zakharove1 2018 & Zakharova2 2018). The diplomatic tension has also caused military tension between the two major international actors involved in the Syrian conflict (Haley 2017 & Zarkharova1 2018).

RESEARCH QUESTIONS

As discussed above, the Syria conflict is complex in nature not only involving the state actor but also other state actors within and outside of the region and many different non-state actor groups. In order to tackle such complexity, the D.I.M.E. (diplomacy, information, military and economic) logic model was used to frame this analysis. Specifically, these authors considered the following research questions to look at what is possible from an adversarial perspective with regards to the Syrian conflict.

Q1: How are Syria and Syrian allies using the YIRTM to weaken the position of the United States?

Q2: Why are state and non-state actors using Syria in the context of the YIRTM to weaken the position of the United States as the world's sole hegemony?

LOGIC MODEL

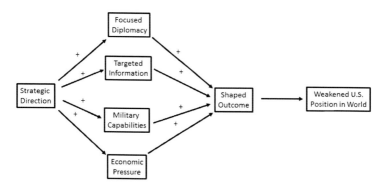

Figure 1. YIRTM.

National power can be measured through diplomacy, information, military, and economic aspects. Shown in Figure 1, the logic model visualizes how an adversary is able to take advantage of four instruments putting pressure on the United States (JP 1-02, 2010, 112). These instruments are useful in shaping outcomes in the world (Weaver1 2015 & Weaver2 2015).

This model begins with the strategic direction of the entity expressly bent on adversely affecting the national security strategy of this country. It begins with direction and guidance by a leader (in this case, Russia and Bashar al-Assad) providing basics on the "who," "what," "where," "when," and "why." With the direction and guidance of the leadership determined, one can then look at the four prevailing instruments as a way to implement tactics, techniques and procedures (TTPs) supportive to one's cause.

The first instrument of national power, diplomacy, is used when those in charge engage with other foreign leaders to implement desired values, interests, and objectives (JP 1-02 2010, 40). This is the most ideal because state and non-state actors can work together to reach a conclusion that can benefit all actors involved. However, diplomacy can also be used as a tool to weaken an adversary. An example would be Russia claiming the United States is furthering the conflict in Syria. Here, Russia is using diplomacy to paint the United States in a negative way, making it more difficult to deal with the Syrian conflict. "The U.S. goal in Syria remains to halt the tragedy that would have ended years ago, if Russia and Iran had not intervened" (Mattis 2018). Russian's power within the United Nations Security Council weakens the United States' ability to diplomatically impact the regime through the UN in any way. "Iranians are in Syria. Iran is propping up the Assad regime with forces, money, weapons and proxies. Part of this overarching problem is we have to address Iran," Mattis (2018) said. "Everywhere you go in the Middle East, where there is instability, you find Iran" (Mattis 2018). The Iranian regime's ability to keep the Assad in power in Syria weakens the United States' ability to provide a smooth transition of power away from the regime.

Targeted information refers to identifying aspects that are vital to national security. This requires means of intelligence collection and knowing what to look for. Jihadist terrorists use both virtual and physical networks around the world to radicalize isolated individuals, exploit vulnerable populations, and inspire direct plots against the homeland (NSS 2017, 10). The Organization for the Prohibition of Chemical Weapons said a Sarin nerve agent or something similar was used in an April 4th, 2017 aerial attack in northern Syria that killed nearly 100 villagers and children. The Trump administration said it had evidence that Syrian President Bashar al-Assad's forces were preparing for another chemical attack and said he would pay a "heavy price" if one were attempted.

The instrument of military power has been used by all sides of the Syrian conflict. Actors like Russia and the United States have the best military capabilities in the world and are using these to test their own systems as well as each other's, without escalating the conflict to a war between one another. The Assad regime's chemical weapon capabilities are what drew the United States into this conflict. Military capabilities are being tested by various actors in the region and could show who has the upper hand in the future. The former United States Secretary of State Rex Tillerson said American troops will remain in Syria long after their fight against the Islamic State is over to ensure that neither Iran nor President Bashar al-Assad will seize control of areas that have been recently liberated. This is to hopefully prevent the mistakes President Obama made during the Iraq war when he withdrew troops before the threat was completely neutralized and failed to stabilize Libya after the North Atlantic Treaty Organization (NATO) airstrikes which led to the overthrow of Colonel Muammar al-Gaddafi in December 2017.

The economic instrument has been used in the region as well. The Syrian regime's bank accounts are extremely low, and money is often associated with power. However, Syria's two biggest allies, Russia and Iran, have been funding them, and selling the Syrians weapons' components. The United States has been supporting various rebel groups in the region as well, which could help unseat President Assad from power. The United States has put economic sanctions on Russia due to its activities in Syria.

METHODOLOGY

The data used to analyze Syria and the other actors involved was collected from unclassified secondary sources for ease of access. Sources for this study were collected from government reports, press releases, and other official documents. Although there are limitations, secondary data provides the important insights to understanding the complexity of the Syrian conflict. Using the York Intelligence Red Team Model (YIRTM), this study was able to show how the Syrian conflict is being waged in regard to the four instruments of national power (D.I.M.E.) and the ways how such conflict weakens the United States.

Figure 2. The Federal Qualitative Secondary Data Case Study Triangulation Model.

The Federal Qualitative Secondary Data Case Study Triangulation Model, shown in Figure 2, helps to ensure data quality in terms of diversity and credibility regarding the Syrian conflict. There are three major areas in the Federal Triangulation Model: (1) plans and systems, (2) documents, legislation, and policy, and (3) press releases, testimony, interviews, and biographies. The first area, plans and systems, focuses on procedures and capabilities that are relevant now. Secondly, documents and policy help to the United States has been unsuccessful in removing Assad and establishing a more stable government.

The United States and its allies continuously accuse Russia of aiding the Syrian regime in committing crimes, specifically the use of chemical weapons. In response, Russia denies the accusations, and warns the U.S. from militarily engaging with Russian and Syrians forces (Zakharova2 2018). As shown in Annex A, Russia has a desire to be the dominate actor in Syria, requesting that the United States provide to Russia a list of suspected chemical sites. For instance, in Annex A, one sees the diplomacy instrument in the Middle East and this suggests that Russia fully recognizes the value and effect of diplomacy in the global hot spot region that it can reshuffle the changing international geopolitics. If the U.S. were to do this, Russia could assert diplomatic control of the situation by handling the inspection of the suspected sites, therefore ensuring any outcome that would benefit Russia in general and the Syrian regime more specifically.

Assad remaining in control of the Syrian government could see an escalation of tensions in the region with the possible expansion of future conflict in the Middle East that could involve Israel and other actors. This will further the proxy war, both militarily and diplomatically, between Russia and the United States, causing even more turmoil in the already unstable region. Through aggressive actions towards Israel, the Syrian regime and its supporters know the U.S. will stand by Israel, drawing the United States deeper into conflict in the Middle East. In doing so, the U.S. will influx more military might into the area, resulting in the diffusion of military presence elsewhere on the planet. The United States, already occupied with multiple other conflicts, will lose an advantage against Russia in other regions within the Middle East. Furthermore, Russia has been and will continue to use the Syrian conflict, and any other conflicts that arise from it, as a means of gathering information on U.S. capabilities. While the full force of the U.S. military is not felt in Syria as of yet, there is high potential that the United States will devote more time, power, and money to the region, especially if Israel is involved, and Russia continues to tighten their grasp in the area.

Iran/Hezbollah

Iran is a Shia country that seeks to be the sole hegemony in the Middle East. The Iranian regime has provided Assad with oil, money, weapons, fighters, everything to maintain power within the region, due to common political goals and interests. It is one of the Assad regime's largest state supporters, both economically and militarily. "The Iranian regime and Russia are providing millions of barrels of oil to this regime in exchange for the movement of hundreds of millions of dollars to the Islamic Revolutionary Guard Corps-Qods Force, and for onward transfer to terrorist organizations such as Hamas and Hizballah" (Office of the Spokesperson 2018). Iran's four main goals in Syria are: (1) protect the Assad regime against opposition, (2) increase its presence and influence in Syria and build weapon-production facilities, (3) maintain Syria as the vital bridge between Iraq and Lebanon, and (4) move closer to the Golan Heights to create another potential front against Israel (Ghaddar 2018, 1). They do this with their proxy group Hezbollah, which has helped them to control Lebanon and, more recently, Syria. Iran uses Hezbollah as a proxy to help support the regime militarily. Iran's strategy has mostly been about filling the vacuum, created mainly by the United States vicariously fighting Assad's forces vis-à-vis support through moderate rebel forces in Syria and other parts of the region and the lack of security that has ensued (Ghaddar 2018, 11).

Iran would eventually like to create a front against Israel who is the ally of the United States' in the region. Geographically, Israel shares its southern border with Syria. If Israel were to fall, this would hurt the United States' influence in the region.

FINDINGS AND CONCLUSION

When looking at Syria's civil war escalation, and all actors involved, it is crucial to consider the impacts on the United States' national security, which specifically includes conflict from state and non-state actors in the region as well as the secretive harboring and spreading of extremist organizations' influence beyond the Middle Eastern perimeter. Inside the Middle Eastern region is an armed conflict involving a multitude of actors that include the Assad regime, insurgent agencies fighting the government and/or each other, all the while state actors such as Russia and Iran have been feeding into this civil war long before it started.

Much of Russia's role in the Syrian conflict is taken to undermine the United States. The first research question looks to find how Syria's allies, in this case, Russia is using the instruments of national power through the Syrian conflict to weaken the United States. Data reflected in Annex A shows that the Syrian conflict serves as a catalyst for Russia who successfully used the diplomatic instrument to move against the U.S. while strengthen allegiances in the Middle Eastern region. By supporting the Assad regime, Russia used its diplomatic power in the Middle East and the UN to gain an advantage against the United States in this part of the world that the U.S. devotes much of its power and time. Diplomacy is being used to protect the Syrian government against moves the U.S. takes in the backdrop of the UN and global politics. Finding an answer to the first research question and determining how the Syrian conflict is being used in relation to the instruments of national power became clear once evidence was found connecting Russia to strong support for the Assad's government. Russia's military capabilities, found in Annex A, are being used in opposition to the goals of the United States by protecting the sovereignty of the Syrian leader. Through the conflict in Syria, Russia is creating a proxy war and gathering information on the United States and its military capabilities. Lastly, Russia's economic interest in Syria further undermines U.S. goals in the Middle East, support and profiting from a very hostile government. Annex A reflects how Russia is using, and will continue to use, the Syrian conflict to weaken the United States.

Regarding the second research question, looking to find why the Syrian conflict is being used in relation to the YIRTM one sees that Syria is an open medium for exerting the instruments of national power against the United States. The Syrian government accepts Russia's support, and creates stronger diplomatic ties in the process. Russia's political presence in the Middle East is a threat to the U.S. and its allies in the region, mainly because

Russia is establishing connections with governments known to be dangerous and destructive. Russia can control the actor and advance its own military goals through the support it gives to the Syrian government. Assad has used the military power given to him by Russia to terrorize his own people. This has complicated efforts in this country where the U.S. has been drawn deeper into Syria and allows Russia to gain information on the military might of the United States. Furthermore, the U.S. becomes stuck in a quagmire that has little political upside. Russia benefits from this by using Syria as a proxy war against the United States to collect information and test its own military power. The conflict also causes the U.S. to spend more money and tying up its military, slowly weakening the nation's strength. Annex A reflects Russia's support of Assad and the continuous denial of malicious intent.

For Russia, Syria is the easiest way to undermine the United States. The U.S. has a heavy presence in the Middle Eastern region due to the fight against terrorism through its support to staunch allies such as Israel and Saudi Arabia, and economic resources that it expends to keep oil moving in the region. Because of this, Russia has utilized diplomatic, military, and economic moves in Syria, fully knowing the United States will be compelled to remain involved. Generally, the U.S. does not interfere in civil wars; however, the inhumane actions taken by the actors in Syria give the United States little choice, as portrayed through the evidence in Annex A. To drag the U.S. into yet another conflict would allow room for other international powers to begin moving against the U.S. to weaken and eventually allow other countries to potentially overtake the United States as a global power.

Assad's ability to form diplomatic ties with Russia, as a world power, and Iran, as a regional actor, has forced the U.S. to deploy troops in the region to arm, train, and assist rebels fighting Assad and his backers. This costs the United States money, and ties up troops in the region. Ultimately, this spreads and strains the United States' military more than it already was. While this may not benefit Syria, this does help its allies in weakening the United States. Iran has used Syria, to establish regional control. The Assad regime could see it in an advantageous position because it does not feel the need to adhere by international laws of warfare, as seen in Annex A. Their chemical weapons use has provided them an edge in terrifying not only its own citizens, but many other nations throughout the region. This lack of fear to use extreme measures is beneficial for the Syrian leadership and the regime's control of Syria. This is how this country is using the instruments of military power.

Iran is adept at implementing the instruments of power referred to in the YIRTM to assert their influence in the region. Their diplomatic ties with Syria have allowed the Iranians to get closer to the Golan Heights, and in the future, potentially create a front against United States' ally, Israel. Iran has helped the Assad regime militarily through their proxy terrorist organization Hezbollah. This group has further assisted Assad as he exercises control of the territory without needing to deploy many Iranian troops. Potentially this affords Iran an upper hand militarily over the United States in this part of the world. Thus, Hezbollah allows Iran to maintain military influence in Syria, without having a large presence of its own. This is also very cost effective for Iran. It is cheaper to fund Hezbollah than to deploy its own conventional military.

The conflict in Syria provides an opportunity for Iran to gain information about United States' weapon capabilities and strategies. This information can be used against the United States in potential direct warfare. Referring to research question one, Iran and Hezbollah are using the YIRTM in Syria, through focused diplomacy with the Assad regime as seen in Annex A, while also using targeted information, and military capabilities within Syria. In referring to research question two, Iran and Hezbollah are using the YIRTM to become the hegemonic power within the Middle East. When turning back to research question one, these authors found that focused diplomacy and military capabilities were the most relevant variables from the YIRTM, and economic pressure was less relevant. Shifting to the Federal Qualitative Secondary Data Case Study Triangulation Model, press releases provided the greatest source of evidence and plans and systems were less relevant and/or not available. When affording consideration to the second research question, these authors found that focused diplomacy, targeted information, and military capabilities were the most relevant variables from the YIRTM, and economic pressure was the least relevant.

ANNEX A

How/Why	D.I.M.E.	Source	Source Type	Date	Page (If applicable)
Bashar al-Assad uses snipers, tanks, and chemical weapons on its own citizens	M	NSS	Government Document	2017	Pg. 10-11
Iran and Russia align with the Assad Regime	D, I, M, E	NATO	Press Release	2018	N/A
Russian companies allegedly sold chemical weapon components to the Syrian government, resulting in sanctions	D, I, M	Sharp	Government Report	2008	Pg. 18
Russia says U.S. is furthering conflict in Syria	D	Zakharova 1	Press Release	Aug-18	N/A
Conflict continues to make U.S. spend on training and arming opposition rebels, mainly to oppose ISIS forces, but similarly to fight against forces hostile to the U.S.	I, M, E	CTEF	Plan	2018	Pg. 3, 14-18
Russia announces their only aim in Syria is to fight back extremist groups and promote peace in accordance with UN Resolution 2254	D, I	Zakharova1	Press Release	Aug-18	N/A
U.S. UN Ambassador blames Bashar, Russia, and Iran for chemical attacks, discusses a new phase of a political solution for the crisis	D	Haley	Press Release	Apr-17	N/A
The Organization for the Prohibition of Chemical Weapons said Sarin nerve agent, or a similar poison gas, was used in an April 4, 2017 aerial attack in Northern Syria that killed nearly 100 villagers	I, M	Security Council	UN Meeting	Nov-17	N/A
U.S. Ambassador Nikki Haley accused Russia of defending Syria, U.S. and Russia not on good terms	D, M	Haley	Press Release	Mar-17	N/A
Russian Minister Lavrov reaffirms support of the Syrian regime	D	The Ministry of	Press Release	Sept-18	N/A

How/ Why	D.I.M.E.	Source	Source Type	Date	Page (If applicable)
		Foreign Affairs of the Russian Federation			
U.S. Secretary of State said American troops will remain in Syria to ensure that neither Iran nor President Bashar Al-Assad of Syria take over areas that have been newly liberated	D, M	U.S. Secretary of State Rex W. Tillerson	Press Release	Jan-18	N/A
Russian UN Ambassador Nebenzya requests the U.S. disclose target sites suspected of being used for storage of chemicals for Russian experts to inspect the sites. Russia warns against "new dangerous steps."	D, I, M	Zakharova 2	Press Release	Sept-18	N/A
France accuses President Bashar Al-Assad's government of using same Sarin gas used on Ghouta, Syria in 2013, Russia denounces reports	D, I	France Foreign Minister Jean-Marc Ayrault	Press Release	Apr-17	N/A
The United States puts economic sanction on Russia and Iran, due to aiding the Assad Regime with thousands of barrels of oils	D, I, E	Office of the Spokesperson	DOD Media Note	November 20, 2018	N/A
UN adopts Resolution 2254, in order to begin planning a peaceful solution in Syria	D	Resolution 2254	Plan	2015	N/A

By looking at the Federal Qualitative Secondary Data Case Study Triangulation Model, government reports and documents provided the greatest source of evidence and plans and systems were less relevant and/or not available.

Finally, both the YIRTM and the Federal Qualitative Secondary Data Case Study Triangulation Model where useful tools to assist these authors in answering their research questions. Future studies might want to make use of primary data collected through surveys or interviews to complement the findings of this study.

REFERENCES

Bolan, Christopher J. 2018. *The Brewing Battle over U.S. Troop Presence in Syria*. Retrieved from https://www.fpri.org/article/2018/08/the-brewing-battle-over-u-s-troop-presence-in-syria/.

Congressional Budget Office. 2018. H.R. 1677, *Caesar Syria Civilian Protection Act of 2018*. Retrieved from https://www.cbo.gov/publication/54590.

Department of State, Department of State. 2018. Briefing on Syria Meeting and U.S. Strategy [Press release]. https://www.state.gov/r/pa/prs/ps/2018/09/286289.htm [accessed on November 14, 2018].

Haley, Nikki. 2017. *Remarks at a UN Security Council Meeting on the Situation in Syria*. Retrieved from https://usun.state.gov/remarks/7755.

JP 1-02. 2010. Department of Defense Dictionary of Military and Associated Terms. Joint Publication 1-02. November 8, 2010.

Lesch, David W. 2005. *The new lion of Damascus: Bashar al-Asad and modern Syria*. New Haven (Conn.): Yale University Press.

Mattis Stresses Geneva Process for Syria, Gives DoD Good Grades for Hu. (n.d.). Retrieved from https://dod.defense.gov/News/Article/Article/1643586/mattis-stresses-geneva-process-for-syria-gives-dod-good-grades-for-hurricane-ef/.

NSS. 2017 National Security Strategy. https://www.whitehouse.gov/wp-content/uploads/2017/12/NSS-Final-12-18-2017-0905.pdf.

Office of the Secretary of Defense. 2018. Department of Defense Budget Fiscal Year (FY) 2019. https://comptroller.defense.gov/Portals/45/Documents/defbudget/fy2019/fy2019_CTEF_JBook_Final.pdf [accessed on October 26, 2018].

Office of the Spokesperson1. 2018. Joint Statement on Syria. Retrieved from https://www.state.gov/r/pa/prs/ps/2018/09/286282.htm.

Office of the Spokesperson2. 2018. Sanctions Announcement on Iran. Retrieved from https://www.state.gov/r/pa/prs/ps/2018/11/287500.htm.

Previewing the Imposition of Chemical and Biological Weapons Control and Warfare Elimination Sanctions on Russia. 2018. https://www.state.gov/r/pa/prs/ps/2018/08/285046.htm [accessed on October 26, 2018].

Security Council Unanimously Adopts Resolution 2254. 2015. *Endorsing Road Map for Peace Process in Syria,* Setting Timetable for Talks | Meetings Coverage and Press Releases. (2015, December 18). https://www.un.org/press/en/2015/sc12171.doc.htm [accessed on October 26, 2018].

Sharp, Jeremy M. 2008. *Syria: Background and U.S. Relations* (p. 18) (United States, Congressional Research Service, Foreign Affairs, Defense, and Trade Division). Washington DC: CRS.

The World Factbook: SYRIA. *2018*, October 17. Retrieved October 26, 2018, from https://www.cia.gov/library/publications/the-worldfactbook/geos/sy.html .

Trump, Donald. 2018, April 13. Statement by President Trump on Syria. Retrieved from https://www.whitehouse.gov/briefingsstatements/statement-president-trump-syria/.

United Nations Security Council. 2017. Government, 'Islamic State' Known to Have Used Gas in Syria, Organization for Prohibition of Chemical Weapons Head Tells Security Council | Meetings Coverage and Press Releases. Retrieved from https://www.un.org/press/en/2017/sc13060.doc.htm.

United States Government, Department of Defense. 2018. Statement by Secretary James N. Mattis on Syria [Press release]. https://dod.defense.gov/News/News-Releases/News-ReleaseView/Article/1493610/statem

ent-by-secretary-james-n-mattis-on-syria/ [accessed on October 26, 2018].

U.S. Department of Defense. 2017. Statement from Pentagon Spokesman Capt. Jeff Davis on U.S. strike in S. Retrieved from https://dod.defense.gov/News/News-Releases/News-ReleaseView/Article/1144598/statement-from-pentagon-spokesman-capt-jeff-davis-on-us-strike-in-syria/ .

U.S. Department of the Treasury. 2018. U.S. Department of the Treasury. Retrieved from https://home.treasury.gov/news/press-releases/sm0410.

Warrick, Joby. 2016. *Black Flags The Rise of ISIS*. London: Transworld.

Weaver1, John M. 2015. The Perils of a Piecemeal Approach to Fighting ISIS in Iraq. Public Administration Review. 75(2) 192-193.

Weaver2, John M. 2015. The Enemy of My Enemy is My Friend…Or Still My Enemy: The Challenge for Senior Civilian and Military Leaders. *International Journal of Leadership in Public Service*. 11(3-4).

Zakharova1, Maria. 2018. Foreign Ministry Spokesperson Maria Zakharova's answer to a media question regarding statements by a US State Department senior official on the Syrian issue. http://www.mid.ru/en/foreign_policy/news/asset_publisher/cKNonkJE02Bw/content/id/3322144 [accessed on October 26, 2018].

Zakharova2, Maria. 2018. Foreign Ministry Spokesperson Maria Zakharova's answer to a media question about the so-called Syrian chemical dossier. Retrieved from http://www.mid.ru/en/foreign_policy/news/asset_publisher/cKNonkJE02Bw/content/id/3339634.

In: Global Intelligence Priorities ISBN: 978-1-53615-836-6
Editors: John Michael Weaver et al. © 2019 Nova Science Publishers, Inc.

Chapter 8

TURKEY - FRIEND OR FOE OF THE UNITED STATES: A QUALITATIVE ASSESSMENT

*Christopher Geer, Jaiden Moul,
Jordan Sowers and Vivian Ferris*
York College, York, Pennsylvania, US

ABSTRACT

Turkey's unique geographic location allows it to exert a greater presence in the European and Middle Eastern regions despite the recent military coup that resulted in instability and shook up its national political regime. Although being a North Atlantic Treaty Organization (NATO) ally, Turkey has not been a reliable one to the United States in the past decade. Set forth in the Integrated Country Strategy by the United States Department of State, the Turkish government is supposed to be improving on their views of human rights and treating individuals with fairness; this investigation found it to be otherwise. The evidence from triangulation of data sources suggests that Turkey has been acting in defiance of these humanitarian ideas. Using the D.I.M.E. model, the analysis revealed how Turkey has been using a modified model to be able to adversely impact the national security of the United States through the instruments of diplomacy, information, military, and economics. Despite its distance from the continental United States, Turkey poises itself in a unique way to the homeland in that its movements with its own ideas and actions directly affect the national security and hegemony of U.S. interests in the Middle East and Europe. With President Erdoğan at the helm, one can follow recent trends in a decline in pro-U.S. and western relations and an incline with its neighbors, Iran and Russia.

LITERATURE REVIEW

The United States is a country in which its foreign policy has greatly influenced the world. A country like Turkey is no exception. Since the conclusion of the Second World War, Turkey has not only remained an ally of the United States in the Eastern European region but also one that bridges influence into the Middle East. Since its introduction into the North Atlantic Treaty Organization in 1952, Turkey has enjoyed a global voice for cooperation for countries both on its borders and across the world (NATO 2012). In recent years, President Erdoğan of Turkey has assumed more assertive presidential powers following a coup that changed the political system of Turkey from a parliamentary system to that of an executive presidential one. Through a mission priority stated by the United States' Department of State, a collective agreement between the United States and Turkey is one of which upholds a "broad range of security and diplomatic challenges in recent years that underscores the importance of rebuilding and maintaining robust and dynamic ties with Ankara… The American and Turkish people enjoy broad and deep ties, stemming from tens of thousands of academic exchanges…" (United States Department of State 2018).

The main objectives of Turkey are like those of most modern developed countries: to remain economically, diplomatically, and militarily strong both domestically as well as abroad. As a member of the North Atlantic Treaty Organization, Turkey has been afforded protection against foreign adversaries under Article 5 which states the concept of collective defense, where if an attack is made against one member of the organization, it is considered an attack against all the member nations (North Atlantic Treaty Organization 2018).

Turkey is no stranger to military coups, but in the recent one of 2016, this one was the most problematic for the United States. A political coup is when a faction or group within a military or branch of the government desires a radical change in the political leadership and attempts to convert the previous administration to the new desired one by those implementing the action. For Turkey's current political landscape, the leadership under the direction of President Erdoğan has been slowly asphyxiating the freedoms and liberties held by both the Turkish citizens and other political entities.

However, following the failed coup of 2016, the trend ultimately seemed to change as the coup was initiated by those within the Turkish military, but not primarily those that were pro-western, and secularist as has been done in the past (Kennedy 2016). Instead it was initiated by those who simply wished to undermine the government led by Erdoğan and to displace him from power. What became of this coup was the placement of the Turkish military under complete control of the Turkish Defense Ministry, a subsection of Erdoğan's government. By doing so, this allowed Erdoğan to begin to purge those who were suspected of being involved in the military coup as well as transferring overall power from the military to the power of President Erdoğan (Kennedy 2016). Following the coup, previous Assembly President Mogens Lykketoft of the United Nations stated, "I strongly condemn the attempt from groups in the armed forces to overthrow the Government of Turkey and express my sincere condolences for the lives lost during the coup" (United Nations 2016). This type of solidarity from a prominent leader of the United Nations as well as continued support from the organization highlights the bond between the two entities and showcases the prominence of cooperation.

The United States and Turkey have a long history, and a complicated relationship. In the 1970s, following a Turkish invasion of Cyprus, the United States imposed an embargo on arms sales to Turkey. This added tension between the two nations, even after the embargo was removed several years later. In the 1980s the nations signed DECA, the Defense and Economic Cooperation Agreement, which allowed the United States access to more than 20 military bases across the nation and for Turkey to purchase modern military equipment. This led to the United States actively using the bases during the Gulf War. The War in Iraq and following conflicts created more tension, as much of Turkey disagreed with the United States' involvement and the Turkish government could not get the vote to allow the United States to attack Iraq from Turkish soil. The "Hood Event," which involved U.S. soldiers capturing and interrogating Turkish soldiers only added to the overall tension between the two countries. Additionally, the unrest and association with the problems in Syria are also a threat to the security of the Middle East overall.

The geographical location of Turkey allows for the state to remain influential in many matters of foreign policy to all its bordering countries. Therefore, it is essential to discuss Turkey's geographic context here.

The country, officially known as the Republic of Turkey, was founded after the Turkish War of Independence and the defeat of the Ottoman Empire. Since then, the country has been experiencing waves of political instability as well as several military coups. As the aforementioned stated, most recently, the Turkish government implemented a change from a parliamentary system to a presidential system in April of 2017 (CIA 2018). Turkey applied to be part of the European Union (EU) and became an official candidate for full membership in 1999. However, the request was denied. Negotiations for membership have stalled since 2016. Yet, Turkey plays a role in the stability of the Middle East as a whole. Spatially, Turkey is farther away from the Atlantic Ocean than any other member nation of NATO. In recent years, there have been critical concerns raised against Turkey. An example of something causing concern is Turkey purchasing missiles from Russia.

By area, Turkey is ranked as the 38th largest country in the world with a total area of 783,562 km^2. Such size puts Turkey as slightly larger than that of Texas (CIA 2018). Turkey's population is 79 million (World Bank 2017). The U.S. Census Bureau's International Program estimates the 2018 population of Turkey to be around 81,257,000, which would make it the 19th largest country by population (Census Bureau 2018). The capital of Turkey is Ankara, which has a population of 5.45 million people. Turkey's population is most dense in the northwestern part of the country, with 20% of its citizens living in Istanbul (around 15 million).

Turkey occupies a unique geographic location that has long played a significant role in its internal matters and regional affairs. According to the World Factbook by the CIA, Turkey is in Southeastern Europe and Southwestern Asia. Such location lends the country being on a natural land bridge at the crossroad of the European, Asian, and African continents. The term of the "Middle East" refers to this unique transcontinental region that has attracted constant outsiders' attention. The country also has so-called European half and Asian half. For a more absolute location, the capital city of Ankara is located at 39° 55'31.9188" N, 32° 51' 58.6332" E.

Turkey is a largely land-based nation-state. Of its total area, only a small segment of about 13,390 km² is water. Turkey shares its 2,626-kilometer borders with eight countries. Starting a counter-clockwise order from the east of the Black Sea, these terrestrial neighbors are Georgia, Armenia, Iran, Iraq, Syria, Cyprus, Greece, and Bulgaria.

The internal landscape is diverse as physical geographic features include a narrow coastal plain, a high central Anatolian plateau, and several mountain ranges dot the landscape. Turkey's terrain is generally considered high as its average elevation of the country is 1,132 meters above sea level. Turkey's highest elevation is Mount Ararat at 5,137 meters, which is on the Far East edge of the country. Mount Ararat is also a historically active volcano but has not erupted since the early 19th century (CIA 2018). The lowest elevation in the country is the Mediterranean Sea shorelines where fertile land is used for agricultural purposes. Several other mountain ranges in Turkey include the Taurus Mountain range in the south, the Anti-Taurus Mountains in the south and the east, and the Pontic Mountain range in the north running along the coast of the Black Sea.

Turkey's mid-latitudinal location dictates its general climatic regions. With its adjacency to the Mediterranean Sea, Turkey is classified as a Mediterranean Climate (Csa) that is characterized by a hot dry summer and cool wet winter. Istanbul is located within this climatic region. The average temperature in Istanbul is 14.1° C, and the average rainfall is 747 millimeters annually. From west to east, Turkey's coastal regions experience milder climates, and further inland climate sees harsher conditions. In the mountains of Anatolia, the climate is a continental cold climate with dry and hot summers. Lastly, the central Anatolia plateau is coded as "Bsk" which is more of a steppe climate that is cold and dry, with dry summers. There is more seasonality and rainfall towards the outer parts of the country, leaving the plateau and other inner areas with less precipitation.

Turkey's coastline is 7,200 kilometers touching the Black Sea and Mediterranean Sea. Turkey also claims territory going out 18 nautical miles; 12 nautical miles in the Black Sea and Mediterranean Sea, and six nautical miles in the Aegean Sea. There is also a fourth sea that is separated from the Black Sea by the land bridge and Istanbul. This is the Sea of Marmara. The seas have varying salinity levels. The Sea of Marmara has the lowest average at 2.2% salinity. The Mediterranean Sea has a 3.8% salinity level, close to the Aegean Sea at 3.9% salinity. The unique sea in terms of salinity is the Black Sea. Its salinity varies. Surface water leaves the Black Sea with a salinity level of 1.7%, and by the time it reaches the Mediterranean Sea the water has a 3.4% salinity rating. The variation in salinity can have serious impacts on the biosphere. The difference in density causes the oxygen from the surface not to reach all the water in the sea. Most marine animals and algae cannot thrive in this section of the Sea.

In addition to the border seas, there are several other water features in the Republic of Turkey. A major water feature is the Bosporus Straight, which divides the city of Istanbul and forms the continental boundary between Asia and Europe. Turkey also is home to the Euphrates River, the longest river in the country, as well as the Tigris and many others. The two largest lakes in Turkey are Lake Van, with a surface area of 3,755 km^2, and Lake Tuz, with a surface area of 1600 km^2.

According to the European Environment Agency, there are many different kinds of land which creates varying soil types. Over 60% of the soil is shallow and moderately shallow. Based on the structure, topography, climate, and soil makeup, most areas of Turkey have a high chance of erosion. However, Turkey has sufficient arable land being used for agricultural purposes (World Bank 2015). Natural land cover is the result of climate conditions. The overall natural landscape is diverse as the country is situated on the major migratory routes for many bird species. Turkey has several natural resources. These include coal, iron ore, copper, and several other metals and precious metals (CIA 2018). Turkey's main exports utilizing these resources are gold, cars, delivery trucks, and knit t-shirts (Observatory of Economic Complexity 2016).

According to the World Bank, only 49% of Turkey's population is of working age, which is down from 83% in the 1970s. This dependency issue is one of the difficulties happening in the country.

Additionally, Turkey is a Muslim-majority country, with over 98% of the population practicing some form of Islam. There has been controversy regarding the denial from the EU to whether or not the Islam majority played a role in it.

Another contribution to the stability of the nation is the ethnic tensions that are rampant, mainly between the Turkish government and the Kurdish people. Around 72.5% of the population are ethnically Turks, 12.7% ethnically Kurds, with the remaining 14.8% ethnically Zaza Kurd, Circassian, Bosniak, Georgian, and other. The tension between the Turks and Kurds began in the 1930s but became an armed conflict in the late 1970s (World Atlas 2016). This ongoing conflict has created major instability in the country, due to the fact the ethnic Kurds were aiming to leave the country to create their own nation.

National power is generally manifested in diplomacy, information, military capabilities, and economic factors which is known as D.I.M.E. In the rapidly changing world of global geopolitics, it is urgent to better understand how a nation state like Turkey could play in defense of the U.S. hegemony. Specifically, the authors asked the following research questions to examine how Turkey is taking on an adversarial role and weakening the United States: (1) How is Turkey a threat to the national security of the United States? (2) Why is Turkey a credible threat to United States' hegemony?

LOGIC MODEL

The D.I.M.E. model is based around the four instruments of national power. With these instruments, they together examine how one may extend their means in one dimension to exert pressure on another country and/or even non-state actors. Emanating from the National Security Act of 1947, all the instruments of national power listed above, except for information, were validated as ways to exert influence over others (Office of the Historian 2018). Other publications have referenced the D.I.M.E., for example, in President Trump's proclamation in the latest National Security Strategy. Historically, mid and upper level personnel at war colleges have also examined such factors and their shaped outcomes and predict the near and midterm impacts. In this chapter, the four instruments of national power were used to turn the concept around and examine how a state actor, Turkey has used these instruments to weaken the position of the United States on global stage.

The York Intelligence Red Team Model (YIRTM), as shown above in Figure 1, shows the start to finish sequence in the whole array of actions that could be taken by Turkey. The model begins with a strategic direction. In relation to Turkey, it allows for the explanation of this country's four means that Turkey has engaged in. The agent who enacts all actions is the state head, President Recep Tayyip Erdoğan. These four directions, in turn, synthesize into one final shaped outcome which can ultimately lead to a weakened position of the United States and can potentially threaten U.S. national security both domestically and abroad.

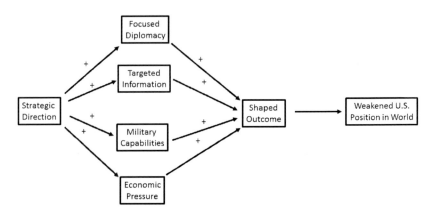

Figure 1. YIRTIM.

The first instrument of national power is diplomacy, in which a state actor uses both its government and the power it possesses both domestically and abroad to influence policy and other states. For this specific model, it is how Turkey's government continues to gauge and use its political strength and increase its globally influence. The consequences of these actions not only affect Turkey but also regional and global actors such as the United States.

The subsequent instrument of national power that a state actor can implement is targeted information. Information is one of these elements that refers to the way a nation uses information to help shape the world towards its own goals and interests. In the sense of this topic at hand, and specifically with regards to Turkey, it applies the methods that it employs to enhance its appearance in international and domestic relations. This instrument tends to also mean intelligence a state possesses and disseminates, giving it the ability to decide for what means it shall be used. The use of targeted information however is not limited as it can use data from other sources such as social media, records from internet providers, telecommunication companies, as well as using information that is taught to generations of individual progression through years of education and schooling.

A country which possesses a powerful and effective military is one that can exert pressure on other countries simply by conducting military exercises in a show of strength, or in other cases engage in humanitarian efforts, multinational wargames, and other military operations. The third instrument of national power includes the military capabilities that a state actor controls at any one time. A military force can be a powerful tool to shape foreign policy as a well as an effective deterrent from a possible conflict arising among other countries especially those contiguous to it. Turkey is situated between Europe and the Middle East, as well as being the land bridge connection between the two areas. Because of this fact, the Turkish military is at a geographical advantage for not only dealing with credible threats like the Islamic State (ISIS), but also with being a deterrent for war that could occur within the Middle East. However, the strategic mobility of the armed forces of Turkey have become "overstretched and likely unsustainable... between the purges, the conflict with the Kurdistan

Workers Party Rebels, and the conflict with the Islamic State" (McLaren & Karasek 2017). This instrument of national power is often seen by most as the one of last resort as a military conflict, no matter how small, places a significant strain on the economy and wellbeing of a country.

Following this, the final instrument of national power is the economic pressure that a state actor can place on other nations. With the ability of either engaging in trade negotiations, to use inducements, tariffs or sanctions, a country could use these as a way to exert influence that could lead to the economic collapse of another country's economy if it isn't strong enough to withstand such actions.

METHODOLOGY

This research is a qualitative in nature. All research data was obtained through open source and secondary data. It is also crucial to pay attention to the fact that the research done is qualitative in its approach, as there was no quantitative data used to support how and why Turkey may be a credible threat to the United States. However, qualitative research requires mechanisms that can ensure the quality of data interpretation and can collect data from multiple sources to avoid personal biases. Triangulation was used to explain where these data came from and what the data is. Since this study looked specifically at Turkey and what has been done, it is crucial to have data coming from other than U.S. government sources.

To further ensure data quality and diversity of data and where they come from, the authors used the Federal Qualitative Secondary Data Case Study Triangulation Model – see Figure 2 below. This model dictated researchers to use multiple publicly available sources to extract data and perform their analyses.

As illustrated below, beginning with the top circle, a case study should focus heavily on government and military plans and system. The authors of this chapter used sources from government and military plans and systems of the Turkish state and analyzed how Turkey and the United States used direct means to guide their actions.

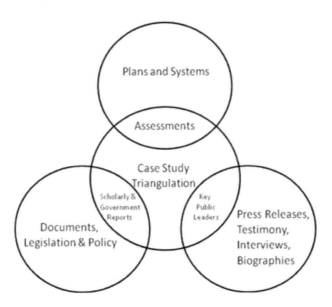

Figure 2. Federal Qualitative Secondary Data Case Study Triangulation Model.

Another group of public data sources are documents, legislation and policy as they are official government documents representing a state's official point of view and public policies. In addition, independent scholarly work includes peer reviewed articles from journals. Related to the Turkish state, the country has a website in which government officials publish short updates on diplomatic and militarized events and actions. Using this website, the authors can research and gain knowledge from Turkish officials directly relative to current events occurring not only around the world, but also within the country of Turkey itself (MFA 2018). It was important that the authors once again not only look at events and statements that may be a direct threat to the United States, but assertions that could lead to actions which could influence a variety of areas throughout the world, leading to secondary consequences that could occur.

The third component of the Triangulation Model generally pertains to oral speeches or statements that have been made by important figures who are influential and includes the likes of politicians, law makers, and high-ranked military personnel. Their speeches, press releases, testimonials, interviews and biographies offer significant additional insights and interpretations of a state's position. The authors found that triangulating in on these sources was a way to be able to provide rich and reliable analysis helping better understanding both Turkey and the U.S.' recent activities.

LIMITATIONS

Qualitative research is often viewed as more subjective and could be seen as more biased, when compared to empirical studies using quantitative techniques. This research project fully recognizes these shortcomings. Therefore, the limitations are discussed below.

First and foremost is the time period that data was collected. The data used was collected over several months ranging from August through December of 2018 and in some occasions, the data went back to five years. While the research included all open source material, the data collected was restricted to those only in the public domain, meaning none were classified. Although completely avoiding biases is impossible, triangulation has been able to reduce the biases substantially. In addition, more weight in this study was afforded to those sources that occurred within the last year.

As is the case with all other qualitative research, it is increasingly difficult to make any generalizing statements beyond this specific study. This synthesis of the presented data is focused around how Turkey could weaken the national security of the United States. It is only based around how it may possibly use diplomacy, targeted information, their military capabilities, and/or economic pressure to do so. Further research may be conducted to look at other means that could be executed by the Turkish government.

When examining secondary data, it becomes apparent that other weaknesses can reside in the cross-sectional design. This is simply recognized because it may be increasingly difficult for one to pick out if there is any biased based information that occurred when the data was originally collected. Moreover, an individual may not be able to determine the collection method for the research (Cross-Sectional 2012). Looking deeper into this, another challenge that can arise is with the interpretation of this cross-sectional design type. The challenge arises because they tend to lack fully inclusive events that happened (Cross-Sectional 2012). Primary sources such as personal observations, non-government interviews, and surveys were not included in this research due to time constrain and cost.

ANALYSIS

This section will look at the implementation of the YIRTM and the use of the Federal Qualitative Secondary Data Case Study Triangulation Model in order to look at what Turkey is doing to weaken the United States. Annex A exhibits a total entry of 27 data sources used in the analysis. By following the D.I.M.E. model, the frequency ranking is 17 for "D," 16 for "M," 11 for "I," and 5 for "E."

As the ranking indicated, Turkey has been proficient at using diplomacy to its advantage. As relations between Turkey and the United States seem to slowly worsen over time, interactions between Turkey and other potential belligrant countries of the U.S. could pose a greater threat to the United States. Stated by the honorary Eliot L. Engel in Congressional Record E1090 (2018), the relationship between Turkey and the United States has been deteriorating in recent times. He stated that he does not believe that the president of Turkey is fully committed to the relationship between the two countries. He underscored this in his speech when he cited numerous occasions where Americans were wrongly held hostage by Turkey. Moreover, Mr. Engel stated that he questions the Turkish government due to its response to failed military coups. A major reason that Mr. Engel thinks the relationship between the two countries is deteriorating is because of the Turkish government's restraints on freedom and democracy. Conversely, the United States relies on these values to be at the core of its being.

On March 13 of 2018, President Trump was delivered a letter that discussed Turkey's rising aggression. In this release (Congressional Record H3582 2018), the honorable Gus Bilirakis stated how Turkey had threatened regional security and United States' interests within the Mediterranean Sea specifically, as well as more broadly in the border region. Mr. Bilirakis also informed the president that the Turkish government continues to "Violate long-standing international law and treaties - a threat to regional security and an impediment to regional interests, stability, and prosperity" (Congressional Record 2018). He suggests that the United States condemns these activities as they have done in the past, as well as call for President Erdoğan's government to show the rest of the world what they are capable of, and willing to stay committed to all international laws.

The authors expand upon this difference by diving back in time, to the final years of the waning Ottoman Empire. During the years before its dissolution in 1920, the government of the Ottoman Empire was commencing a systematic genocide against the Armenian people within its borders (The Ottoman Empire 2016). Following the creation of the Republic of Turkey, the leadership of the country has continually refused to acknowledge the genocide of 1.3 million Armenians that had taken place in Turkey. The refusal of acknowledgement by Turkey and President Erdoğan, highlights the contrast of the value of all human rights that the United States possesses and desires to see within Turkey.

Using the Federal Qualitative Secondary Data Case Study Triangulation Model, the authors were able to further expand on the point that Turkey and the United States are not seeing eye-to-eye on issues regarding human rights. Using an official Turkish government website in which government officials are able to publish short press releases regarding a variety of topics, one is able to find a relatively recent statement in which Turkey bashes the United States for its ending of financial support towards the United Nations Relief and Works Agency for Palestinian Refugees, while stating that they are "determined to continue to make every effort to support the Agency" (MFA 2018). This program benefits Palestinian refugees in offering support through means of education, health care, and employment opportunities. In this statement, Turkey expresses its strong disapproval of the United States' decision to withdrawal contributions to the organization. As this does not necessarily pose a direct threat to the national security of the United States, it does cause an increase in tension between the two countries which can, as mentioned before, have secondary consequences. Essentially, the more that tensions are exacerbated between Turkey and the United States, the more relations could increase for the better between Turkey and the opposition of the United States, to include such prominent actors such as Russia and Iran.

A subsequent thought one should keep in mind is the idea of pro and anti-state actor forces present within the Turkish government. From even within the Turkish military, there lies sects of high-ranking members who follow different ideologies which are aimed at steering the country towards a beneficiary for military support; these two are the Atlanticists and Eurasianists who seek to an align Turkey's strategic interests towards the United States and NATO, and a Russian dominated relationship, respectfully (Jacinto 2017). For the consequences of any action, one must speculate as to the effects of Turkey on what can happen if it should fall back and continues to rely on NATO and the United States for support or if it changes course and looks towards Russia for support.

Turkish leaders have used the military instrument of national power to achieve its desired effects. On May 4, 2017, U.S. Senator Roger Wicker cited the political instability of the Turkish government in a congressional hearing (Congressional Record S2770 2017). He expressed his concerns of how following the referendum to remove the ceremonial position of president and abolish the position of Prime Minister, the executive presidency becomes the sole source of power within Turkey even allowing the president to dissolve the assembly and call elections at a whim, centralizing power around one individual for what can be a lifetime of rule. Concurring with this notion, the executive presidency under Erdoğan has been curtailing the powers and rights of all other organizations and individuals while strengthening his own. Although very alarming, the Turkish people did vote for these changes in April of 2018, which passed with a narrow 51% majority. Wicker also said that hours after the defeat of the July 2016 military coup, the government was firing individuals, and revoking professional licenses. As many as 100,000 individuals were arrested or detained without due process (Congressional Record S2770 2017). Of the many individuals that were arrested following the coup, over 50,000 of them are facing criminal charges (Kenyon 2017). The government has also been closing news outlets and putting journalists behind bars, revoking the rights of freedom of speech and assembly as well. In addition to information through media outlets being limited by the Turkish government, Turkey's closing of schools and universities as well as the dismissal of over 17,000 academicians from the period following the failed military coup in July 2016 to February 2017 is having an effect as well (O'Dea 2016). With the essence of knowledge hindering the truth to the people of Turkey, the government is targeting the specific information that is being released and taught to its citizens. Simultaneously, it is strengthening the values that it deems necessary, as thousands of individuals have been detained from various ministries within the Turkish Government including the Ministry of Health, Agriculture and Livestock, and Sports (Kennedy 2016). In his closing remarks, Wicker stated that it is hard to imagine a relationship between Turkey and the United States continuing in a prolonged state of emergency as well as with weakened democratic institutions (Congressional Record S2770 2017).

As seen in Annex A, Turkey was able to use targeted information in multiple scenarios to advance its position. When examining the targeted information, it is easy to see that it is mostly executed in conjunction with military efforts. With the rising of personal power under Erdoğan following the coup of 2016, specific information can be applied by Erdoğan and his government to control what information is disseminated to the people of Turkey as well as understanding the road ahead. Turkey can use targeted information as an instrument of national power which allows it to shape its own mission on a global scale by influencing nearby and other global power countries. Turkey is promoting or limiting the ideas that the government wishes to spread about this country both domestically and abroad such as closing many newspapers and arresting journalists following the coup of 2016.

Since its founding in 2001, the Justice and Development Party (AKP) in Turkey has had a strong "traditional Islamic core but has also tried to widen its electoral base to include broad segments of Turkish society..." (O'Dea 2016). Being the political party of President Erdoğan, this party has gained influence and since being elected, Erdoğan's grip on Turkey has become more and more powerful as he has found ways to extend the reaches of his government.

Following the July 2016 military coup, both Erdoğan's Justice and Development Party as well as opposition parties, who usually are adversaries, rallied together around the strength of Erdoğan in a cross-party rally. Both parties broadcasted speeches in support of Erdoğan and his vision for Turkey. Following this coup however, Turkey shut down major media outlets such as Facebook, Twitter, and YouTube within the country to limit the spread of information that could portray Erdoğan unfavorably across the nation (O'Dea 2016).

As stated in Congressional Record H3582, (2018) Turkey seemingly intimidated the United States into a sense of silence through a cause of denial about the Armenian Genocide. The record also stated how Turkey has been imprisoning a significant number of journalists who dare to speak out against the government. President Erdoğan's bodyguards also brutally assaulted a group of peaceful protesters within Washington D.C. (Congressional Record H3582). Such actions as those listed above are simply not the actions that a true ally would carry out. When examining the Gross Domestic Product (GDP) of Turkey, they rank 18th in the world. When examining it closer, it is increasingly easy to see the pitfalls. Examples such as the unemployment rate haven risen to 10.8%, and the inflation rate jumping to a 15-year high, go together and helps one see the instability that the country is experiencing with global effects (Trading Economics 2018).

Next, Turkey has shown a proclivity moving towards acquiring military equipment. Likewise, it is using its armed forces, making good use of this component of the YIRTM. The Turkish military stands at a precipice in its history, as for a large majority of its existence as a nation, it remained the deciding factor in the style of government it possessed. Previously in Turkey's history, coups were initiated by the military to diminish the power of the executive branch of government (Basaran 2016). However, the July 2016 coup which ultimately failed, led the military to be placed under control by the Turkish Defense Ministry, under direct command from President Erdoğan (Kennedy 2016). This style is like that of the United States as the president is the commander in chief of the military; for Turkey, this is a symbol for a change in pro-western leaning military operations. Following the massive purges initiated by Erdoğan after the 2016 coup, a large majority of the secular leadership was removed from power and as a result, foreign policy is solely in the hands of Erdoğan and his government. This serves in contrast to U.S. and Turkish relations as Turkey is "forging a path politically 'that is not dependent upon the West' harking 'back to the days of the Ottoman Empire' as it is attempting to become 'a self-confident regional power'" (McLaren & Karasek 2017).

The Turkish military stands as a conventionally sound military fighting force, ranking within the top twenty of active militaries on the planet. For Turkey in the Middle East, its military is one of those at the highest state of readiness for combat. It is estimated to have over 350,000 men in active military service with another 350,000 men in its reserve forces (Global Fire Power 2018). Regarding Turkey's military and their militaristic relations within the Middle East, the authors once again used the Federal Qualitative Secondary Data Case Triangulation Model to assess the Syrian conflict and how Turkey's military activities could have adverse effects on the relationship of the United States and Turkey. Looking at this topic, the authors used sources to investigate government and military plans and systems of the Turkish state, which could effectively bring harm to the United States either by direct means or by secondary consequences of their actions.

An example of secondary consequences can be found in the Syrian conflict. A country embroiled in a civil war since 2011, Syria is primarily split into two sides with each one gaining backing from countries throughout the world. Turkey has taken the side of President Assad and the Syrian government, subsequently putting them in an unofficial alliance with Russia and Iran; two countries of which have rising tensions with the United States.

One may argue that tensions between the United States and Turkey are not as bad as they seem due to the agreement between the two countries that the ISIS threat needs to be held in check, with both countries going as far as to launch their own campaigns against the Islamic State. As this is a positive stance for the two countries to take together, Turkey has also launched its own military campaigns against the Kurds. Turkish Kurds are an ethnic group, who largely identify as Sunni within the Middle East with numbers estimated at 14 million. The United States has backed the Kurds and given support when it is needed. Conversely, Turkey has a history of prosecuting this ethnic group. President Erdoğan has been dismayed about the U.S. support and made threatening statement against the United States with an "Ottoman slap" if it continues to support the Kurds in Syria (Congressional Record H3582 2018).

Following the Syrian government's victory over rebel forces in Aleppo, Syria in 2016, Turkish officials met in Moscow along with Iranian officials to come to a consensus on the actions in Syria going forward (Sisk 2016). As this is seemingly unrelated to the United States in that it did not directly jeopardize the national security of the U.S., however, there are secondary consequences that can come from these military plans or strategies from among these three countries regarding Syria. In one scenario, Turkish, Russian, and Iranian operations could potentially interfere with U.S. operations in Syria in the future. This has the potential to start an unintended conflict because the United States historically supports moderate rebels attempting to overthrow the Syrian government. In a more long-term scenario, this alliance could create conditions that might see Turkey, Russia, and Iran as allies for years to come. This alliance has the potential to make any type of military action in the Middle East by the United States increasingly more difficult and jeopardizes relations with Turkey.

What's more is that there exists a problem from within the Turkish military following the failed coup of 2016, of which President Erdoğan began to purge those that were suspected having a hand in the coup, dismissing over 1,400 military personnel in the first month alone after the overthrow attempt. President Erdoğan possesses the power to not only control the leadership within the military but also with placing the Turkish military under control of the Turkish Defense Ministry (Kennedy 2016).

With the purchase of the S-400 missile system, one of the world's most advanced air defense systems from Russia, the Turkish military upgraded both its offensive and defensive capabilities, affording it the ability to project its military prowess into the Middle East as a dominant armed force (Aydin 2018). For a third time, the authors were able to apply the Federal Qualitative Secondary Data Case Study Triangulation Model by finding transcripts of open interview sources with President Erdoğan. Using this part of the model in the research to show how Turkey is a credible threat to the United States, a 2018 Bloomberg interview was used. In the interview, President Erdoğan sat down to answer a variety of questions, some of which regarding relations and conflicts between Turkey and the United States (Demokan & Ant 2018). Referring to the decreasing relations between Turkey and the U.S. and a byproduct being increasing the strength of relations between Turkey and Russia, President Erdoğan was asked about sanctions that may be placed on Turkey by the United States should Turkey purchase the S-400 missile system from Russia. When pressed about the topic, Erdoğan addressed these sanctions by stating, "Right now as it is known we are a country which is a member of NATO. The Secretary General of NATO, Mr. Stoltenberg, said about the decision Turkey has taken, regards S-400s that 'it is our ally's own choice, they can make such a decision.' At the moment we have the freedom, the independence to buy our defense needs from allies, from any country. If we can't go and get it from the U.S., if the Senate is not allowing this, or Congress is not allowing this, are we not going to find a solution for ourselves" (Demokan & Ant 2018). Once again this is a prime example of how souring relations between the United States and Turkey are pushing the latter to turn towards other options outside of assistance from the former. Why the purchase of this missile system is a dire threat to the national security of the United States is that if Turkey and the U.S. were to become involved in either a proxy war or a direct military conflict, the missile system would wreak havoc on U.S. warplanes and shield Turkey from attack directly minimizing offensive military action by the U.S.

Turkey's military launched several operations into Iraq and Syria against remnants of the Islamic State, one of which was Operation Euphrates Shield, which lasted from August 24, 2016 to March 31, 2017 (Yesiltas et al. 2018). This operation resulted in a significant victory for both the Turkish military as well as Western forces such as the United States. The true outcry of this operation highlights two key points: (1) the cooperation and aspirations for the elimination of the Islamic State with U.S. backing, and (2) the problematic entrance of Russia into the mix. In the early days of January 2017, Russian warplanes launched airstrikes in support of Operation Euphrates Shield in their first military cooperation mission with Turkey

(Gordon & Schmitt 2018). The United States often sees Russia as an adversary, especially in the region of the Middle East. If Turkey were to foment an alliance with Russia, this would pose an immediate and potentially dangerous credible threat to U.S. hegemony in the region.

Finally, although the economic component is ranked as the last, with only five for the frequency, Turkey still includes the economic instrument of power to increase its presence within the region and on the global stage. In 2014, Turkey established its first foreign military base in Qatar on the promise that this nation could also station army personnel and aircraft in Turkey (Akpinar et al. 2017). Turkey initiated this after the power vacuum that the United States left as it began to extricate the number of military personnel in its ongoing conflicts with Iraq and Afghanistan. With the increase in relations among other countries with Turkey, the idea that a joint military coalition or force could be assembled among the consortium of other countries in the Middle East could potentially leave the United States not only without cooperative allies, but also use of military bases and supply points for its military forces. This in turn would increase the threat to U.S. national security and interests directly in the Middle Eastern region. The possibility of this happening however is slim, as without the financial and military backing of the United States, any significant military operation in the Middle East by Turkey would not be as successful without aid. In fiscal year 2017, the trade relationship between Turkey and the United States approached almost $20 billion. Additionally, the U.S. Department of States' Integrated Country Plan predicts that if Turkey continues its economic path, it would become a top ten world economy by 2023 (United States Department of State 2018). Because of the value of this trade relationship, either Turkey would remain an ally of the United States and aid in its foreign interests to promote its own or seek aid from other countries such as Russia or Iran. This would lead to a decline in U.S. hegemony in the area as well as increasing the threat that the Middle East poses to U.S. national security.

FINDINGS AND CONCLUSION

As discussed in the previous analysis section, despite Turkey's distant location away from the U.S., Turkey's recent activities have serious implications to the national interests of the United States. The tumultuous relationship between the state actor, Turkey, and the U.S. can be traced back since becoming a member of the North American Treaty Organization in 1952 and continues to show signs of sporadic unpredictableness (NATO 2012). Although surviving and tightening power following a failed military coup, the stability of the Turkish government is called into question as to what is in store for it in the foreseeable future. Due to the history of Turkey having multiple coups, like the one in 2016, the notion that another political plot may happen at any time cannot be dismissed. As a result, the United States must find a way to ensure the political stability of Turkey for it to remain as an ally. If a political plot were to become successful and overthrow President Erdoğan, the U.S. could find itself with another adversary in the Middle East.

By purchasing the S-400 missile system from Russia, the United States is unsure of what Turkey's true intentions are. By not purchasing arms from the U.S., this could be a twofold situation: (1) either the government of Turkey simply desires to outfit its military arsenal with the most advanced weaponry, or (2) sees the sale of arms by Russia as a step towards an ever increasing yet problematic relationship for the United States. Likewise, this could possibly decrease U.S. hegemonic influence in the region as well as limiting U.S. interests more broadly. By purchasing this system, the Turkish State improved their military capabilities both offensively and defensively. Supported by the evidence made by many congressional members, Turkey is starting to become a big question mark because President Erdoğan is letting many different global relationships fall by the wayside, like that of the United States.

Turkey is a pivotal country to the United States with its strategic location straddling Asia, Europe, and Middle East. Thus, geographically, Turkey can be a suitable location for U.S. troops stationed there such as at Incirlik Air

Base (Wertheimer 2016). However, this military advantage to the U.S. can only be guaranteed when Turkey is an ally of the United States.

Turkey plays an important role in the regional security around the Mediterranean Sea. Turkey has been violating multiple international laws that have been long-standing in the world. In conjunction with cited political instability within the Turkish government, the challenges in this country will significantly hinder its regional influence.

Turkey's military is still a potent threat, despite the fact that President Erdoğan removed many military leaders following the coup of 2016. It is reported that almost 38% of its generals and 8% of officers were sacked between March and September of 2016 by President Erdoğan (Jacinto 2017). Turkey, however, is still becoming a strong military power beyond its regional role as it continues to climb the ladder in rankings. The military has been seen typically as the deciding factor as to which government system will become more influential. It possesses one of the largest military forces in the Middle East (Global Fire Power 2018). Turkey developed its first military base abroad in 2014, which found its home in Qatar, is a great example of Turkey's global rise (Akpinar et al. 2017). Such military power projected abroad was in part because the United States is thinning its military presence in the Middle East and allowing for other powers to establish a more prominent presence.

Turkey could be seen as a national security threat to the United States due to its political structure and ignorance to international law. The relationship between the United States and Turkey has been deteriorating for quite some time and shows no signs of improving any time soon. Its immediate military threat is insignificant compared to the overall U.S. military strength in the Middle East and Mediterranean Sea region, but this could change over time. However, compounded with other factors, such as if Turkey were to align itself militarily with Russia creating a Middle Eastern coalition with Iran, or back out of NATO, the threat to the national security of U.S. interests will be quite real.

Turkey is a credible threat towards the national security of the United States because of the thawing of diplomatic relations. Turkey continually falters in its foreign policy by sending mixed signals. Examples such as not improving human rights within the country as stated by the Integrated Country Strategy and holding journalists hostage can be viewed as an uncivil act by other nations (United States Department of State 2018). Turkey has been able to use its diplomacy to achieve ends which risk the national security of the United States. By purchasing the S-400 missile system from Russia, Turkey not only improved its military prowess, but also highlighted the use of diplomacy to build relations with neighboring countries to collectively pose a significant threat to U.S. power in the region. Also, information can be continued possibly using this against the United States if President Erdoğan was to disseminate false claims.

To summarize, Turkey is a credible threat to the United States based off the diplomatic efforts with regional nation states that are not aligned with the United States and running counter to U.S. interests and desires; there is no telling what turn Turkey will do next, and where that road may lead. As a nation, Turkey is seemingly in its own world, and is paying grievance to countries in their region and allies abroad. While examining these elements it is also important to pay slight dividends to targeted information. Within the collection of information, President Erdoğan can consume material, but then disseminate it however he wishes, with possible personal biases behind it as he is now the executive President of Turkey and wields a significant amount of power. The United States and Turkey do not have the same goals and visions on the global stage. Despite the fact that the Integrated Country Strategy strives for a series of cooperative missions and ideas to be shared by both state actors, the U.S. is mainly in the dark when it comes to Turkey's actions (United States Department of State 2018). President Erdoğan ultimately has the final say in most matters regarding the Turkish state and its military, putting the United States at a realm of uncertainty to what ends Turkey will go to carry out its specific goals and visions.

Moreover, with acquiring missile capabilities now through a purchase from Russia, the Turkish military may not presently be viewed as a major threat to the United States. However, combining this instrument with the use of diplomacy, the Turkish state has the potential to wreak havoc on the United States' influence in the Middle East and possibly beyond.

ANNEX A.

How/Why	D.I.M.E	Source	Source Type	Date	Page (if applicable)
Honorary Eliot L. Engel in a speech of New York In the House of Representatives	D	Congressional Record E1090	Testimony	July - 18	N/A
American Hellenic Institute letter to President Trump regarding Turkish Aggression	D	Congressional Record E307	Testimony	Mar - 18	N/A
Roger Wicker and Speech on Turkish parliamentary reform concerns	D	Congressional Record S2770	Testimony	May - 17	N/A
Interview with Deborah Amos from NPR about failed Turkish Military Coup	D, M	Wertheimer	Interview	July - 18	N/A
Where is Turkey Heading?	D, I	Kemal	Systems	2017	N/A
Turkey Ruling, Political Parties Rally Together After Coup	D, I	O'Dea	Systems	Jul - 2016	N/A
A Year after the Failed Military Coup in Turkey, a Summary	D, I	Kenyon	Systems	Aug - 2017	N/A
Turkish Foreign Policy and the Qatar Crisis	D, I, M	Aras, Akpinar	Systems	Aug - 2017	4-6
Turkey Coup: Who was behind Turkey coup attempt?	D, I	Basaran	Press Release	Jul - 2016	N/A
Between East and West: Strategic Potential Analysis of Turkey & Debating Turkey's Rising Power Status	D, I, M	McLaren, Karasek	Plans	Jul - 2017	69, 76
Attitudes toward Structure of the Turkish Military	M	Ugurlu	Systems	Aug- 2016	N/A
Integrated Country Strategy	D, I, M, E	United States Department of State	Policy	2018	2, 7, 10
Operation Euphrates Shield: Implementation and lessons learned	M	Yesiltas, Sere, Ozcelik	Plans	2017	23-31
Airstrikes by Russia Buttress Turkey in Battle vs. ISIS	M	Gordon, Scmitt	Plans	2017	N/A
Changing Role and Position of Turkish Armed Forces in Turkish Foreign Policy	D, M	Aydin	Documents	2018	N/A

Annex A. (Continued)

How/Why	D.I.M.E	Source	Source Type	Date	Page (if applicable)
Turkey's Post-Coup Purge and Erdoğan's Private Army	D, M	Jacinto	Interview	2017	N/A
Turkish Military Strength	M, E	Global Firepower	Systems	2018	N/A
A Month After Turkey's Failed Coup, Taking Stock Of A Sweeping Purge	D, M	Kennedy	Plans	Aug-2016	N/A
After Failed Coup, Turkey Brings Military Further Under Government Control	I, M	Kennedy	Plans	Jul - 2016	N/A
Gross Domestic Product of Turkey	E	Trading Economics	Systems	2018	N/A
US Sidelined as Russia, Turkey, Iran Plot Syria's Fate	D	Sisk	Interview	2016	N/A
103rd Anniversary of The Armenian Genocide	I	Congressional Record H3582	Testimony	Apr - 2018	N/A
Transcript: Turkey's President on Monetary Policy, Politics	E	Ant, Demokan	Interview	May - 2018	N/A
Republic of Turkey Ministry of Foreign Affairs Press Releases	D, I, M, E	Turkish Ministry of Foreign Affairs	Policy	2018	N/A
State vs. Academy in turkey: Academy Under Surveillance	I	Surveillance and Society	Interview	2018	N/A
Turkey Coup Attempt Leaves President Erdoğan With Uncertain Grip on Country	I, M	Wertheimer	Interview	Jul - 2016	N/A
Assessing International Fallout from Failed Military Coup	M	Wertheimer	Interview	Jul - 2016	N/A

The possibility of Turkey creating a military coalition, continually purchasing weapons, and seeking other foreign relations in the name of their national security could lead to a detrimental direction to the United States' position in the region.

Turkey poses a significant existential threat to U.S. hegemony in the region by using economic measures as another sharp instrument undercutting the U.S. power. Although the country does not provide the United States with many goods or services, it is sure that the U.S can be a benefactor in its rising economic development. Targeted information could continue to be employed disseminating negative information about the United States.

All of the above suggest the National Security Council (NSC) and the Intelligence Community (IC) need to focus efforts on zeroing in on how the diplomacy in Turkey continues to falter between it and the United States. For the near and foreseeable future, U.S. intelligence agencies should take special interest in ensuring that Turkey is not continuing to acquire military aid from Russia and be accountable and, more importantly, as a global actor willing to follow international laws and norms of behavior. The U.S. should also make constant efforts warning Turkey to treat U.S. citizens abroad with the utmost respect, in addition to its own citizens. Moving forward, more in-depth research could investigate the interactions between the two states.

REFERENCES

Anonymous. 2017. "State vs. Academy in Turkey: Academy Under Surveillance." *Surveillance and Society* 550-556. https://web.b.ebscohost.com/ehost/pdfviewer/pdfviewer?vid=1&sid=80f48e08-75d7-4cdf-b7c7de150b737b55%40sessionmgr120.

Akpinar, Pinar, and Bülent Aras. 2017. *"Turkish Foreign Policy and the Qatar Crisis."* Istanbul: Istanbul Policy. Accessed November 2, 2018. Center. https://www.researchgate.net/profile/Pinar_Akpinar2/publication/319059837_Turkish_Foreign_Policy_and_the_Qatar_Crisis/links/5

98d9aab0f7e9b07d22bc3f6/Turkish-Foreign-Policy-and-the-Qatar-Crisis.pdf.

Aydin, Selcuk. 2018, February 26. *"The Changing Role and Position of Turkish Armed Forces in Turkish Foreign Policy."* Accessed on November 1, 2018. Defense-In-Depth: https://defenceindepth.co/2018/02/26/the-changing-role-and-position-of-turkish-armed-forces-in-turkish-foreign-policy/.

Basaran, Ezgi. 2016. *"Turkey Coup: Who was Behind Turkey Coup Attempt."* British Broadcasting Company News. Accessed on September 13, 2018. https://www.bbc.com/news/world-europe-36815476.

Census Bureau. "International Programs, International Data Base." *Region Summary - U.S. Census Bureau*, 27 June 2011. www.census.gov/datatools/demo/idb/region.php?N=%2BResults%2B&T=13&A=separate&RT=0&Y=2018&R=-1&C=TU.

CIA.gov. "The World Factbook: TURKEY." *Central Intelligence Agency*, Central Intelligence Agency. Accessed October 23, 2018. www.cia.gov/library/publications/the-world-factbook/geos/tu.html.

Congressional Record E307. 2018. *American Hellenic Institute Letter to President Trump Regarding Turkeys Continued Aggressive Actions in The Eastern Mediterranean.* Congressional Record. Accessed September 3, 2018. https://www.gpo.gov/fdsys/pkg/CREC-2018-03-13/pdf/CREC-2018-03-13-pt1-PgE307-2.pdf.

Congressional Record E1090. 2018. *United States-Turkey Relationship.* Congress: Congressional Record. Accessed September 23, 2018. https://www.gpo.gov/fdsys/pkg/CREC-2018-07-26/pdf/CREC-2018-07-26-pt1-PgE1090-4.pdf.

Congressional Record S2769. 2017. *Turkey.* Retrieved from Congressional Record - Senate. Accessed October 3, 2018. https://www.gpo.gov/fdsys/pkg/CREC-2017-05-04/pdf/CREC-2017-05-04-pt1-PgS2769-2.pdf.

Congressional Record H3582. 2018. *103rd Anniversary of The Armenian Genocide.* Congressional Record- House. Accessed September 30, 2018. https://www.congress.gov/crec/2018/04/26/CREC-2018-04-26-pt1-PgH3582-3.pdf.

Cross-Sectional. 2012. *Cross-Sectional Studies*. Accessed November 27, 2018. https://www.healthknowledge.org.uk/public-healthtextbook/research-methods/1a-epidemiology/cs-as-is.

Demokan, Simin, and Onur Ant. 2019. "Transcript: Turkey's President on Monetary Policy, Politics." *Bloomberg Economics*. Accessed October 3, 2018. https://www.bloomberg.com/news/articles/2018-05-15/transcript-turkey-s-president-on-monetary-policy-politics.

Findlay, Justin. World Atlas. 2016, October 18. "*The Ethnic Groups of Turkey.*" https://www.worldatlas.com/articles/the-ethnic-groups-of-turkey.html.

Global Fire Power. 2018. "*Turkey Military Strength.*" Global Fire Power: Strength in Numbers. Accessed October 2, 2018. https://www.globalfirepower.com/country-military-strength-detail.asp?countryid=turkey.

Gordon, Michael., and Eric Schmitt. 2017. "Airstrikes by Russia Buttress Turkey in Battle vs. ISIS." *The New York Times*. Accessed September 6, 2018. https://www.nytimes.com/2017/01/08/us/politics/russiaturkey-syria-airstrikes-isis.html.

Jacinto, Leela. 2017. "Turkey's Post-Coup Purge and Erdogan's Private Army." *Foreign-Policy*. Accessed November 3, 2018. https://foreignpolicy.com/2017/07/13/turkeys-post-coup-purge-and-erdogans-private-army-sadat-perincek-gulen/.

Karasek, Tomáš., and Lauren McLaren. 2017. "*Between East and West: Strategic Potential Analysis of Turkey & Debating Turkey's Rising Power Status.*" University of Glasgow. Accessed October 29, 2018. https://is.cuni.cz/webapps/zzp/download/120279918.

Kennedy, Merrit. 2016. "*After Failed Coup, Turkey Brings Military Further Under Government Control.*" National Public Radio. Accessed September 23, 2018. https://www.npr.org/sections/thetwo-way/2016/07/31/488119346/after-failed-coup-turkey-brings-military-further-under-government-control.

Kennedy, Merrit. 2016. *A Month After Turkey's Failed Coup, Taking Stock Of A Sweeping Purge*. National Public Radio. Accessed November 2, 2018. https://www.npr.org/sections/thetwo-way/2016/08/20/49067798

9/a-month-after-turkeys-failed-coup-taking-stock-of-a-sweeping-purge.

Kenyon, Peter. 2017, July 16. *"A Year Later, A Divided Turkey Remembers Failed Coup Attempt."* Accessed September 20, 2018. National Public Radio. https://www.npr.org/sections/parallels/2017/07/16/537549673/a-year-later-a-divided-turkey-remembers-failed-coup-attempt.

MFA. 2018. *"Republic of Turkey Ministry of Foreign Affairs."* Accessed October 23, 2018. http://www.mfa.gov.tr/default.en.mfa.

NATO. 2012. *"The Historic Document Confirming Greece and Turkey Joining NATO."* Accessed October 4, 2018. https://www.nato.int/docu/review/2012/turkey-greece/greece-turkey-membership/en/index.htm.

New Zealand History. 2016, January 13. *"The Ottoman Empire."* Accessed October 9, 2018. https://nzhistory.govt.nz/war/ottomanempire/collapse.

Observatory of Economic Complexity. (n.d.). Turkey - OEC. Accessed September 26, 2018. https://atlas.media.mit.edu/en/profile/country/tur/

O'Dea, M. 2016. Turkey Ruling, Opposition Parties Rally Together After Coup. *Fortune.com*, 1-1. Accessed October 27, 2018. https://web.b.ebscohost.com/ehost/detail/detail?vid=0&sid=c2db723a-1304-4c47-98b595aa7a61b871%40sessionmgr103&bdata=JnNpdGU9ZWhvc3Qt bGl2ZSZzY29wZT1zaXRl#AN=117020131&db=bth.

Office of the Historian. 2018. "National Security Act of 1947." Accessed October 22, 2018. https://history.state.gov/milestones/1945-1952/national-security-act.

Oke, Kemal. 2017. "Where is Turkey Heading?" *South East Europe Review*, 223-245. Accessed October 31, 2018. https://web.b.ebscohost.com/ehost/detail/detail?vid=0&sid=cb4e83a4-fa0c-497c-9237-ef3639da85a1%40sessionmgr120&bdata=JnNpdGU9ZWhvc3QtbGl2 ZSZzY29wZT1zaXRl#AN=129456567&db=sih.

Sisk, Richard. 2016, December. *"US Sidelined as Russia, Turkey, Iran Plot Syria's Fate."* Military.com Accessed September24, 2018. https://www.military.com/daily-news/2016/12/21/us-sidelined-russia-turkey-iran-plot-syrias-fate.html.

Trading Economics. 2018. *"Turkey GDP."* Accessed September 30, 2018. Trading Economics Turkey GDP: https://tradingeconomics.com/turkey/gdp.

The World Bank Group. *"Turkey."* Turkey | Data. Accessed September 25, 2018. data.worldbank.org/country/turkey?view=chart.

United Nations News. 2016. *"UN officials condemn attempt to overthrow Turkish Government."* UN News. Accessed October 1, 2018. https://news.un.org/en/story/2016/07/534572-un-officials-condemn-attempt-overthrow-turkish-government.

United States Department of State. 2018. *"Integrated Country Strategy: Turkey."* Accessed October 12, 2018. www.state.gov: https://www.state.gov/documents/organization/285064.pdf.

Wertheimer, Linda. 2016. *"Turkey Coup Attempt Leaves President Erdogan with Uncertain Grip on Country."* Interview. Weekend Edition Saturday of National Public Radio. Accessed September 20, 2018. https://web.b.ebscohost.com/ehost/detail/detail?vid=0&sid=099e2fcc-387d-4ed8-be18e486d59f333c%40sessionmgr120&bdata=JnNpdGU9ZWhvc3QtbGl2ZSZzY29wZT1zaXRl#AN=6XN201607161312&db=nfh.

Wertheimer, Linda. 2016. *"Assessing International Fallout from Failed Military Turkey Coup."* Interview. Weekend Edition Saturday of National Public Radio. Accessed September 20, 2018. https://web.b.ebscohost.com/ehost/detail/detail?vid=0&sid=f51ee70e-bc28-4438-a7f4-c00208058c86%40sessionmgr103&bdata=JnNpdGU9ZWhvc3QtbGl2ZSZzY29wZT1zaXRl#AN=6XN201607161209&db=nfh.

Yellkikalan, Nazan., Erdal Aydin, and Unzule Kurt. 2017. *"Impact on Economic Growth of Technological Progress in the Turkey Economy: Empirical Analysis on Political and Financial Stability Channel."* Canadian Center of Science and Education. Accessed November 1, 2018. https://mpra.ub.uni-muenchen.de/73255/1/MPRA_paper_73255.pdf.

Yesiltas, Murat., Merve Seren, and Necdet Ozelik. 2017. *"Operation Euphrates Shield Implementation and Lessons Learned."* SETA Publication. Accessed November 2, 2018. https://setav.org/en/assets/uploads/2017/11/R97_Euphrates.pdf.

In: Global Intelligence Priorities ISBN: 978-1-53615-836-6
Editors: John Michael Weaver et al. © 2019 Nova Science Publishers, Inc.

Chapter 9

IS INDIA A U.S. ALLY TO "THE CHINA THREAT"? A QUALITATIVE ASSESSMENT

Jason Guo
Case Western Reserve University,
Cleveland, Ohio, US

ABSTRACT

The China challenge is considered by the current Trump administration as a top national security issue. In order to contain China, the U.S. has been searching for strategies to counterbalance China's power, so it can continue to be the global hegemony. One of strategies is to have a partner located within the broad geographic region. The U.S. has long hoped for India to be its ally in the region especially as India is the world's largest democracy located nearby China. Would India be an ally of the U.S. in the coming years hedging against Chinese influence? Using a qualitative research approach and collected data from unclassified sources, this chapter focused on the two current "hot spot" issues standing between the

U.S. and China: the "Belt and Road Initiative" (BRI) and the South China Sea as case studies and investigated complex spatial-temporal relationship among the trio entities – the U.S., China, and India. It was concluded that an ally like India will most likely not succeed because of its long historical pattern on its foreign relations. Despite of India's recent leaning toward to the U.S., India's "non-alignment" tenet of foreign policy has played an important role that will dictate the nation state of India stands at a neutral standpoint in the newly dubbed Indo-Pacific region. In addition, this chapter also outlines the strategies that China has been exercising to undercut India's role as a regional competitor.

INTRODUCTION

In the most recent *National Security Strategy* by the Trump administration, China is listed as one of the top five main national security threats – a revisionist power to the United States (NSS 2017). Such a statement stems from China's recent rapid economic growth and expanded national influence within and beyond East Asia and on the global stage. Such language used in a strategic document like the NSS is a significant deviation of the U.S.' foreign policy on China. The tension has escalated; an example includes the on-going trade war between the two nations and serves as a good example of global power competition which might be one of the greatest in the 21st century. As the Trump administration takes the U.S. on a different direction than the past on its China policy, can the U.S. turn to another big country, India that is located in the same broad geographic region, for assistance winning the power game of the century? Will India answer the U.S. call for being an ally? These questions are important to help untangle the quagmire among the trio of international relations. This chapter focuses the "Belt and Road Initiatives" (hereafter BRI) launched by China in 2013 and the South China Sea as case studies and investigates the complex relationships among the three big countries in the world today and what the potential future relationship might be. Taking a qualitative approach, the D.I.M.E. (diplomacy, information, military, and economic) conceptual model (JP 1-02 2010, 112; Weaver 2015) was used to frame the current trio relationship. In doing so, future national powers and the inter-relationship were analyzed and projected.

Case 1. The Belt and Road Initiative

The BRI is China's ambition for a more integrated economic cooperation through a transregional railway network (The Word Bank 2018). It takes after the idea of China's ancient major land-based trading network, the "Silk Road" from 200 BC. The difference is that today's BRI will expand and cover a much greater geographic area. The land portion of the BRI follows the "Silk Road" route connecting China to South Asia, Central Asia, and then northward to Europe. Its newly added marine portion, once it leaves China, links China with Southeast Asia, the Persian Gulf States, Northern Africa, and back to Europe. In total, the initiative covers some 65 countries which comprise 62% of population, 30% of world Gross Domestic Product (GDP), and 75% of known energy reserves (The World Bank 2018). It is estimated that China's BRI will cost China more than $1 trillion (Sherwood 2018).

China's old "Silk Road" plays a significant role in China's open-up contacting with outside of the world since the Han Dynasty. The "Silk Road" is literally a trans-Asian trading highway. It allowed ancient Chinese merchants exchanging goods ranging from silk, of course, tea, and spices, and diffusing ideas and cultures throughout the route for over two thousand years all way to Rome. Started at Xi'an, the original "Silk Road" stretches across 4,000 miles (approximately 6,400 kilometers) through various landscapes connecting ancient port cities such as Zanzibar, Alexandria, Muscat, and Goa (UNESCO, 2019). The Chang'an-Tianshan Corridor of the "Silk Road" today was established as a World Heritage Site by the United Nations Educational, Scientific, and Cultural Organization (UNESCO). The influence of the "Silk Road" has a lasting influence and is still being truly felt today.

In September 2013, Chinese President Xi Jinping announced the BRI as a new national project to "promote the economic prosperity of the countries along the Belt and Road and regional economic cooperation, strengthen exchanges and mutual learning between different civilizations, and promote world peace and development" (Xi 2015). The initiative contains two physical portions: a land route and a maritime route. The land route will largely rely on existing cities, towns, and settlements of the old "Silk Road" but will move across Eurasia. The marine portion aims to take advantage of coastal locations by including large marine trading ports. Figure 1 by Pomeroy (2019) on next page shows these integrated coastal port cities: Indonesia's capital Jakarta, global transshipping hub Singapore, India's Kolkata, Sri Lanka's capital city Colombo, Pakistan's southwestern Gwadar, global city Athens of Greece, Italy's Venice, the European Union's major logistic and economic center Rotterdam, and the world's largest inland port Duisburg located in Germany's Rhine-Ruhrot heartland. It is China's major geo-economic measure whose goal is to create a modern global city-based trade network by such massive transportation infrastructure affecting a total urban population of nearly 140 million people – see Table 1 in Annex A. On the note of the global financial system, China can further develop its national economy and internationalize the renminbi (RMB). In addition, other economic corridor projects are designed by China to further expand China's impact inside of its neighbors and partners. Two examples of these additional economic corridor projects are the China-Pakistan Economic Corridor (CPEC) and the Bangladesh-China-India-Myanmar Economic Corridor. Through development approach, these Chinese projects carry huge impact well beyond its economic arena.

The United States' response to China's BRI is strong and worrisome. In these American perspectives, it is argued that the BRI "could threat the very foundations of Washington's post-WWII hegemony" (Cavanna 2018) and "a deliberate attempt to economically marginalize the United States, to create a Eurasian sphere of influence, or as a pretext for expanding China's overseas military presence" (Chance, 2016). Although they do recognize that the BRI aims to stabilize "China's western peripheries, rekindle its economy, propel non-Western international economic institutions, gain influence in other countries, and diversify trade suppliers/routes" but it does so "circumventing the U.S. pivot to Asia." Ely Ratner, Vice-President and

Director of Studies at the Center for a New American Security which is a Washington-based think tank, states that China's BRI is an "Economic coercion has become a fundamental part of Chinese economic statecraft and has had a chilling demonstration effect on the world" (Shi & Churchill 2018).

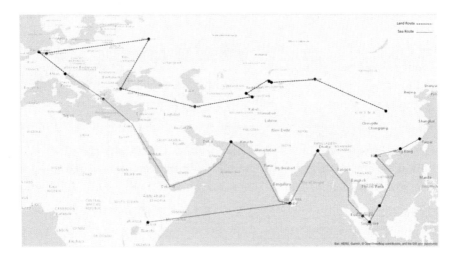

Figure 1. Distribution of Cities along the BRI.

Case 2. South China Sea Territorial Dispute

The South China Sea is an English name referring to a marginal sea in the southern Pacific Ocean. As the largest sea body after the five oceans, the South China Sea is a major international water with many marine features including islands, rocks, shoals, reefs, and islets. For over the last 25 years, this international water has been contentious and encapsulates as many as five countries located adjacent within the region and a few more outside of the area leading to constant disputes continuously challenging global peace.

The South China Sea is located to the south of China's southern border, east of Vietnam, and west of the Philippines. Because of its central location among these three countries and near a few others, the marine boundaries for these nations have long been disputed. The countries involved encompass China, Taiwan, Vietnam, the Philippines, and Malaysia. One of the disputed areas that China and Vietnam both claimed is the Paracel Islands. China and Philippines are in dispute about the Scarborough Reef located to the northeast. Another intensely disputed area is the Spratly Islands among the nations of China, Taiwan, Malaysia, the Philippines, Vietnam, and Brunei. Named after British whaling captain Richard Spratly, it is an archipelago covering 425,000 km^2 in area consisting of several large rocks in an arc shape and they are only surfaced in low tides. Being an archipelago presents a quite challenge in terms of how many rocks there are; should only those bigger rocks be counted? If so, how big?

Regardless the simple question of how many and size related questions and in general, the South China Sea is natural resource abundant. The U.S. Energy Information Administration estimates that there are approximately 11 billion barrels of oil reserves and 190 trillion cubic feet of natural gas reserves throughout the South China Sea (2013). The predicted amount of natural resources within the South China Sea makes the Spratly Islands the perfect location to begin to harvest the natural resources coveted by these developing countries as they are seeking natural resources such as oil, natural gas, fisheries, and trade routes for economic development. All of these countries have been building up development on the various parts of islands, including China. It is reported that China has been undertaking extensive island building and has constructed military bases. It is also reported that, over the years, China has increased its military presence throughout the South China Sea with the militarization of the land that China claims among the Spratly Islands and frequent military vessels throughout the region. Because of geographic proximity to southern China where China's Economic Exporting Zones (EEZs) are located, China not only sees itself with a legitimate right of use but also for the purpose of southern national border defense on these waters. However, countries such as the Philippines have concerns and are fearful of China's increasing military presence among the islands. The U.S. strongly disagrees with it in that the U.S. views China's dominance in the South China Sea and in all other near seas along the entire west Pacific as a strategic threat weakening the U.S. hegemony. This concern is well described by Navy Admiral Philip Davidson who writes "China is now capable of controlling the South China Sea in all scenarios short of war with the United States" (O'Rourke 2018).

China's BRI, along with China's persistent engagement in the South China Sea, make the U.S. feel pressure and great threat and power challenge. In order to contain China and solve the China challenge, the U.S. is vehemently seeking allies who can help it win this greatest power competition. This study used the D.I.M.E. (diplomacy, information, military, and economic elements of national power) conceptual framework to examine the two hot spots that have been stressing the U.S.-China relations because of the framework's suitability and dynamic nature that can best capture the fluidity of the U.S.- China relationship.

An additional theoretical construct used was the York Intelligence Red Team Model (YIRTM) to complement the D.I.M.E. instruments. Depicted in Figure 1, the YIRTM is specifically designed around the D.I.M.E. logic model. It was used to explore and investigate relationships among the variables, the directions of each national power's element, and the shaped outcomes (Weaver & Pomeroy 2018, 6).

Q1: How is China using its political, economic, and military capabilities in the context of YITRM to weaken or diminish the U.S. hegemony in the Indo-Pacific region?

Q2: In the greatest century power competition, will India be a U.S. strategic partner in the Indo-Pacific region counterbalancing the China influence? And why?

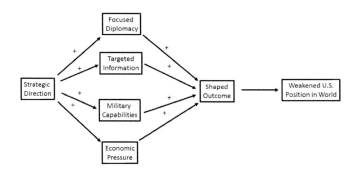

Figure 2. YIRTM.

As shown above, the YIRTM evaluates the strategic direction of a cause-effect relationship. In this case, weakened U.S. position is the shaped outcome of certain behaviors in the four specific instruments. Comprehensive understanding of those relationships provides the leader within a state vital information for creating strategies to overcome adverse effects threatening the national security strategy of the United States.

Diplomacy is the first element a country has for its national power. If it is used effectively, it can easily advance a country's values and national interests and of course, is a best tool a country could have to avoid any warfare which would cause loss of life and assets that could become damaged and or destroyed. This direction of diplomatic policies and maneuvers is critical as a leader engages others in order to foster conditions favorable to their cause not only regionally but also globally (Weaver & Pomeroy 2018, 6). Diplomacy requires a country not only to examine its internal affairs but also the impact by its diplomatic policies, treaties, recognition, negotiations, and international forums beyond its homeland. Often, these diplomatic policies carry regional and global impacts. On September 3rd, 2018, President Xi Jinping addressed the Forum on African-Chinese Cooperation where he spoke of partnerships and achievements between China and various African countries. President Xi's speech continued to strengthen China's relationship with the African nations; as a result, the U.S. influence is being marginalized (Zhuxi & Yaochun, 2018).

Information is the second element that refers to the way a nation's leaders use it to influence its people and it can exert great power in the global environment (Farlin, 2014). Some examples are a variety of communication resources, spokespersons, media and different venues for announcement and press releases. Communication technology-based information today has rapidly been improved and will continuously advance. Whoever uses it can leverage the purpose, legitimize and/or delegitimize messages through social media (Weaver & Pomeroy 2018, 7). Political propaganda is one type of information that can be easily flourished among social media and in advertisements. Such information can misinform different issues and can advance various organizations and entities' goals by supporting their own image or defaming someone else. One of the quintessential examples of

Is India a U.S. Ally to "The China Threat"? 233

those apps within in Chinese society is WeChat. WeChat is used for almost every aspect of the day but has complied with the Chinese government when requesting information from the application. WeChat cannot guarantee that its users' information will be protected for privacy away from Chinese government and officials (Grigg 2018). One of consequences of such tight government control of social media could directly influence their own citizen's views and to undermine other countries.

The military is the third element of national power. It establishes the defense and power of a nation through size and composition of all armed service branches and the use of military force, field combat operations, and peacekeeping engagement and force presence overseas. A military protects a nation for national security overtly and covertly. It consists of military defense capabilities, communications, intelligence, and surveillance systems. A country's technology level directly links to pull from the strength of its national military power.

Figure 3. Federal Qualitative Secondary Data Case Study Triangulation Model.

The economic component is the last element of national power. It can include the likes of trade policies, fiscal and monetary policies and regulations, tariffs and embargos, and aid. Using one or a combination of two or more are often used by a country to exert its influence. By leveraging a state's domestic markets, trade policies and financial investments, countries are able to join and shape the global geopolitical landscape to their own designs.

A synergy among these four instruments is necessary to ensure a country's national power. For any adversaries of a country, they can equally be employed to weaken that country's national power. According to Figure 2, the intent of this research was to understand the dilemma of the U.S.-China-India relations. The use of the YIRTM model enabled the investigation process to drill down into each of the three countries, their crisscross relations, and how those relations can help either alleviate or increase the U.S. global hegemony which is what the two prevailing research questions intended to answer earlier. For instance, who is most likely behind these, why they are occurring, and what might be next from China's perspective (Mastapeter 2008).

The core component of the model is a case study approach. A case study is conducive in accommodating complex causal relations but it needs substantial high-quality data to support the arrival of a conclusion (Starman 2013, 37; Creswell 2008). The Federal Qualitative Secondary Data Case Study Triangulation Model (hereafter Federal Model) was used for this purpose (Weaver 2015). As illustrated above, this model provides the needed guidelines to triangulate multiple data sources and assure only those credible data were used for analysis triangulation. Triangulation focuses on tactics, techniques, and procedures (TTPs) from the variety of data sources. For example, plans and systems, government reports, legislation and policy, press release, testimony, interviews, and biographies. Key public leaders are an important data provider. Scholarly work is also included as an important data source as they provide independent points of view. The final component gravitates to a balance in the triangulation process to ensure the data quality and validity of data interpretation.

A qualitative research must address validity issue. This was completed through variable checks in terms of what each variable measure and how each is measured (Jaeger 1993, 384). Although these specific validity procedures are subjective, triangulation procedure minimized the validity problem as much as possible (Jaeger 1993, 80).

An emphasis was also afforded to the topic of reliability. The researchers often use consistency in their approach to similar projects to ensure reliability because consistency is the key to conducting reliable research (Creswell 2008, 190). The use of the D.I.M.E. conceptual model measuring the four instruments of national power and consistent use in the implementation of the YIRTM and the Federal Model make sure the impact of validity was achieved and thus a maximum of reliability was realized.

LIMITATIONS

First of all, the temporal scope of this research was limited to a three-year period from 2015 to the end of 2018. More weight was assigned to the data in the latter time because of immediate relevance to what is studied.

Second, it should be noted that primary data was not used in this research project. Only secondary data in the public domain was collected and used for analysis. Other limitations from secondary data emanate from the implementation of a cross-sectional design. Due to the reliance on secondary data, it is often difficult for one to understand whether bias existed from how the data was originally collected (Cross-Sectional 2012).

Thirdly, it also should be noted that other variables outside of the YIRTM could impact and influence a study like this as changes rise. For example, these include legacy trade agreements and treaties, and sophistication of technology. Future studies might also consider these to build upon the results of this study. It must be noted that it is difficult to generalize beyond the study at hand for any qualitative research.

Lastly, the results from this research is confirmatory research and in a contributory fashion helping expanding efforts looking at a major threat in the context of the YIRTM; challenges can also spring up regarding cross-sectional design when interpreting results in part based on bias issues and the lack of full inclusion of all relevant events (Cross-Sectional 2012). Future studies might consider these research techniques to either reconstruct the study or to complement its findings as additional information becomes available.

ANALYSIS

This section provides an in-depth analysis that is based on the D.I.M.E., and the YIRTM model under the guidance of the Federal Model. First and foremost, the Indo-Pacific Region must be defined and examined to contextualize the analysis. Then, the exhibited diplomacy, information, military, and economic elements in the two hot spot case studies in the trio state actors are offered. Lastly, the between and among relations and the common myths are comprehensively analyzed.

Define the Indo-Pacific Region

While the name change of the Pacific Command to the Indo-Pacific Command may come as a shock to the public, many top officials have referred to the region as Indo-Pacific and it was used in the most recent National Security Strategy (NSS 2017). The Indo-Pacific Region is a newly used concept that geographically encompasses the southern tropical Indian Ocean and the western and central Pacific Ocean. It is often used by tropical physical geographers as it is in fact a biogeography realm with a significant value in high species richness. It comprises of extensive coastal land areas, islands, seas, and straits. Countries included in this region are Eastern Asian state actors like China, Japan, Oceanian country of Australia, southern Asian country of India, and the U.S., although it is geographically distant, but is historically involved especially after WWII. In order to contain China's rising influence, the Trump Administration has endorsed the "Indo-Pacific" region. However, such endorsement conflicts with where the marine portion of the BRI covers and the South China Sea territorial dispute includes, therefore, it has become a major area of battleground in the U.S.- China power competition. Japanese Prime Minister Shinzo Abe and India's Prime

Minister Modi have publicly showed their support on the U.S. "Indo-Pacific Strategy" (Chen 2018).

Belt and Road Initiative

China's new BRI has an emphasis of laying high speed rail for trains as the main transportation form creating the transcontinental geo-economic region. Through this supposed highly-efficient transportation network, the BRI will establish a comprehensive land-maritime freight transportation network connecting China with South Asia, the Association of Southeast Asian Nations (ASEAN), East Africa, and Europe (Cavanna 2018). China has already spent approximately $21 billion in their first steps by building new ports in various countries who have joined onto China's BRI and invested about $340 billion in construction contracts (Sherwood 2018).

Throughout the last five years, the BRI has been used as a major economic instrument by the Chinese government and made considerable progress in connecting less and least economically connected state actors to a global economic structure. Obe and Kishimoto (2019) reported that while Japan pulled out from the shinkansen-style high-speed rail project in Thailand, China filled in the void by constructing a high-speed project in northern Thailand and will continue to reach Bangkok and further southward to Singapore, which is an entrépot occupying a strategic location in transcontinental shipping. In Pakistan, China has opened a new train route between Lanzhou, the capital of China's northwestern province of Gansu, and Islamabad, Pakistan (曹家寧 2018a) and opened rail and sea freight service routes from China's Yunnan Province to Karachi, Pakistan's largest city (Sherwood 2018). In connecting the northern Africa region, Ethiopia contracted with the Ethio-Djibouti Railways to China in October 2012 and Kenya signed the joint agreement with China in May 2014 (Sherwood 2018). Furthermore, China has been successful in establishing two new train routes with Moscow as President Xi continues to expand and further the BRI (曹家寧 2018b). China has funded massive infrastructure projects for some who are globally, peripherally, and economically connected to countries like Kazakhstan who otherwise cannot get much financial investment and support. With the BRI, such countries are now part of the "joint projects" of being linked to the global economy (Watts 2018). The attraction of global connectivity is vital for state actors like this. Another example of such is that, in spite of far out in the South America, Chile decided to join China's BRI to deepen the two countries' trade relations (Sherwood 2018).

The BRI is not without resistance and obstacles. Oppositions include the U.S. and several other countries since mid-2017. One major obstacle is the partnership China has secured with the Philippines, advancing the BRI. In November 2018, Chinese President Xi Jinping visited Philippine President Rodrigo Duterte where they both reached a bilateral agreement to work together both on the BRI and solve the dispute over the South China Sea (曹家宁 2018c). The agreement between China and the Philippines ushers in a new period of cooperation between the two countries. China's state media has been vigorously publishing news releases and articles about the BRI successful agreement with the Philippines. The new partnership between China and the Philippines works to strengthen the BRI a paradox to U.S. interests. The opposition that the U.S. and other countries have against the BRI will continue to be tested and challenged by Chinese influence gaining partners and allies to promote and expand the BRI. For example, one states that the initiative will promote, "mutual respect, equity and justice, and win-win cooperation and join hands with all parties in building a clean and beautiful community of shared future for humankind featuring enduring peace, universal security, common prosperity, and openness and inclusiveness" (Ministry of Foreign Affairs of the People's Republic of China 2014). With this perspective, many analysts are hesitant about the potential for China to manipulate the political and economic situation while others see this as an opportunity for China to establish stability and peace throughout the region.

David Dollar (2015), a senior fellow at the Brookings Institute, argues that with China attempting to establish diplomatic relations and build allies in the region will allow China to compete with the U.S. on a different level; this competition will improve the global economy and allow both parties to establish stronger relations in the Indo-Pacific region. Furthermore, Dollar believes that the establishment of the Asian Infrastructure Investment Bank (AIIB) will allow for more development within the region where the World Bank has failed to provide monetary support for infrastructural development in some of the world's most underdeveloped countries (Dollar 2015). Other analysts, Meltzer (2018) and Watts (2018) agree that the BRI will provide a "win-win" situation for the U.S. and China as U.S. businesses will realize benefits from it. However, there are other opinions that believe that China is using the BRI and AIIB to further its own geopolitical goals and interests. Australia is currently unsure of the implications of the BRI; it is concerned with China taking control of the region (Banerjee 2018). Another issue is that China will usurp the U.S., who has historically maintained stability in the region (Xu 2018). With the interpretation of the BRI's economic initiatives (an instrument of national power), another major argument about the BRI is that China is using a "debt-trap diplomacy" method to cajole countries to sign onto agreements (Chellaney 2017a). This stance was also supported by Professor Brahma Chellaney. He states that China is utilizing methods that ensure that countries cannot pay back debts to loans that China has provided for projects; as a result, China will then cancel the debt in exchange for various agreements. This tactic has provided China diplomatic leverage over countries that are in debt to China (Dollar 2015).

This then begs the question on the reputation of the U.S.' role in the Indo-Pacific region. Historically, the U.S. has maintained peace and stability and has over time repeated its desire to maintain respect for sovereignty and independence (NSS 2017). A growing international Chinese presence should be a major concern of the United States as China continues to extend its influence and network beyond Asia. This is a powerful economic tactic that China is able to utilize against U.S. interests. One primary example is that China is also utilizing this economic influence to also grow the capacity of its military presence beyond the Indo-Pacific region. In 2015, China established a military base in Djibouti, a critical geographical location along the maritime path (Panda 2015). This is a critical sign to the rest of the Indo-Pacific region and the U.S. that China is ready to expand and exert its influence internationally.

While recognizing China's rising role and global influence, many analysts have been mistakenly referring to the BRI as "China's Marshall Plan" (Shen & Chan 2018). However, the Marshall Plan was implemented by the U.S. during a time of crisis following World War II and exported the notions of a free market and democracy. These are ideals that many ordinary citizens found very attractive for their respective countries. As stated within United States Agency for International Development's (USAID's) 2018-2022 report, the threat of China is not a light one and the U.S. should be wary of the influence that China poses in the region but should also not over-react in light of Chinese ambitions. Unlike the Marshall Plan, China does not have the values that ordinary citizens desire. Not too many citizens are protesting or lobbying for a state-controlled system and one party to decide on all domestic and international issues. When trying to understand China's policies and grand strategy, it is vital to the U.S.' interest to not to overreact to China's growing influence and presence for there is not as large of a threat as many other analysts have presented it to be.

South China Sea

Before understanding how China could potentially dominate and destabilize the region, one must understand how the South China Sea is defined by the United Nations Convention of the Law of the Sea (UNCLOS) – an international treaty adopted in 1982. The first important part of the South China Sea is "rocks," which are defined as the following: "Rocks which cannot sustain human habitation or economic life of their own shall have no exclusive economic zone (EEZ) or continental shelf" (Davidson & Davidson 1997). Many of the "islands" that countries such as China and Vietnam have claimed are not islands by UNCLOS definition. They are rather just a rock. This is an extremely important clarification since rocks do not generate EEZs-- only territorial waters. This will be crucial to remember when analyzing recent U.S. operations within the South China Sea.

The next part of UNCLOS that is quite relevant is low-tide elevations. "A low-tide elevation is a naturally formed area of land which is surrounded by and above water at low tide but submerged at high tide. Where a low-tide elevation is situated wholly or partly at a distance not exceeding the breadth of the territorial sea from the mainland or an island, the low-water line on that elevation may be used as the baseline for measuring the breadth of the territorial sea" (Davidson & Davidson 1997). Once again, the South China Sea is littered with many low-tide elevations that do not generate territorial waters or an EEZs. Lastly, there are islands, which are classified as the following by UNCLOS as, "a naturally formed area of land, surrounded by water, which is above water at high tide (Davidson & Davidson 1997). Islands do generate both territorial waters and EEZs. However, this does not matter in the situation of the South China Sea since the arbitration ruling of the International Court of Justice ruled that all of the land features in the South China Sea are not capable of generating any extended maritime zones or EEZs (The Hague 2016). However, a common misunderstanding of the arbitration is that China is "breaking the law" and the ruling provides leverage for the Philippines (O'Rourke 2018). This is not the case since arbitrations do not hold any actual judicial power on any country but provides administrative support.

It was noted that at the Shangri-La Dialogue by He Lei, Vice President of the Academy of Military Science of the Chinese People's Liberation Army, that the South China Sea is a routine discussion item in recent years with all countries in the disputes (ZX 2018). For instance, on August 3rd, 2018, China and the ten-member states of ASEAN drafted a code of conduct (COC) that these countries have verbally agreed to temporarily after two years of negotiation (Wong & Lo 2018). It is important to know that this is not the first time China began this kind of discussion on the South China Sea. The earliest such attempt was in 1995. While it may seem as though the situation may have simmered down following the draft of a code of conduct between ten ASEAN countries and China, the U.S. cannot let its guard down now especially in contentious times such as today's.

A crucial part of the U.S.' role in the Indo-Pacific Region is the continuous and frequent Freedom of Navigation Operations (FONOP). On March 23rd, 2018, a FONOP was conducted throughout the Spratly Islands (Ali & Blanchard 2018). The purpose of a FONOP is to curtail excessive claims by other countries and is not only utilized against China, but with other countries all around the world in accordance with UNCLOS. Lieutenant Commander Nicole Schwegman, a spokeswoman for U.S. Pacific Fleet stated that, "We [U.S. Navy] conduct routine and regular freedom of navigation operations, as we have done in the past and will continue to do in the future" (Ali & Blanchard 2018). While the U.S. Navy has been able to present itself as fearless and powerful to the rest of the world, the Chinese have not taken FONOPs by the U.S. lightly. It is important to recognize that China does not like to bow out or turn away from a challenge. On April 12, 2018, Chinese President Xi Jinping announced the largest review of the Navy since 1949 (ZD 2018). This is a clear sign to the United States that China is not going to demilitarize the South China Sea anytime soon despite the agreements with ASEAN. The growing military activity in the region is concerned with the rest of the international community and is indirectly challenging the international authority that the U.S. is dominant. China is using the South China Sea as a testing ground to see how far they can go militarily and diplomatically without crossing a line. If the U.S. does not utilize the tools such as a FONOP, China will continue to push the limits of international order and undermine the system that the U.S. has established (Swaine et al. 2013, 38).

Despite the presence and refocusing of the National Defense Strategy, the Indo-Pacific is in *de facto* of the domination and control by China. The recent name change of the Pacific Command to the Indo-Pacific Command by the U.S. Defense Department showcases the U.S. military clout in order to counter and contain the growing power of China, as Admiral Phil Davison states that "... and the credibility of the combat power within U.S. Pacific Command... To our allies here in the Indo-Pacific, you will have no better ally. To our partners, I look forward to advancing our partnership in a way that serves our mutual interested" (Davidson 2018). In order for the South China Sea to achieve peace, the U.S. cannot solely rely on the military instrument and must be ready to support and uphold international regulations if the U.S. hopes to maintain its hegemony on the rule-based international system.

Sino-Indo-U.S. Relations

As the China-U.S. relationship is becoming tenser, India has been brought in to the discussion as part of the U.S. NSS. Is India's growing influence large enough in the Indo-Pacific region to counter-balance China? Such conversations mainly take place among lawmakers and officials. The former Secretary of Defense, James Mattis, was extremely interested in the role India might play in the Indo-Pacific region and a possible partnership that can be formed between the two democracies (2018).

Overall, the U.S. struggles to understand India's policy of non-alignment especially if it believes that India will be a player in the U.S.' grand strategy. India, the second most populous country in the world, is a dominant country in the South Asia Region. It is the world's largest federation. Since India's independence, its first Prime Minister, Jawaharlal Nehru, established a foundation for India's foreign policy of conservative and permanent non-alignment and aspiration for India to be an independent sovereign state. This policy has held a historical root for India's foreign policy and was reiterated in Prime Minister Narendra Modi's speech at the Shangri La Dialogue in 2018 (Modi 2018). As the keynote speaker, Modi focused on India's stance of non-alignment within the international community. His position is rooted in India historically choosing the third path by holding a stance that does not push India to one side. Modi uses language through his remarks to acknowledge all the connections that India has established among the U.S., China, Russia, and the ASEAN countries. He specifically adds "And by no means do we consider it as directed against any country" when he was discussing a nation seeking to dominate—hinting at China in the Indo-Pacific region. Modi's statements are all carefully chosen in order to neither favor any country nor attack any one specific treading the line between global superpowers. His remarks were a reminder to the international community that India holds a mutual position on its foreign relations and is a friend to all countries and does not choose one side as established by Nehru in 1947 (Modi 2018).

Nehru's legacy shines through many top officials of India's government. India's leader, President Pranab Mukherjee, stated at a conference in 2015 that, "Pandit Nehru, the architect of India's policies in the early decades of independent India's journey, firmly enshrined these goals in our country's quest for fulfilling its destiny as an independent nation" (Shri Yashwant Sinha 2003). It is clear that Nehru and his successors have followed the middle-ground stance on the independent nature of India. It would be a fool's errand if the U.S. believes they could override decades of precedent that has led India's foreign policy (Sridharan 2017, 60).

Therefore, India's foreign policy has historically been one of that avoids conflict. However, it is important to note that while India did side with the former Soviet Union during the Cold War because this was primarily to counter Pakistan when the U.S. allied with India's rival. Nevertheless, India has avoided being one-dimensional, but rather remains open and flexible to all countries. Nehru's leadership early on in India's modern history has allowed India to pursue this third path of international relations instead of choosing one side over the other. It is historically suggestive that India will not select the United States over China (Bussiére & Arnaud 2008, 15). As Nehru continues to state, "India is too big a country herself to be bound down to any country, however big it may be" (Nanda 1990, 41). Following decades of British rule, India will not be the pawn of any country, but instead shall be an innovative, independent country that creates its own foreign policy. The U.S. should not and cannot expect to influence India's foreign policy especially with the precedent and influence Nehru's policy still holds in India today.

The misinterpretation of India's foreign policy has led to many false assumptions and could disappoint many U.S. officials who do not understand India's stance of non-alignment. Understanding this policy is the key to gaining insight into India's growing partnership with China and the different global design that India and the U.S. envision. In December 2018, China and India conducted their first joint army tactical coordination called "Hand-in-Hand" (Li 2018). The joint initiative between China and India focuses on counter-terrorism and comradery between the two Asian powerhouses. Furthermore, the two countries have begun to build and develop a stronger relationship. Indian Defense Minister Nirmala Sitharaman invited Chinese State Councilor and Defense Minister General

Wei Fenghe to India to continue to bolster and develop the Sino-Indian relationship. The meeting between the two top officials signifies a changing perspective between the two countries. Although India still has many differing opinions running contrary to China, their relations still remain uncertain, but it is clear that India is not ready to be a countering force against China that shares a border and much closer to the U.S.

A "Natural Partner or Ally?"

Exploring if India can be a U.S. partner in the Indo-Pacific Region had been tried before. On March 2, 2006, President George W. Bush met with India's Prime Minister Singh to discuss a multitude of political issues ranging from nuclear proliferation to economic cooperation (Bush 2006). President Bush stated, "India in the 21st century is a natural partner of the United States because we are brothers in the cause of human liberty" (Bush 2006). This is the first time a U.S. president referred to India as a "natural partner." Shortly after President Bush, President Barack Obama in 2009 met with Prime Minister Singh as well. During this meeting, Obama stated that, "India today is a rising and responsible global power. In Asia, Indian leadership is expanding prosperity and the security across the region. And the United States welcomes and encourages India's leadership role in helping to shape the rise of a stable, peaceful, and prosperous Asia" (Yurou 2018). President Obama went further by stating that, "the United States and India are natural allies not just around counterterrorism issues, but on a whole host of issues" (Yurou 2018). Obama expressed that he believed that the two countries are "natural allies" and the U.S. hopes to use India to vicariously counter China's growth but is mistaken to utilize simple rhetoric. It would be in the U.S.' best interest to reiterate the shared opinion of past U.S. presidents regarding India's vital role and influence within the Indo-Pacific region.

While past presidents have attempted to coax India into the grand strategy of the U.S., the U.S. seems to still be unaware of the differing worldviews with their "natural ally." India treads the line of non-alignment in order to prevent a unipolar global system and instead leans toward to support an "open, inclusive, and multipolar world" (Sakhuja 2018). However, the U.S. has enjoyed a unipolar world that is dominant by itself, especially since the Soviet Union's disintegration in early 1990s. The value of the U.S. hegemony is fundamentally a disagreement against India's "multipolar" worldview. It primarily established global system by the U.S. that is operated on the international rules-based system since the end of World War II—makes the U.S. a global hegemon. This is a fundamental philosophical difference between these two "natural allies." Though, the U.S. and India do share the idea of free markets. When economic development is pertinent to their own domestic economies, the two countries have differing goals. The U.S.' intention is to use the U.S. economy for "defending against threats from state-led economies" so that the U.S. will remain as the "world's premier economic actor" (NSS 2017) whereas India's top priority is to improve and strengthen their overall economy. One could almost argue that India does not utilize its economy in order to gain dominance over other countries.

There are recent events and developments that may misguide officials and some analysts believe that India is allying itself with the United States because of the revitalization of the Quadrilateral Strategic Dialogue (the Quad). The Quad is comprised of the U.S., Japan, Australia, and India. Within the Quad, Australia and Japan are both official allies of the U.S. while India is only a partner of the United States. This caveat means that the Quad is only an alignment of values among four democracies in the Indo-Pacific region and not an alliance (Banerjee, 2018). India and the U.S. are not formal allies; they are only "Major Defense Partners" which commits the U.S. to sharing technology information at the same level as close allies (NSS 2017). The agreements and actions between the U.S. and India may seem like they are allies, but only have formally agreed to "Next Step in Strategic Partnership" (NSSP) initiative leaving the relationship only as a partnership. The Quad has initiated in multilateral discussions among the four democracies which may seem like these countries are banding together to take on China, but it is merely a "natural mutation of international relations" (Banerjee 2018). Zhiqun Zhu who is Professor of Political Science and International Relations at Bucknell University lists three reasons on why the Quad will "unlikely to become reality" (2018). He argues that (1) all four countries have no consensus on the common approach on China; (2) China's BRI is inclusive and seeking for multilateral collaborations; and (3) the U.S. may not want to cast huge investment overseas because Trump's "America First" policy (2018).

India-China Quagmire

India and China have had border disputes in the past which has affected China's relations with India and Pakistan. Many people in the U.S. believe that this is enough for India to join the U.S. against China, but this may not be the case as India does want to talk to China on improving its trade relationship with China. China is India's largest trading partner with a total bilateral trade of $84.4 billion, a leap from $38 billion in 2007-2008.

In 1950, India was the first non-socialist country to establish diplomatic relations with China. Despite the two countries having disputes between each other in the past, within the 21st century, China and India have had numerous top governmental official visits and held many high-level meetings from state and provincial levels to further establish positive diplomatic relations between the two countries. These visits and meetings have strengthened ties with China and in 2008, China replaced the U.S. as India's largest trading partner while India continues to grow it its economic influence (Bussiére & Arnaud 2008, 11). These growing relationships between two major influences in the Indo-Pacific region are growing closer at a time when the U.S. wishes that India would formally align itself with the United States. The U.S is misinformed if it believes that India will prioritize its values over its interests.

There are two major parties of India's government, the Bharatiya Janata Party (BJP) and Indian National Congress (INC) as well as many of the other smaller political parties. Many of these parties publish their goals and stances on many policy issues, but many of them lack detail or any opinion in foreign policy. The INC, which was the ruling party until the BJP with

Prime Minister Modi took power in 2014, have a short section in their plan focused on foreign policy, and specifically states that "We expect to proceed with our mutual efforts with China to work through established instruments towards a resolution of differences of perception about the border and the Line of Actual Control (LAC), even as our economic cooperation and multilateral cooperation continue to grow" (Indian National Congress 2014).

The INC's plans show the willingness of India to work with China to overcome many of the conflicts and pursue agreements to benefit both sides. The BJP, the ruling party of India, even wrote that India's, "foreign policy will be based on best National interests" (Bharatiya Janata Party Manifesto 2014). The BJP has been true to their word especially with the communication between Indian and Chinese officials to strengthen economic and diplomatic relations to bolster the domestic economy and standards of living. As of now, India's national interest does not view China as a threat and to the U.S.' distaste and India will not weaken its relationship with China.

The U.S. would be mistaken if it believes that India is fearful of China's growing dominance in the Indo-Pacific region. On the contrary, India is rising to the occasion to match China's economic power and hopes to establish stronger bilateral trade agreements. Where it may seem unclear to U.S. officials, there are the numerous disputes between China and India such as territorial disputes that have lasted since 1962, China's massive investment in India's rival, Pakistan, the growing trade deficit, and China's trade policy making the Chinese market difficult to enter (Kronstadt 2017). However, during discussions between the two countries, India is willing and hopes to overcome these conflicts and is actively seeking to establish a mutually beneficial bilateral trade agreement. The Chinese perspective is very similar as well. China has acknowledged how both countries would benefit tremendously from Free Trade Agreements and how both countries have grown to become powerful countries within the Indo-Pacific region.

The Enemy of My Enemy is My Friend?

India's famous ancient strategist, Kautilya, wrote the Arthashastra, an ancient Sanskrit that discussed economics, statecraft, and military politics and has been instrumental to Ancient India's development. One of the most famous quotes from this ancient text is, "the enemy of my enemy is my friend" (Lai 2011). It is used to describe international relations between neighboring countries seeing each other as threats, but the countries neighboring those around them were allies. With a rapidly changing and developing international system, it only seems logical and natural that both the U.S. and India should be friends to their common adversary, China. However, both the U.S. and India share a common "frenemy" relationship with China. Both India and the U.S. benefit heavily from trade and business with China. With a view of China as a threat only depends on one's view or perspective (Lai 2011, 22).

If China were to act out illogically and act in a way that upset both the U.S. and India deeply enough, then the two countries would most likely come together to counter China. China has fully recognized this and played its cards well and has not done anything to pump and drive these two democracies together. Until China lashes out, the U.S. can put its hopes on India becoming an ally to the side. India will remain as an independent power of the Indo-Pacific by sticking with its own unique foreign policy that could be a model to other developing countries.

The interactions between the Chinese and Indian government highlights an interesting relation in terms of both tension and diplomacy. In spite of the tensions between these two economic powers, it is also possible that with stronger economic ties, India and China may be able to look past some of their previous disagreements or even settle the border disputes because continuing to develop their national economies is the top priority.

Conclusion

Several main conclusions can be drawn and they are: (1) China's BRI is used by Chinese government as its economic and political instruments to weaken and diminish the U.S. hegemony in the Indo-Pacific region; the South China Sea is a China's testing ground for military element showcasing current Chinese military capabilities competing against that of the U.S.; the diplomacy instrument is also used in both hot spot cases by China facilitating China's positions. Secondly (2) in the greatest century power competition, the perception held by the U.S. that India will be an ally and strategic partner in the Indo-Pacific region to counter-balance China is most likely false because of India's historical foundation of "non-alignment" policy and deeply-woven economic relationships with China.

"The China threat" refers to China's recent embracing of its ascending and expanded global influence beyond the limits of Asia competing with the U.S. global hegemony. The United States has made strides in how it has confronted China during this current administration. While China has been pinpointed as one of the U.S.' greatest potential threats of the Trump Administration, it is unavoidable that China has become one of this nation's strongest economic partners affecting ordinary American daily lives. This interdependent relationship has made it especially difficult for the U.S. to be able to make abrupt separation actions against China in the realm of economics. It is very clear when analyzing the South China Sea territorial disputes, BRI, and complex Sino-Indo-U.S. relations that China has successfully manipulated all instruments of a national power - diplomatic, information, military and economic to its own causes in the Indo-Pacific Region and thus undermining the U.S.' hegemony. Whether India could come to the U.S. rescue counter balancing the China influence in the Indo-Pacific Region remains questionable, though, this analysis suggests it is unlikely.

ANNEX A

Table 1. Cities Included in the BRI

Index	City	Country	2018 City Population (million)	Land or Sea
1	Almaty	Kazakhstan	1.523	Land
2	Athens	Greece	3.000	Sea
3	Bishkek	Kyrgyzstan	1.000	Land
4	Colombo	Sri Lanka	2.000	Sea
5	Duisburg	Germany	0.500	Land
6	Dushanbe	Tajikistan	9.110	Land
7	Fuzhou	China	7.660	Sea
8	Guangzhou	China	13.000	Sea
9	Gwadar	Pakistan	0.264	Sea
10	Hanoi	Vietnam	7.588	Sea
11	Istanbul	Turkey	14.900	Land
12	Jakarta	Indonesia	10.000	Sea
13	Kolkata	India	5.202	Sea
14	Kuala Lumpur	Malaysia	7.800	Sea
15	Moscow	Russia	12.190	Land
16	Nairobi	Kenya	4.556	Sea
17	Rotterdam	Netherlands	1.009	Land
18	Samarkand	Uzbekistan	3.652	Land
19	Singapore	Singapore	5.800	Sea
20	Tehran	Iran	8.400	Land
21	Urumqi	China	2.900	Land
22	Venice	Italy	0.636	Sea
23	Xi'an	China	12.900	Land
		Total	135.590	

It is fair to recommend that the U.S. should be innovatively utilizing the four instruments of nation power to diffuse the growing competition tension with China in the Indo-Pacific Region. Although India may seem as a logical ally to the U.S. in the region, it would be the U.S.' folly to believe that India is ready to play a significant role at the global stage counterbalancing the

"Dragon of the East." The Quad could be another mechanism that the U.S. could utilize to win the power game against China, but as India is not yet prepared to handle the potential stress caused by such alignment, the Quad cannot contain Chinese actions and strategies. The Indo-Pacific Region will continue to become the epicenter of the world both for the rest of the century economically and politically. With time, China's BRI and its involvement in the South China Sea can be better assessed.

References

Abe, Shinzo. 2007, August 22. "Confluence of the Two Seas." Speech by H. E. Mr. Shinzo Abe, Prime Minister of Japan, at the Parliament of the Republic of India. Ministry of Foreign Affairs of Japan. Accessed October 20, 2018. https://www.mofa.go.jp/region/asia-paci/pmv0708/speech-2.html .

Ali, Idrees, and Ben Blanchard. 2018. "Exclusive: U.S. Warship Sails near Disputed South China Sea Island, Officials Say." *Reuters*, March 23. Accessed October 20, 2018. https://www.reuters.com/article/us-usa-china-southchinasea/exclusive-u-s-warship-sails-near-disputed-south-china-sea-island-officials-say-idUSKBN1GZ0VY

Banerjee, Somen. 2018. "Whither 'Quad' – Alliance or Alignment." Vivekananda International Foundation. Accessed Octobe 23, 2018. https://www.vifindia.org/article/2018/march/07/whither-quad-alliance-or-alignment .

"Bharatiya Janata Party Manifesto." 2014. AccessDecember 27, 2018. https://www.bjp.org/images/pdf_2014/full_manifesto_english_07.04.2014.pdf .

Bush, George W. 2006. "President's Visit to India and Pakistan." Accessed October 21, 2018. https://georgewbushwhitehouse.archives.gov/infocus/india-pakistan/

Bussiére, Matthieu, and Arnaud Mehl. 2008. *"China's and India's Roles in Global Trade and Finance: Twin Titans for the New Millennium?"* Accessed October 19, 2018. http://www.ecb.europa.eu.

Cao, Jianing (曹家宁), ed. 2018. "Chinese Defense Minister to Visit India."China Military Online, August 21. Accessed October 21, 2018. http://eng.mod.gov.cn/news/2018-08/21/content_4823013.htm .

———. 2018b. "China, Philippines Agree to Upgrade Ties, Jointly Build Belt and Road-Belt and Road Portal." *Xinhua News Agency.* 2018. https://eng.yidaiyilu.gov.cn/qwyw/rdxw/72302.htm .

———. 2018c. "New Freight Route Links China, Pakistan-Belt and Road Portal." *Xinhua News Agency.* 2018. https://eng.yidaiyilu.gov.cn/qwyw/rdxw/69571.htm .

Cavanna, Thomas P. 2018. "What Does China's Belt and Road Initiative Mean for US Grand Strategy?" *The Diplomat,* June 5. Accessed October 20, 2018. https://thediplomat.com/2018/06/what-does-chinas-belt-and-road-initiative-mean-for-us-grand-strategy/

Chance, Alex. 2016. "American Perspective on the Belt and Road Initiative: Sources of Concern, Possibilities for US-China Coopeartion." Institute for China-American Studies. Accessed January 11, 2019. https://chinaus-icas.org/wp-content/uploads/2017/02/American-Perspectives-on-the-Belt-and-Road-Initiative.pdf

Chellaney, Brahma. 2017. "China's Debt-Trap Diplomacy" Project Syndicate, January 23. Accessed October 20, 2018. https://www.project-syndicate.org/commentary/china-one-belt-one-road-loans-debt-by-brahma-chellaney-2017-01?barrier=accesspaylog .

Chen, Dingding. 2018. "The Indo-Pacific Strategy: A Background Analysis". ISPI – Istituto per Gli Studi di Politica Intenationale. Accessed January 13, 2019. https://www.ispionline.it/it/pubblicazione/indo-pacific-strategy-background-analysis-20714.

Cogliati-Bantz, Vincent P. 2016. "The South China Sea Arbitration (the Republic of the Philippines V. the People'S Republic of China)" *The International Journal of Marine and Coastal Law,* 31(2016): 759-774. https://doi.org/10.1163/15718085-12341421 .

Creswell, John W. 2008. *Research Design: Qualitative, Quantititve, and Mixed methods Approaches.* Thousand Oaks, CA: SAGE Publications.

Davidson, J. S., and J. S. Davidson. 1997. "United Nations Convention on the Law of the Sea Act 1996 (UNCLOS)." *The International Journal of*

Marine and Coastal Law 12 (3): 404–12. https://doi.org/10.1163/157 18089720491594.

Dollar, David. 2015. "China's Rise as a Regional and Global Power: The AIIB and the 'One Belt, One Road'" *The Brookings Institure*, July 15. Accessed October 20, 2018. https://doi.org/10.1073/pnas.0703993104.

Eder, Thomas. 2018. "Mapping the Belt and Road Initiative: This Is Where We Stand." Mercator Institute for China Studies, July 6. Accessed January 6, 2019. https://www.merics.org/en/bri-tracker/mapping-the-belt-and-road-initiative. .

Farlin, Jeff. 2014. "Instruments of National Power: How American Earned Independence."United States Army War College. Accessed January 11, 2019. http://publications.armywarcollege.edu/pubs/87.pdf. .

Grigg, Angus. 2018. "WeChat's Privacy Issues Mean You Should Delete China's No. 1 Messaging App." *Financial Times*. 2018. https://www.afr.com/news/world/asia/wechats-privacy-issues-mean-you-should-delete-chinas-no1-messaging-app-20180221-h0wgct .

"India-China Bilateral Relations Political Relations." 2017. *Ministry of External Affairs.* https://www.mea.gov.in/Portal/ForeignRelation/China_October_2017.pdf .

"Indian National Congress Manifesto." 2014. www.incmanifesto.in. JP1-02. 2010. Department of Fedense Dictionalry of Military and Assoaited Terms. *Joint Publication* 1-02. November 8, 2010.

Kronstadt, Alan K. 2017. "India-U.S. Relations; issues for Congress." Congressional Research Service. Accessed October 30, 2018. http://www.crs.gov.

Lai, David. 2011. *The United States and China in Power Transition.* Strategic Studies Institute of Carsile, Pennsylvania, US: U.S. Army War College.

Li, Jiayao, ed. 2018. "China-India Joint Army Exercise Enters Tactical Coordination Phase" China Military Online, December 18. http://eng.mod.gov.cn/news/2018-12/18/content_4832433.htm.

Mattis, James. 2018. *"Opening Remarks at the U.S.-India 2+2 Dialogue."* U.S. Department of State. 2018. Accessed October 20, 2018. https://www.state.gov/secretary/remarks/2018/09/285728.htm .

Mattis, James N., and John Chipman. 2018. *"Remarks by Secretary Mattis at Plenary Session of the 2018 Shangri-La Dialogue."* U.S. Department of Defense, June 2. AccessedOctober 22, 2018. https://dod.defense.gov/News/Transcripts/Transcript-View/Article/1538599/remarks-by-secretary-mattis-at-plenary-session-of-the-2018-shangri-la-dialogue/.

Mastapeter, Craig. 2008, December. The Instrument of National Power: Achieving the Strategic Advantage in a Changing World. Thesis for Master of Arts in Security Studies at the Naval Postgraduate School. Monterey, California. Accessed December 20, 2018. https://apps.dtic.mil/dtic/tr/fulltext/u2/a493955.pdf.

Ministry of National Defense of the People's Republic of China. 2018. "Chinese Defense Minister to Visit India - Ministry of National Defense." http://eng.mod.gov.cn/news/2018-08/21/content_4823013.htm.

Meltzer, Joshua P. 2018. *"China's One Belt One Road Initiative: A View from the United States."* The Brookings Institution, 1–6. Accessed October 22, 2018. https://www.brookings.edu/research/chinas-one-belt-one-road-initiative-a-view-from-the-united-states/.

Modi, Narendra. 2018. "Prime Minister's Keynote Address at Shangri La Dialogue Press Information Bureau Government of India Prime Minister's Office."

Nana, Bal R. 1990. *India Foreign Policy: They Nehru Years.* London: Sangam Nehru Memorial Museum and Library.

Obe, Mit Suru and Marimi Kishimoto. 2019. *"Why China Is Deternmined to Connect Southeast Asia by Rai'."* Nikkei Asian Review, January 9. Accessed January 13. https://asia.nikkei.com/Spotlight/Cover-Story/Why-China-is-determined-to-connect-Southeast-Asia-by-rail.

O'Rourke, Ronald. 2018. "China's Actions in South and East China Seas: Implications for U.S. Interests-Background and Issues for Congress" Accessed October 23, 2018. https://www.hsdl.org/?abstract&did=813476.

Panda, Ankit. 2015. "India Plucks a Pearl from China's 'String' in Bangladesh." *The Diplomat.* https://thediplomat.com/2015/06/india-plucks-a-pearl-from-chinas-string-in-bangladesh/.

Pejsova, Eva. 2018. *"The Indo-Pacific: A Passage to Europe?"* European Union Institute for Security Studies, April 25. Accessed October 20. https://doi.org/10.2815/56656 .

Shen, Simon, and Wilson Chan. 2018. "A Comparative Study of the Belt and Road Initiative and the Marshall Plan." *Palgrave Communications* 4 (1): 32. Accessed October 23, 2018. https://doi.org/10.1057/s41599-018-0077-9.

Sherwood, Dave. 2018. "Chile to Join China's Belt and Road Initiative." *Reuters*, November 1. Accessed January 13, 2019. https://www.reuters.com/article/us-chile-china/chile-to-join-chinas-belt-and-road-initiative-idUSKCN1N65YD.

Shi Jiangtao and Owen Churchill. 2018. "US Competes with China's 'Belt and Road Initiative' with US$113 Million Asian Investment Programme." *South China Morning Post*, July 30. Updated on August 2. Accessed January 10, 2019. https://www.scmp.com/news/china/economy/article/2157381/us-competes-chinas-belt-and-road-initiative-new-asian-investment.

"Shri Pranab Mukherjee: Former President of India." 2015. http://pranabmukherjee.nic.in/sp300915.html..

Sridharan, Eswaran. 2017. "Where Is India Headed? Possible Future Directions in Indian Foreign Policy." *International Affairs* 93 (1): 51–68. https://doi.org/10.1093/ia/iiw008 .

Starman, Adrijana B. 2013. "The Case Study as a Type of Qualitative Research." *Journal of Contemporary Educational Studies*, 1/2013: 28-43. Accessed January 11, 2019. http://www.sodobnapedagogika.net/wp-content/uploads/2013/03/Star man1.pdf

Swaine, Michael D, Mike M Mochizuki, Michael L Brown, Paul S Giarra, Douglas H Paal, Rachel Esplin Odell, Raymond Lu, Oliver Palmer, and Xu Ren. 2013. *"China's Military & The US- Japan Alliance in 2030: A Strategic Net Assessment."* Carnegie Endowment for International Peace. https://carnegieendowment.org/files/net_assessment_full.pdf .

The Hague. 2016. *"The South China Sea Arbitration (the Republic of the Philippines V. the People'S Republic of China,"* no. July: 1–11. https://doi.org/10.1163/15718085-12341421.

The State Council - The People's Republic of China. 2015."Full Text: Action Plan on the Belt and Road Initiative." Accessed October 15, 2018. http://english.gov.cn/archive/publications/2015/03/30/content_281475080249035.htm

The Whitehouse Office of the Press Secretary. 2009. *"Remarks by President Obama and Prime Minister Singh of India in Joint Press Conference."* Accessed October 20, 2018.. https://obamawhitehouse.archives.gov/the-press-office/remarks-president-obama-and-prime-minister-singh-india-joint-press-conference .

The World Bank. 2018, March 29. "Belt and Road Initiative." Accessed January 7, 2019. https://www.worldbank.org/en/topic/regionalintegration/brief/belt-and-road-initiative .

Trump, Donald J. 2017. *"The National Security Strategy United States of America,"* 68. https://www.whitehouse.gov/wpcontent/uploads/2017/12/NSS-Final-12-18-2017-0905.pdf.

UNESCO. "About the Silk Road | SILK ROADS." n.d. United Nations Educational, Scientific, and Cultural Organization. Accessed January 7, 2019. https://en.unesco.org/silkroad/about-silk-road.

United Nations. 2013. Oceans & Law of the Sea . Division for Ocean Affairs and the Law of the Sea, October 29. Accessed October 25, 2018. http://www.un.org/depts/los/convention_agreements/convention_declarations.htm#China Upon ratification.

U.S. Energy Information Administration. 2013. "South China Sea." Accessed October 15, 2018.https://www.eia.gov/beta/international/analysis_includes/regions_of_interest/South_China_Sea/south_china_sea.pdf.

U.S. Pacific Command. 2018. *"U.S. Indo-Pacific Command Holds Change of Command Ceremony."* U.S. Indo-Pacific Command (USINDOPACOM), May 30. Accessed January 14, 2019. http://www.pacom.mil/Media/News/News-Article-View/Article/1535776/us-indo-pacific-command-holds-change-of-command-ceremony/.

Vijay Sakhuja. 2018. *"Is 'Democratic Quad' a Viable Construct?"* Vivekananda International Foundation. 2018. https://www.vifindia.org/2018/july/02/is-democratic-quad-a-viable-construct.

Weaver, John M. 2015. The Enemy of My Enemy if My Friend... Or Still My Enemy: The Challenge for Senor Civilian and Military Leaders. *International Journal of Leadership in Public Service*, 11(3-4).

Weaver, John M. and Jennifer M. Pomeroy, ed. 2018. *Intelligence Analysis: Unclassified Area & Point Estimates (And Other Intelligence Related Topics)*. New York: Nova Science Publishers, Inc.

Wong, Catherine, and Kinling Lo. 2018. "China and Asean Reach 'Milestone' Draft Deal on South China Sea Code of Conduct." *South China Morning Post*, August 2. Updated on August 7, 2018. Accessed October 12, 2018. https://www.scmp.com/news/china/diplomacy-defence/article/2158017/china-and-asean-reach-milestone-draft-deal-south-china.

Xu, Shanpin. 2018. "Why Australia Is Cautious about the Belt and Road." *China Daily*, Feburary 9. 2018. Accessed October 18, 2018. http://www.chinadaily.com.cn/a/201802/09/WS5a7cdbc8a3106e7dcc13baa0.html.

Yurou. 2018. "Chinese Defense Minister to Visit India This Year." *Xinhua News Agency*, July 26. Accessed October 20, 2018. http://www.xinhuanet.com/english/2018-07/26/c_137350147.htm

ZD. 2018. "China Focus: President Xi Reviews Navy in South China Sea." *Xinhua News Agency*, April 13. Accessed October 20, 2018. http://www.xinhuanet.com/english/2018-04/13/c_137106984.htm.

Zhu, Zhiqun. 2018. "Can the Quad Counter China's Belt and Road Initiative?" *The Diplomat*, March 14. Accessed January 14. https://thediplomat.com/2018/03/can-the-quad-counter-chinas-belt-and-road-initiative/.

ZX, ed. 2018. "Deployment of Defensive Facilities on S. China Sea Islands Legitimate, Says Chinese Military Official" *Xinhua News Agency*, June 2. Accessed October 20, 2018. http://www.xinhuanet.com/english/2018-06/02/c_137225661.htm.

In: Global Intelligence Priorities ISBN: 978-1-53615-836-6
Editors: John Michael Weaver et al. © 2019 Nova Science Publishers, Inc.

Chapter 10

MONSTERS OF THE MIDDLE EAST: ISIL'S PERPETUAL PURSUIT FOR POWER (A QUALITATIVE ASSESSMENT)

Alexis Hart and Brielle Schultz
York College, York, Pennsylvania, US

ABSTRACT

The United States still regards the Islamic State of Iraq and the Levant (ISIL) as a prominent threat to its national security and has come up with priority actions for its defeat of Jihadist terrorists. With the help of its strong intelligence department and its contemporary recruitment tactics, ISIL is able to spread its influence with little effort. Although they do not have any formal diplomatic connections with outside countries, they are able to still perform at their highest level without having to rely on other people. ISIL also directs their attention to creating a brotherhood which in turn attracts the people who are classified as lone wolves to gain control of the territories that they lost. The United States has become accustomed to other terrorist groups who were not as economically advanced making ISIL a harder target. The United States' goal by 2022 is to contribute to the defeat of ISIL and its branches through the mobilization of a Global Coalition. Although the United States has made efforts in trying to prevent

ISIL's influence, the terrorist group continues to adapt to challenges or policies that prevent them from growing. ISIL has proven to be a deadly force that will go to extremes for its cause. ISIL's overall purpose is to gain enough power to be recognized as a formidable group that has taken over a nation and will stop at no end to spread their extremist views across the world.

LITERATURE REVIEW

This literature review consists of ISIL's historical development, its effective recruitment, powerful intelligence department, and organizational reaction to set up the scene of this chapter.

Historical Development

The Islamic State of Iraq and the Levant (ISIL) is the most feared terrorist group in the contemporary world. It started as an offshoot of well-known terrorist group al-Qaeda that was led by Abu Musab al Zarqawi. It was a small army of radicals striving for world domination with no remorse for the bloodshed of anyone, including other Muslims. Osama bin Laden, later rising as the leader of al-Qaeda, did not approve of the extreme violent acts on Muslims and had his second chief in command, Ayman al-Zawahiri, send Zarqawi a letter to tone down the attacks after the killing of sixty Muslims at a Jordanian wedding using suicide bombers (Townsend 2017). After ignoring the letter, Zarqawi released a video claiming himself as the leader of the al-Qaeda division in Iraq and committed to creating an Islamic State (Townsend 2017).

Musab al Zarqawi was killed after one of his followers turned against him and led American forces to the leader's safe house to drop two bombs and killed all five members inside the building. The killing of Zarqawi did adversely impact al-Qaeda's presence in Iraq. Although the core of the group was diminished, and its leader was gone, Zarqawi's ideas lived on and the group continued to actively grow into the Islamic State. With a black flag as its symbol, this emerging group stayed undercover from the United States' priorities until al-Qaeda started to fall (Townsend 2017).

A dual leadership structure began to emerge from the rummage including Abu Umar al Baghdadi from Iraq and Abu Ayyub al-Masri from Egypt (Nance and Engle 2016). After American counterintelligence sifted through al-Qaeda's attempt to hide the dual leadership structure, both leaders were killed in a subsequent American led airstrike. Once again, ISIL struggled to gain strength. Eventually, after a strong American presence in Iraq, al-Qaeda began battling to keep its presence. Once realizing its shrinking abilities, the al-Qaeda division in Iraq packed up and moved to Syria, officially naming themselves ISIL or the Islamic State. Despite the constant change of authority, the Islamic State persisted in brutally attacking weak points in Iraq (Nance & Engle 2016).

Finally, around 2013, ISIL started attacking other rebel groups to assert its dominance in the region. In June 2014, it declared itself a universal caliphate and its leader, Abu Bakr Baghdadi, the caliph. The Islamic State also claimed that the caliphate holds the religious, political, and military power over all Muslims across the world (Xingang et al. 2017). The group was starting to take extreme measures to assert its presence and instill fear throughout the world with more frequent and gruesome attacks. They charged into the city of Raqqa, Syria, and declared it the capital of the Islamic State; this was one of its first major movements towards domination of the region. In an interview with Matthew Heineman, he explains how the once prosperous Raqqa was now a breeding ground for the terrorist group, "...because ISIL had completely blacked out the city from the rest of the world. No information was coming in; no information was going out" (West 2017). Raqqa's citizens' lives changed as they had to make the decision to stay in the ISIL claimed city or flee.

RECRUITMENT

Once the group conquered its first major city, its momentum continued, and the name ISIL was spoken around the world. Currently, branches of the

Islamic State have spread to many countries, including Libya, Nigeria, and Afghanistan and its influence has reached areas in North America, South Asia, and other places in the world (Xingang et al. 2017). Many "lone wolf" adolescent minds are being manipulated across the globe to join the organization. Recruiting is one of ISIL's main priorities for expansion. One of the main resources ISIL uses to spread its message across the world is social media. (Moore 2015). The Brookings Institute stated in 2014 the amount of ISIL Twitter accounts was between 46,000 and 90,000 and it was found that English was the primary language in many of these accounts with many followers (Moore 2015.) This has sparked many individualized attacks in areas of the world where ISIL is not dominant. Before ISIL, terrorist groups had to recruit by word of mouth and through the use of persuasive verbal communications; ISIL has since turned computer screens and cell phones into training camps viewable by sympathizers in cities and countries all over the world. People no longer have to live in a foreign city or understand a foreign language to join this war (Moore 2015). The development of social media propaganda has brought major concerns to nations trying to contain ISIL.

Numerous amounts of sympathizers from around the globe are convinced and travel thousands of miles to join the terror movement while others are striking in the name of ISIL in its home communities. There are also those who travel overseas to train with ISIL and eventually return home to plan and carry out attacks. Many secluded people around the world are intrigued by ISIL's sense of brotherhood and fearless stance against the strongest countries in the world (Moore 2015). The spread of Islamophobia and the dislike, or prejudice of Islam or Muslims in the west, also encourages malleable minds to begin to develop a proclivity in the interest into a jihadist life. ISIL uses other countries' fear of attacks to fuel its movement.

INTELLIGENCE

The Islamic State has a highly developed intelligence department named Emni. First discovered in captured documents after the death of Haji Bakr, the architect of Emni, who gained his leadership while plotting with Abu Bakr al-Baghdadi when they were both imprisoned in Camp Bucca from 2004-2008. This sector of the Islamic State is in charge of many factors that contribute to the success of the spread of the Islamic State and its ideology. Emni gathers intelligence on Iraq and Syria, areas ISIL intends to conquer, people living in the "Islamic State," attacks on ISIL, and other areas of interest. Many Iraqi former Baathists were emergent as leaders in the organization, even in Syria, who had brought with them and the tradecraft and intelligence operations they had practiced in Saddam Hussein's government (Speckhard & Yayla 2016). For having limited land, money, and resources, Emni is a very capable and advanced group of jihadists.

Emni also has a very important role in recruiting for the Islamic State. They are responsible for strategically spreading propaganda and fear not only inside the Islamic State but also beyond its borders world-wide. They actively feed ISIL media centers with video, pictures, and information of operations and external attacks. Foreign fighters travel to train with Emni so they can deploy back to their home countries to collect intelligence and prepare for the command to attack. Out of the many new recruits ISIL gains every day, Emni is required to collect intelligence on all new prospects, most importantly those who are foreign without a referral from someone already in the state. Captured documents in Aleppo reveal that the Emni keeps detailed lists and personnel files on the foreign fighters that join its movement, including letters of application detailing levels of religious knowledge, former military training and terrorism references, including telephone numbers, and even one's hobbies (Speckhard & Yayla 2016). It is very important for Emni to make sure there are no insider threats revealing secrets to its larger enemies.

Emni's other priorities include keeping track of Syrian refugees fleeing the area from violence. The group is deploying troops to countries like Turkey to spy and recruit the refugees. Also, duties of members in Turkey include the regulation of logistics services to ensure the safe, undercover travel of recruits and equipment. Other logistics responsibilities include the trade of oil, wheat, and slaves. Not only is Emni in charge of all intelligence gathering and logistics support, the group also does the more specialized violent acts such as assassinations, kidnappings, and bartering for hostage. Emni members are known as the best within ISIL's organization and are hand-picked based on loyalty. Protecting intelligence and all covert actions performed by ISIL is a significant component in keeping Emni a threatening subsection within this organization.

REACTIONS

Due to the immense amount of attacks that were occurring, ISIL had been brought to the national stage in the countries that have been affected by it. As these countries began to combat ISIL's activities, one of the first groups to emerge was the Global Coalition. Established in September of 2014, the Global Coalition currently has 79 member organizations. Of those member organizations, 23 have over 9,000 troops within Iraq and Syria with the goal of defeating ISIL. The Coalition has trained 90,000 Iraqi Security Force members. There have been 8,200 tons of military equipment donated to these efforts as well (U.S. Department of State 2017).

The Coalition has a Foreign Terrorist Fighter Working Group that is co-led by The Netherlands, Turkey, and the United States. This group serves as a platform for an international governmental approach. These countries aim at supporting working together and capacity-building; they are creating a structure to have a law-abiding community who obeys the code of behavior that is set by the government. With the help of partners, obligations and recommendations that were previously laid out in the United Nations Security Council Resolution 2178 are made and put forward. This resolution requires that "countries must take the proper steps to counter foreign terrorist fighters, expanding obligations under international law, and strengthening international measures that prevent foreign terrorist fighters from traveling, disrupt financial support to foreign terrorist fighters, and further strengthen international and regional cooperation mechanisms" (The Global Coalition 2018). The Coalition has also formed a Counter-Daesh finance group; Daesh is another word for describing ISIL. This group is planning to shut down all forms of financial aid to Daesh, which includes all funds ISIL has raised from kidnapping for ransom, illicit trade in stolen cultural heritage artifacts, and its sales of natural resources (The Global Coalition 2018).

Over the few years that this coalition has been in effect there have been countless courses of action taken. 62% of the terrain that ISIL had once controlled in Iraq and 30% of the terrain in Syria has been subsequently liberated. ISIL has lost more than 90% of its total territory that they had occupied in the past, which in turn resulted in 7.3 million people being liberated (Manjana Pecht 2016). ISIL's numbers are down by more than half since ISIL's peak in the year 2014. As of October of 2017, ISIL's propaganda yield was 85% less than it was in August 2015. The Coalition has conducted over 19,000 airstrikes, targeting more than 2,600 energy targets, and more than 25 bulk cash storage sites (Manjana Pecht 2016). Throughout the past three years the Coalition has targeted about 30 Daesh banks and financial centers, which allowed them to destroy over tens of millions of dollars of the organization's money. It is said that 80% of the funds ISIL was able to gain over the years was attributed to them conquering territories, replicating the functions of a state, collecting taxes from citizens, and using tariffs from the people under its control (Mansour & Al-Hashimi 2018). As a result, over 3.7 million people have been able to return to their homes in Iraq.

There have been four milestones that the Global Coalition has been taking fighting against ISIL. The first one was the secured Syria-Turkey border in November 2016. Next was the European Union that was able to adopt a Passenger Name Recognition Protocol to aid in security against the foreign fighters that are traveling abroad. Also, 31 Non-European members have worked on implementing better traveler screening measures. Lastly, countries are enacting measures through the United Nations Security Council Resolution 2178 (mentioned previously) to strengthen its response and abilities to go against foreign fighters and related crimes (The Global Coalition 2018).

There are also other organizations that have helped in the efforts to end ISIL. In 2017, the Bureau of Political-Military Affairs gave over $800 million in security aid to the Global Coalition partners and separated over $104 million in regular and specialized funding to help stabilize the most recent liberated areas of Iraq and Syria. Prime Minister Abadi and the Government of Iraq gave a $500 million pledge to the support of stabilization programs in liberated areas. This has created a program that has the ability to enter these areas to clean up the explosives that are purposely left behind in liberated areas. The U.S. State Department has also allocated money to this cause. They have given over $167 million for conventional arms destructive programs in Syria and Iraq. With the help of these programs there have been over 7.9 million square meters of explosive contaminated land cleared since April of 2016 (Strike 2018). Syrian Democratic Forces are fighting to liberate the remaining held territories that ISIL possesses, specifically in Eastern Syria; by doing this, they are also aiming to capture and secure control of the Syria-Iraq Border. One of the main reasons countries continue to fund this program is because ISIL has not been able to reclaim any areas that they have lost in coalition-supported operations (Blanchard & Humud 2018). The United States was the main leader in a Coalition that began to use airstrikes against ISIL in the country of Iraq on August 7th of 2014 and was then able to expand it to Syria in September of 2014. On October 15th of that same year, the United States decided to name the operation "Operation Inherent Resolve," and throughout the next year this operation was able to realize over 8,000 airstrikes between the countries of Syria and Iraq (Glenn 2018). In June 2018, the Coalition Political Directors decided to have a meeting in Morocco and they were able as a group to raise $90 million for the stabilization program in Northeast Syria (The Global Coalition 2018).

RESEARCH QUESTIONS

After affording consideration to the literature review, several variables, most notably diplomacy, information, military and economic (D.I.M.E.) were considered to analyze the potential impact of these on a shaped outcome weakening U.S. global hegemony. Specifically, these authors considered the following research questions to look at what the current status and development of ISIL mean to the immediate future from an adversarial perspective with regards to the Islamic State (ISIL).

Q1: How does ISIL weaken the position of the United States as the world's sole hegemony?
Q2: Why should actions by ISIL be considered as a way to weaken the position of the United States as the world's sole hegemony?

LOGIC MODEL

The authors have used a logic model for their analysis to come to a detailed conclusion based on diplomacy, information, military, and economic (D.I.M.E.) means. Many credible journals and peer reviewed chapters have used the D.I.M.E. instruments to study state, non-state actors and relationships between them. Instruments such as D.I.M.E. have been used throughout intelligence communities to help understand national security issues.

The authors also incorporated the use of the York Intelligence Red Team Model (YIRTM). As shown in Figure 1, this model provides a visual representation of the components that exist within the conflict. The YIRTM uses diplomacy, information, military, and economic means to shape an outcome and eventually devise the best plan to weaken any actions brought forth by United States pertaining to ISIL. Starting with strategic direction of ISIL, actors must organize its strategies for its main goal: to establish a caliphate that has influence throughout the entire world. With proper direction, ISIL can accomplish all aspects of the strategic direction step including basics on the questions "who," "what," "where," "when," "how," and "why." By setting fundamental building blocks in ISIL's strategic direction, authority figures can accurately use the next four steps to advance.

The starting point is with focused diplomacy and the international relationships ISIL has. Since there are no direct relationships between states and ISIL, the authors have looked at countries that have turned a blind eye to terrorist activities performed by ISIL and its affiliates. Diplomacy is a major part of a strategic and successful plan to establish ISIL's Caliphate. Unfortunately, being a well-known violent terrorist group, ISIL has found some difficulties which leads to attacking cities to claim them as territories. Little foreign relationships pose challenges on the group such as a lack of support or trade relationships. Establishing stronger relationships will benefit ISIL in its quest for world influence.

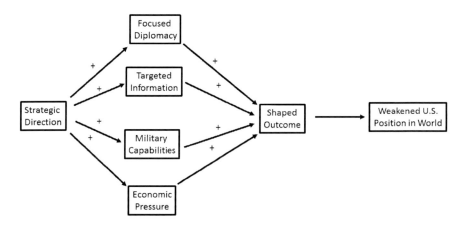

Figure 1. YIRTM.

Next, information creates a smarter and stronger non-state actor that have planned attacks more effectively. Not only is it an amalgam of information in bulk, but the sorting and investigating detailed sources for authentication. ISIL has a strong intelligence component that is actively investigating and making it easier for leaders to plan attacks with a higher success rate. Information is a very basic but important concept that if ISIL did not pay attention to, it would lead them going into an attack blind. By providing false but plausible messaging, especially through social media, ISIL can weaken the United States' strategy. This inexpensive and effective tactic has raised concerns for the United States because of how seemingly benign and easy it is to overlook. Information can be passed in a variety of ways; many of the United States' citizens are being influenced by ISIL everyday due to information that is spread over the internet. This also is an important weak spot for the U.S. because ISIL is advancing its influencing while on a completely different war front. Not only is the incoming information important to ISIL's intelligence, but outgoing information has the power to influence recruits in other countries as well.

The military component is one of ISIL's strongest components due to its soldiers' resilience and devotion for the cause. Every member has the mentality to die regarding whatever cost it takes to advance ISIL in the world, which is a significant and threatening force for the United States. "A crucial means by which ISIL leverages pragmatic factors is by presenting ISIL as a highly capable, adaptable and ruthless military force" (Ingram 2015). ISIL has a very violent history when it comes to its military and trains its soldiers to conduct less organized attacks than its enemies, and "ISIL communiqués have flaunted its application of a full spectrum of combat operations, including terrorism (suicide attacks), guerrilla tactics (hit-and-run ambushes) and conventional warfare (artillery)" (Ingram 2015). These types of attacks instill fear not only where ISIL is located but also in its sphere of influence.

Economics is also a major part to success of ISIL's mission. Without money, ISIL could not pay its troops or for any supplies that contribute to its achievements. Although it is important to note that most attacks by ISIL are much cheaper than any military strategies the United States uses. Not being part of a country might cause a struggle for a terrorist group, but ISIL has little in terms of economic adversaries. "In 2015, for example, the self-proclaimed Islamic State (also known as ISIL) had a budget of up to $1.7 billion, according to a study by King's College London and the accounting company Ernst & Young, making it the world's richest terrorist group" (Neumann 2017). ISIL is very creative when hiding its money by not acquiring and using bank accounts for high authority figures, but rather by using much lower ranking, unnoticeable members' accounts (Neumann 2017). "Even large and legitimate transactions are carried out in cash, which means that most people never interact with the international financial system at all. As a result, few of the financial transactions of terrorist groups appear on bank statements" (Neumann 2017). ISIL's strong economy is a significant factor enabling ISIL to launch its activities weakening the United States' strength and power within and beyond the Middle East region.

METHODOLOGY

The authors have gathered secondary data and used a case study methodology for their analysis. All data used in this assessment came from secondary data that were available in the public domain so unclassified but yet reliable sources were used. Using triangulation as a strategy considering multiple sources through data collection, as shown in Figure 2 below, the authors were able to examine and connect all data resources and corroborate interpretations to arrive at an accurate conclusion.

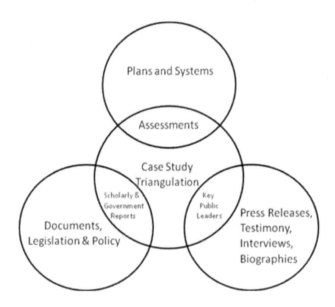

Figure 2. Federal Qualitative Secondary Data Case Study Triangulation Model.

Figure 2 outlines how multiple sources of secondary data were utilized to create a balanced and effective data network for studying a particular state and non-state actors in the richest manner. Starting with the plans and systems portion, the authors studied and looked at the future of ISIL as well as how the terror group will use its systems to weaken United States' efforts. The future of ISIL affords attention to its pursuit for power which includes reclaiming any lost territory and spreading its influence. ISIL will also focus on recruitment in the western world, "ISIL propagandists are often able to use media reports from Western sources mixed in with its own graphic messages to whip up religious or nationalist fervor" (Bloom & Damon 2018) because this will ensure the future ISIL will be a stronger Islamic State that can eventually reach lone wolves in every part of the world building networks of terror. To further accomplish world influence, ISIL must adapt its systems to defeat the United States' efforts in preventing radical recruitment in the West. Already, social media sites have acted against the searching of ISIL related accounts. ISIL adapted quickly now using telegrams to covertly recruit throughout the world. "For example, Telegram was used to recruit and coordinate attacks in France and Brussels, and unlike other encrypted messaging platforms such as WhatsApp (used by the 2017 Westminster, UK attacker Khalid Masood). Because Telegram cannot be traced after an attack (Bloom & Damon 2018) it therefore makes prevention more difficult. Telegram is a free speech social media site. ISIL's quick adoption of this social media shows ISIL's flexibility and a sense of excellent understanding of technology persistently implementing efforts to successfully gain new recruits.

The second component of the triangulation model is the use of documents, legislation, and policies to glean from the data about how ISIL poses a threat to many other areas in the world. These include many policies put through other countries for its citizens' protection. It includes credible sources like government reports collected including the National Security Strategy, the Joint Strategic Plan, and the International Center for the Study of Violent Extremism. Scholarly research work was also used as secondary data because they provide points of view that are independent to governmental sources. These sources provided the authors with the most reliable and least biased forms of secondary data that led to an accurate analysis.

The last component consists of secondary data collected from interviews, press releases, testimonies and biographies from key leaders because they play important roles in decision-making. It is extremely important to emphasize the preaching of ISIL key leaders and its influence. Many members of ISIL strongly believe in what its administration has taught them, and continue to influence others to join the group. Most statements made by opposing countries anger ISIL and fuel its fire to increase attacks. More specifically statements made by the Department of Defense, Department of Homeland Security, U.S. Intelligence Community, and many other departments of the United States irritate leaders of ISIL. It is important to not only study the proclamations of the U.S for ISIL's intelligence but also look into how ISIL is using its key leaders to impact the world.

The authors stress the point that validity with secondary data is limited. By not personally conducting interviews of ISIL leaders and select departments of the United States there could never be a definite conclusion. The authors have intensively studied and cross-checked the coding of all data used in this chapter.

LIMITATIONS

This research analysis has been exclusively derived from secondary data. Therefore, several limitations of a qualitative approach need to be noted. The first is, due to the limitations of secondary data, selected variables may be limited. Second, the study period only covers a five-year period from 2013 to October of 2018. Such limited time may stipulate the dynamic nature of intelligence which is always changing. The emerging of new data leads to a time restriction when synthesizing the data and proceeding with interpretations. Findings may not be as updated so therefore might be less relevant to the current time. As time moves forward since the research for this analysis was conducted, ISIL has had new developments and attacks that could be added to the analysis.

In addition, secondary data was recorded from multiple academic journals, including the International Center for the Study of Violent Extremism, and government reports so more precise examination of ISIL's pursuit for power can be unfolded. Primary sources would be good sources of data but due to time and cost constraints they were excluded from the study. Data coming from primary sources such as interviews and surveys could be used for a more thorough conclusion regading future research.

Since no part of the authors' conclusion was solely based on data collected first hand, there are certain limitation factors to the relevance of data. Data was collected and analyzed to the authors' standards to avoid being biased. All data used by the authors is believed to be dependable and helped in making their final judgment.

ANALYSIS

Since 2014, ISIL has taken major strides in becoming a world stage terrorist organization and continues to hold that title well into 2019. This section will examine how ISIL has used its capabilities to weaken the United States on a global scale and from what has happened, some recommendations for the future will also be addressed. The evidence collected to support the analysis results and conclusions is located in Annex A. Annex A contains a total of 14 data sources. The tally of coding frequency yielded the following: "I" for 11 times, "M" for 10 times, "E" for seven times, and "D" for six times. Such frequency ranking suggested a variant model of I.M.E.D. from the original D.I.M.E. instruments. Based on this evidence it suggests that ISIL is predominantly focused on the diplomatic, economic, and military components of the YIRTM to fight against the United States. Likewise, ISIL has adapted to the obstacles that the United States government has thrown at it and will continue to make attempts at self-proliferation thereby becoming a larger scale terrorist organization.

The citizens of the United States are becoming more susceptible to messaging and being persuaded to join the ISIL movement (Haque & Yu 2016). ISIL does not just recruit in the Middle East; they have expanded to a more global approach to gain fighters. They have continued to use social media tactics and videos to persuade the common man to become part of the "brotherhood." The people who seem to be the most impressionable to these ideas are "the everyday young people who are in social transition, on the margins of society, or amidst a crisis of identity" (Haque & Yu 2016). Some researchers argue that there is a correlation between the optimal amounts of freedom American citizens have, which leads to a lack of individual identity.

Westerners tend to underscore the value of individualism, but in turn this can tend to equate to loneliness (Haque & Yu 2016). This does not only occur in the United States; ISIL has taken an even grander scale approach. One example of this is shown in Norway where two girls were approached about Islam by an extremist, which in turn led them to subsequently move to Syria and begin "breeding" new ISIL members (Stergiou 2018).

As countries began to liberate areas where ISIL was present, it started to leave rigged explosives behind as a tactic to inflict casualties to the people who were returning to their villages. By doing this, ISIL plans to regain lost ground and regenerate places to plot new attacks. The two main locations where this occurs are Iraq and Syria. The Global Coalition has decided to partner with the government of Iraq to try and work to make the cities safer. They "help to clear neighborhoods of mines and remnants of war, restore basic municipal services like electricity, water, education, and health" (The Global Coalition 2018). ISIL will continue to do this because of the fatalities that Americans suffer. In 2017, the Bureau of Political-Military Affairs allocated over $800 million in security aid to the Global Coalition partners and provided over $104 million in regular and specialized funding to help stabilize the most recent liberated areas of Iraq and Syria. Prime Minister Abadi and the government of Iraq gave a $500 million pledge to the support of stabilization programs in liberated areas. This has created a program that has the ability to enter these areas to clean up the explosives that are purposely left behind in liberated areas. The State Department has also allocated money to this cause. They have spent over $167 million for conventional arms destruction programs in Syria and Iraq (U.S Department of State Official Blog 2018).

A major instrument used in ISIL's survival and help it thrive is its finances. They were ahead of the game even before becoming one of the major terrorist groups in the world. David Cohen, who was the U.S. Treasury Under Secretary for Terrorism and Financial Intelligence stated that ISIL was "The best-funded terrorist organization we've confronted" (Stergiou 2016). It is estimated that ISIL generated significant revenue totaling between $70 and $200 million a year from illegal activities. By June of 2010, ISIL had acquired shares in the Iraqi oil industry, controlled many gas stations in the northern part of the country, and were actively taking money from industry contractors. It was speculated that most of its revenue came from five main sources: illicit proceeds from occupation territory, kidnapping for ransom, donations including by or through non-profit organizations, material support, and lastly fundraising through modern communication networks like social media (Stergiou 2016). The United States has taken steps aimed to stop this process and has been successful (The Global Coalition 2018). The Global Coalition has been able to strike around 30 banks and financial centers that ISIL was using (Restricting Daesh Access to Finance and Funding 2017). As illustrated, the financial capabilities of ISIL have successfully weakened the United States because they have never had to experience financial difficulties or cash problem funding the organizational operations.

Due to the fact that ISIL has experienced some territorial contraction, they begin to migrate to other places. With such movement, ISIL can spread its radical views and gain more members to continue its growth as an organization. They have begun to expand more into Syria because they have lost much of its property in Iraq due to liberation programs. The Global Coalition has begun to enhance traveler screening programs in order to curb and/or stop the flow of foreign terrorist fighters into surrounding countries (ostensibly as refugees), which in turn will impede the flow of terrorism and could in time hinder its recruitment process [Impeding the Flow of Foreign Terrorist Fighters (FTFS) 2017]. This has resulted in an increase in its activity in Europe, Yemen, and Egypt of the northeastern Africa. This is detrimental to the United States because these expanded locations pose more difficulties for the United States' intelligence services that begin to lose track of the majority of them.

Over the past three years, the number of ISIL members has decreased at a steady rate. As a result of forfeiting ground, they are also losing members as the immense number of airstrikes upon the ISIL territories is beginning to take a toll on its numbers. In mid-2014, it was believed that ISIL had around 31,500 foreign fighters and by early 2016 it had dropped to about 25,000 (Glenn 2016). One problem confronting the United States is when dealing with the decline in population; ISIL is beginning to become more focused on secondary affiliates instead of core members. One of the most powerful affiliate or alliance members to ISIL is located in Libya with an approximate estimate of around 6,500 fighters (Glenn 2016).

ISIL is believed to have variegated extremists' beliefs. One of the main ideas behind their violent actions subscribes to the notion to go against and destroy Islam's enemies. The main views see the people of the west and the people of the Jewish faith as enemies because they are "regarded as being engaged in a cultural, economic, and military onslaught that seeks to destroy the religion of Islam" (Haykel 2016). ISIL specifically is a representation of and aims to become the mold of the classical model of Islam that existed throughout the seventh century. Moreover, its beliefs are based on Salafism, Salafi Jihadism, and Wahhabism. They aim to restore the caliphate of early Islam and all Muslims must feel compelled to do this in the eyes of ISIL.

ISIL has many recruitment tactics. Facebook and YouTube are the most frequently used social media by the human population and ISIL has started to target these social media platforms specifically. These "platforms [are] as magnets that have attracted thousands of views, comments, forums, and post" (Awam 2016). ISIL began a YouTube campaign that is worth one billion dollars centered on young Muslims joining ISIL. An example of a popular video showcases ISIL militants giving sweets to children. ISIL also created a phone app titled "The Dawn of Glad Tidings." This was centered on the updates of the activities in which they are taking part. It was, however, detected and suspended as an app. The United States therefore needs to continue to monitor social media forums like these in order to counter ISIL's information in a timely manner so campaigns to reduce the amount of people joining ISIL can take place to hinder its recruitment tactics (Awam 2016).

ISIL's main Intelligence component, Emni, has a large influence on the D.I.M.E instruments used in the YIRTM. As exhibited in Annex A, "I" has a highest frequency of 11 and usurped the three other instruments. Mostly focused on the information and military components, all of Emni's actions help each faction of ISIL in becoming a more successful terrorist group. Emni was created to gather information and process it so ISIL could advance and eventually challenge other state and non-state actors. "Among its many tasks, the Emni actively controls and monitors the flow of ISIL's logistical support operations inside Turkey that have been crucial to its operations, including the flow of materials used for explosives (igniters, chemicals, fertilizers, cables, et cetera that have been funded through Turkey to ISIL) and other deliveries critical to them" (Speckhard & Yayla 2016). Emni is an enabler that will continue to focus on information acquisition to gain control of weapons and land so eventually it can grow its ranks (military), another intimidating factor endemic to ISIL. Emni is also responsible for military recruitment and investigations, making sure they are constantly growing and welcoming faithful jihadists. This department of ISIL also actively trains its military to return to its homeland and conduct attacks. "It is now understood that Emni trained operatives carried out the 2015 Paris café, stadium, and nightclub attacks as well as recruited the cadres for and built the bombs used in the 2016 Brussels airport and metro attacks" (Speckhard & Yayla 2016). The adeptness of Emni weakens the U.S position because of its inexperience with intelligent terrorist groups.

There are many other priorities and responsibilities of Emni that focus on weakening its competitors. This strengthens its military units to have a more focused mission. Duties, for example, include investigating its own members to make sure there are no insider threats, thus ensuring that the United States and other predators are not infiltrating its units. "On the technical side, its computers are also monitored in a low-tech manner for internet history and with free downloadable apps that allow monitors to know if banned sites are being accessed" (Speckhard & Yayla 2016). Emni ensures all its members are trustworthy so they can conduct successful attacks and instill fear globally. What is more is that Emni also strategically plans its military tactics, where "The Emni top leaders identify who among Western ISIL cadres is to be sent back. They choose targets and organize logistics for operatives, including paying smugglers to get them to Europe and, according to European intelligence documents, in at least one case, sending Western Union transfers" (Speckhard & Yayla 2016). This tactic makes sure attacks are being carried out by the most trustworthy and loyal military members that will not raise suspicion in western territories and will not fail. The complexity and sophistication of Emni's priorities is setting is a monumental threat to the United States because even though extremists are looked at as unorganized, ISIL strategically plans and conducts massive, coordinated, and violent attacks.

Since ISIL has no direct diplomatic relationships with other countries, they must rely on nations who tolerate its organization and do not make a formidable effort in trying to inhibit its actions. This includes one of the birth places where ISIL emerged: Syria. "In 2009, the Iraqi government accused the Syrian government of harboring terrorist cells, an allegation that Syrian officials denied" (Stanford 2017). ISIL feels comfortable in its homeland but is still striving to crosspollinate into other locations throughout the globe. This has a major impact on the diplomacy and economics of many international relationships on whether they should foster trade and income generation benefiting this terror group. Moreover, ISIL also receives support from other non-state actors in the region."ISIL's success in capturing Iraqi cities depended on the military expertise and local connections of the Baathists; without help from members of JRTN (Men of the Army of the Naqshbandia Order), many experts believe that ISIL would not be nearly as effective" (Stanford 2017). This challenges the United States and its allies because the joining of non-state actors is extremely dangerous as it is sub-national which allows new unmonitored trading relationships and the emergence of more capable economic affairs for this terror organization.

ISIL's financial structure heavily affects its economic and diplomatic components. Along with many other fundraising techniques, many ISIL sympathizers and supporters from other countries have funded operations. Initially, "ISIL relied heavily on monetary support from donors in Syria, Saudi Arabia, Kuwait and Jordan" (Stanford 2017). This further shows its international connections and influence in other areas which can severely threaten enemies. In the past, ISIL also made its money by selling oil from land they seized. "As of September 2014, experts estimated that ISIL sold oil for 20-35 USD per barrel, earning between $1 million and $2 million in revenue per day" (Stanford 2017). Money is also generated by illegal activities like kidnapping and the seizing of cities and banks within them. ISIL's economy plays a monumental part in its successful attacks and the more money ISIL receives the more powerful they become.

ISIL's main strategy includes land acquisition, the spread of fear, and influencing the world through its terror attacks. Over the past five years, ISIL has conducted many attacks that have spread fear, changed, and challenged the world. This has raised tensions among ISIL and other countries and has overall affected this terror organization's diplomatic strategies. Attacks are not just centralized in the Middle East but are also being carried out by citizens of other countries who pledge allegiance to the group and who are angered by their home country's actions.

Attacks are also being performed by ISIL's military component including major ones all the world in 2017. ISIL is known for its persistence and determination, "The Iraqi Prime Minister Haider al Abadi declared victory over the Islamic State in Iraq on December 9, 2017. But ISIL was still inspiring and carrying out attacks all over the world, including New York City" (Glann 2016). ISIL's resilience and increase of attacks within the past year has shown it to be a formidable fighting force bent on weakening the U.S. position.

Social media is the most influential tool. In ISIL's case, most of its influencers come from posts and videos on social media. The internet is used by people of all ages worldwide and specifically is used to target those angry men who can easily be misguided into joining the jihadist life. "Social learning theory asserts that individuals learn deviant behavior from other groups, which may lead to extremist learning that is categorized by association, definitions, differential reinforcement, and imitation" (Awan 2017). Influencing young minds creates a positive foundation for a loyal ISIL military member. Trustworthy recruits strengthen ISIL's operators (military) which can intimidate enemies because of how resilient members are. Social media is where ISIL gathers and disseminates information. "Terrorists use the internet for psychological warfare, publicity, propaganda, fundraising, recruitment, networking, sharing information and planning" (Awan 2017). This threat underscores serious problems for the U.S due to the inability to prevent social media use.

Even though the United States cannot stop social media completely, they have been making headways into efforts to limit the influencing of posts by ISIL and its affiliates. "As social media platforms like Twitter and Facebook progressively have been policed resulting in aggressive account monitoring and deletions, Telegram remains ISIL's primary platform for disseminating propaganda and recruiting new members" (Bloom & Daymon 2018). Quick adaptation showing the flexibility of ISIL is a significant wake up call for the United States. Unlike other terrorist organizations, ISIL is efficiently organized and intelligent. "By creating online spaces that encourage group identity, shared opinions, and dominant ideologies, while exploiting individuals' need to be a part of the group, ISIL sustains user engagement on the platform" (Bloom & Daymon 2018). The social media app, Telegram, prides itself on free speech which makes it harder to take down and easier for ISIL to spread its ideology across the world. ISIL updates its messages and shows its sensitivity and knowledge about communication technology and global current events. The resilience and ability to adapt quickly to foreign restrictions shows the U.S. that ISIL is still a fighting force persistently weakening its enemies.

FINDINGS AND CONCLUSION

After considerable research and evaluation of the data gathered on ISIL, it is concluded that this terror organization's pursuit for power will continue through violent actions towards threatening state powers. Though the U.S. responses may stir up ISIL and cause more violent attacks, in employing sophisticated and effective recruitment acts and its mobility of migrating towards new territories, ISIL will remain as a formidable terrorist group globally. Despite western efforts of curtailing ISIL, this non-state actor has exhibited resilience in its spread of its ideology worldwide.

The first research question asks how ISIL is making and effort to weaken the United States' position with elements provided in YIRTM. By exporting information about its ideology and goals, ISIL will likely seek connections to many "lone wolves" worldwide to either travel to join the organization or take matters into their own hands influenced and supported by ISIL to launch attacks on the homeland soils harming citizens of the United States. By using social media platforms, ISIL easily reaches billions of people without having to leave a computer screen. The more information they are able to proliferate, the more likely it is that ISIL will attract sympathetic people to and thereby willing to join its cause, resulting in a bigger and broader terror military capability. The violent acts of ISIL's troops are a significant threat to the United States as attacks can happen at any time without much warning. ISIL's illegal activities have made them one of the richest terrorist groups in the modern day. This economic strength best facilitates ISIL's daily operations and continuing growth but intimidate the U.S. national security and private citizens. Every advancement ISIL makes is one step further weakening the U.S. global leadership. Although massive strikes on ISIL by the United States have seemed to weaken the group, ISIL remains as a most competent and a resilient non-state actor that could rise in popularity once again.

The second research question asks why ISIL is weakening the position of the United States' hegemony power. When looking at the YIRTM model, it is evident that ISIL has limited direct ties with any country or group, for example, a minor connection with the Houthi Rebels, but there are countries that have decided to turn a blind eye to its violent actions which aids ISIL in gaining sanctuary to plot and perform future attacks. It does, however, hinder its success because it makes it harder for them to foment relationships and create enduring partners. Due to the fact that ISIL has a strong intelligence component, they have an immense amount of information that is being filtered into its organization all with the desire for it to weaken the United States while seeking greater support and power throughout the world.

The military and economic instruments play a very significant role in ISIL's success as a terror group. They have devout members who will do their best for its cause. ISIL often chooses to attack business related facilities or centers that carry economic importance and therefore are classified as one of the best economic terrorist groups of all time. Such targets have presented enormous challenge to the United States to prevent.

ANNEX A

How/Why	D.I.M.E	Source	Source Type	Date	Page (if applicable)
U.S citizens are susceptible to being persuaded to join the ISIL movement	D, I, M	Yu & Haque	Academic Journal	February 2016	1
Global Coalitions is having an impact on ISIL's migration	D, I, M, E	The Global Coalition	Systems	May 2018	N/A
Global Coalition is having an impact on ISIL population numbers	D, I, M, E	Glenn	Academic Journal	March 2016	1
ISIL is attacking other groups in order to assert their dominance	I, M	West	Interview	2017	N/A
ISIL's Recruitment tactics spreading	I, M	Awan	Academic Journal	April 1 2017	139
ISIL's Intelligence Committee Emni's capabilities	I, M	Speckyard & Yayla	Academic Journal	December 2016	1
Emni's Priorities on how to be successful	I, M	Speckhard & Yayla	Academic Journal	December 2016	1
The Global Coalition Counter-Daesh finance program impacting ISIL capabilities	I, E	The Global Coalition	Systems	May 2017	N/A
The Stabilization Programs of ISIL liberated areas	D, E	Office of the Spokesperson	Press Release	March 2017	1
International ISIL relationships	D, E	Stanford University	Academic Journal	October 2017	1
ISIL's Financial Plan impacting their success	D, E	Stanford University	Academic Journal	October 2017	1
ISIL's social media platform to target potential members	I, M	Society	Academic Journal	April 2017	139 - 140
Beliefs of the Members of ISIL	I, M	Xinggang & Wentao & Yulong	Academic Journal	2017	139 - 147
ISIL adaptations from U.S restrictions	I, M, E	Orbis	Academic Journal	2018	1

In conclusion, ISIL is most likely going to recapture lost territory and regain power with the continuing to use subversion and the effective use of information, military, and economic tactics with little use in diplomacy to hold onto power. Using the two models that are complement each other, it is fairly conclude that ISIL as the monsters of the Middle East are resilient, formidable, and still the most influential non-state actor in the world today threatening the U.S. national security and ordinary American citizens.

REFERENCES

Al-Hashimi, Hisham. & Renad, Mansour. (2018, January 17). "*ISIS Is Still in Business.*" Accessed September 28, 2018. https://www.chathamhouse.org/expert/comment/isis-still-business.

Awan, Imran. (2017). "Cyber-Extremism: Isis and the Power of Social Media." *Society, 54*(2), 138–149.

Blanchard, Christopher M. & Carla, E Humud. (2018, September 25). "*The Islamic State and U.S. Policy.*" Accessed September 23, 2018. https://fas.org/sgp/crs/mideast/ R43612.pdf.

Bloom, Mia. & Chelsea, Daymon. (2018). "Assessing the Future Threat: ISIS's Virtual Caliphate." *Orbis, 62*(3), 372–388.

Cassman, D. (2017, October 23). "*The Islamic State. Stanford University: Mapping Militant Organizations.*" Accessed on September 23, 2018. http://web.stanford.edu/group/mappingmilitants/cgi-bin/groups/view/1.

Chris, Townsend. (2018). "*The Violent Rise of ISIS.*" 20-23. New York, NY: Enslow Publishing. https://ebookcentral.proquest.com/lib/ycp/reader.action?ppg=20&doc ID=5428901&tm=1537834213127.

Cornish, Audie. (2018). "'*Two Sisters' Follows Norwegian Teenagers Who Left Home to Join ISIS Fighters in Syria.*" Accessed October 20, 2018. http://go.galegroup.com/ps/i.do?p=OVIC&u=ycp_main&id=GALE%7CA533946420&v=2.1&it= r&sid= summon.

Department of State, U.S. (2018, July 12). "*Meeting of Foreign Ministers of the Global Coalition to Defeat ISIS at NATO HQ.*" Accessed October 10, 2018. https:// www.state.gov/r/pa/prs/ps/2018/07/284052.htm.

Department of State, U.S. (2017, March 22). "*The Global Coalition to Defeat ISIS.*" https://www.state.gov/s/seci/.

Global Coalition. (2018). "*Mission Tackling Daeshs Financing and Funding.*" Accessed September 26, 2018. http://theglobalcoalition.org/en/mission-en/#tackling-daeshs-financing-and-funding.

Global Coalition. (2018). "*Mission Stablising Liberated Areas.*" Accessed September 27, 2018. http://theglobalcoalition.org/en/stabilising-liberated-areas/?lang=en.

Global Coalition. (2018). "*Countering Daesh's Propaganda.*" Accessed September 26, 2018. http://theglobalcoalition.org/en/countering-daeshs-propaganda/?lang=en.

Global Coalition. (2018). "*Mission Military Progress.*" Accessed September 27, 2018. http://theglobalcoalition.org/en/military-progress/?lang=en.

Global Coalition. (2018). "*Impeding the Flow of Foreign Terrorist Fighters (FTFS).*" Accessed on September 28, 2018. http://theglobalcoalition.org/en/preventing-the-flow-foreign-fighters/.

Gatehouse, Jonathon. (2016). Making a Terrorist: While Disorganized Authorities Have Fumbled Investigations Powerful ISIS Recruitment Efforts Have Created a 'Jihadi-mania' in Some Corners of Europe. *Maclean's*, *129*(14), 26. Accessed on September 23, 2018. http://link.galegroup.com/apps/doc/A448685907/OVIC?u=ycp_main&sid=OVIC&xid=3ab287b7.

Glenn, Cameron. (2018, June 18). "*Timeline: The Rise, Spread and Fall of the Islamic State*" https://www.wilsoncenter.org/article/timeline-the-rise-spread-and-fall-the-islamic-state.

Haykel, Bernard. (2016, October 21). "ISIS and Al-Qaeda-What Are They Thinking? Understanding the Adversary." *The Annals of the American Academy of Political and Social Science*, *668*(1).

Ingram, Haroro J. (2015). "The strategic logic of Islamic State information operations." *Australian Journal of International Affairs*, *69*(6), 729–752.

Moore, Johnnie. (2015). "Isis on the Recruitment Trail." *USA Today Magazine*, *144*(2842), 22–23.

Nance, Malcolm. (2016). *Defeating ISIS: Who They Are, How They Fight, What They Believe*, Skyhorse Publishing, ProQuest Ebook Central. https://ebookcentral.proquest. com/lib/ycp/detail.action?docID=5304584.

Neumann, Peter R. (2017). "Don't Follow the Money." *Foreign Affairs*, 96(4), 93–102.

NSS. (2017). *National Security Strategy*. Accessed September 15, 2018. https://www. whitehouse.gov/sites/default/files/docs/2015_national_security_strateg y.pdf.

Pecht, Manjana. (2016, January 29). "International Responses to ISIS (and Why They Are Failing). Accessed October 12, 2018. https://www.sipri. org/commentary/essay/2016/international-responses-isis-and-why-they-are-failing.

Speckhard, Aanne. & Ahmet, S Yayla. (2016, December 03). "The ISIS Emni: The Inner Workings and Origins of ISIS's Intelligence Apparatus. The International Center for the Study of Violent Extremism." *Perspectives on Terrorism.*, *11*(1), 2-16.

Stergio, Dimitrios. (2016). "ISIS Political Economy: Financing a Terror State." *Journal of Money Laundering Control.*, 189-207.

Strike, Andrew. (2018, January 25). "*How the State Department's PM Bureau Supports the Global Coalition to Defeat ISIS.* Accessed October 18, 2018. https://blogs.state.gov/stories/2018/01/25/en/how-statedepartment-s-pm-bureau-supports-global-coalition-defeat-isis A.

'Two Sisters Follow Norwegian Teenagers Who Left Home to Join ISIS in Syria [Interview by A. Shapiro]. 2018, April 3. Accessed October 15, 2018. https://www.npr.org/2018/04/03/599240721/two-sisters-follow snorwegian-teenagers-who-left-home-to-join-isis-fighters-in-s.

U.S Department of State, U.S. Agency for International Development. (2018). Joint Strategic Plan FY 2018-2022. Accessed September 15, 2018. https://www.state.gov/ documents/organization/277156.pdf.

Wang, Xingang., Wentao, Zhang. & Yulong, Yang. (2017). "Ideology, Global Strategy, and Development of the Islamic State and Its Influence on China's "One Belt, One Road" Initiative." *Journal of Global South Studies.*, *34*(2), 139-155.

West, Dennis. & West, Joan M. (2017). "Seeking the Truth About Raqqa: An Interview with Matthew Heineman. Accessed October 3, 2018. https://web.b.ebscohost. com/ehost/detail/detail?vid=0&sid=42e832e4-3954-4ebd-a02c-b90f8dbc34f4%40sessionmgr102&bdata=JnNpdG U9ZWhvc3QtbGl2ZSSZzY29wZT1zaXRl#AN=124993569&db=a9h.

Yu, Seong Hun. & Omar, Sultan Haque. (2016). "Vulnerabilities among young Westerners Joining ISIS." *Brown University. Child & Adolescent Behavior Letter*, *32*(2), 1–6.

In: Global Intelligence Priorities
Editors: John Michael Weaver et al. © 2019 Nova Science Publishers, Inc.
ISBN: 978-1-53615-836-6

Chapter 11

PROMINENT CYBER SECURITY ISSUES FOR THE UNITED STATES: A QUALITATIVE ASSESSMENT

Nathan McDowell, Ethan Walker and Matthew Meyers
York College, York, Pennsylvania, US

ABSTRACT

The United States is seen to be not only defending itself constantly from cyber-attacks but also falling behind in the cyber security world. Several definitions from accredited organizations define cyber-attack as a form of a computer virus that can perplex financial records, shut off power grids, or even damage nuclear reactors. The research conducted made use of the Federal Qualitative Secondary Data Case Study Triangulation Model to ensure the use of viable sources in order to help comprehend and demonstrate how cyber-attacks threaten the cyber world of the United States. Within the United States, both public and private networks are deemed as vulnerable targets to these types of attacks from both state and non-state actors (Trump 2017). The two state actors heavily focused on, North Korea and Russia, have earned their titles for their past and frequent cyber-attacking events that occurred during the study's time period examined in this chapter. In conclusion it is found that both state actors,

North Korea and Russia, exploit cyber-attacks on the United States to obtain mainly information but also economical gains. The likelihood of a decrease in cyber-attacks on the United States is highly improbably. With the election of the current President of the United States, Donald J. Trump has taken many new actions to emphasize cyber security (Trump 2017). The overall concept of cyber security in this chapter will be focusing on the diplomatic, informational, military, and economic impacts that affect the national security of the U.S. and how Russia and North Korea play major roles in the world of cyber.

LITERATURE REVIEW

Cyber space is a critical information infrastructure network that directly influences a country's national security, economic development and daily life at personal level. The United States has been experiencing malicious cyber-attacks and had large amounts of sensitive information being exploited by foreign attackers who are adversaries of the U.S. in the recent years. Put simply, the U.S.' cyber space is not secure. How to keep the U.S. cyber infrastructure less vulnerable to hostile enemies remains as one of the biggest challenges the U.S. intelligence community faces.

The attackers to the U.S. cyber space include state and non-state actors and the geographic scope of attacks is worldwide. Russia and North Korea are two such state actors that have been actively launching their cyber-attacks on the United States to acquire government documents and stealing copious amounts of information (Center for Strategic & International Studies 2018). Many non-state actors also play major roles as shown in many recent events. A leading example of a non-state actor would be the hacking group called Anonymous who claims responsibility for information leaks, denial-of-service attacks, and even sometimes attacks centered on national security affairs (Sigholm 2013). With the increasing capability of non-state actors using cyber acquired information to form organized criminal groups, they can easily hurt industries both private and state-run. Such acts are impactful and have ripple effects bringing an urgent need for nation states to quickly and more aptly equip their cyberspace operations with better protection (Sigholm 2013).

The pattern of the cyber-attacks within the past five years on the United States were focused on such areas as civilians' financials, media outlets, critical infrastructures such as power grids, and elections. In 2006, it was estimated that there were 5,503 cyber security incidents reported by federal agencies within the United States, while in 2014 there was an estimate of around 67,168 which is a major jump in incidences by a factor of over one thousand times in cyber security events (GAO 2015). Such a dramatic increase has remained as a major characteristic in recent years (Bair et al. 2017, 327). For example, in 2017, malware attacks were carried out by WannaCry, Petya, NotPetya, and Bad Rabbit affecting not only the United States but also other state actors of other industrialized nations as well (Jasper 2017).

As a result of such cyber-attacks, economic loss is monumental on the victim side. The scope of where these cyber-attacks took place has been widened. Equifax, a receiver of a malware attack in 2017, is one of the nation's top three major credit-reporting agencies and this attack exposed over $143 million American consumers' personal information (Federal Trade Commission 2017). In June of 2015, the Commissioner of the Internal Revenue Service (IRS) reported that over 100,000 tax accounts have been compromised which saw the release of Social Security information as well as dates of birth and even street addresses of Americans due to cyber-security breaches (GAO 2015). Not only was the IRS attacked but also so was the United States Postal Service, which saw the compromise of more than 800,000 of its employees' information (GAO 2015).

The 2017 National Security Strategy (NSS) of the United States of America is a fifty-five-page document shaped by the executive branch of the United States government that is intended for Congress, to which it outlines many national security concerns and possible solutions. This was affirmed by the signature of President Trump on December 18, 2017 to which he promises to put the safety and wellbeing of the citizens of this country first. The following notions within the National Security Strategy see this as: protecting the homeland, promoting American prosperity, preserving peace through strength, and advancing American influence (NSS 2017). The NSS specifically lists cyber security as a top national security concern by pointing to two major state attackers, North Korea and Russia. The NSS further discusses how large-scale attacks have the capability to harm American citizens through manipulation of global markets and even adversely impacting national defenses raising top level threats for now and for the next several years to come (National Security Strategy 2017).

According to the 2017 NSS, the Department of Defense is taking a major lead in the defense of the country in cyber security as well as other aspects pertaining to the defense of the United States. The Department of Defense states that that they are heavily impacted by cyber security threats as was evident in the Department of Defense Cyber Strategy of 2018. It states that it is due to an influx of advancing technology that creates new challenges for the department every day. Since 2013, the U.S Department of Defense has been significantly expanding its Cyber Command (Sigholm 2013). The Department of Defense's current objectives, according to the Cyber Strategy document, is to build a more lethal joint force, compete and deter in cyberspace, strengthen alliances and attract new partnerships that reform the department and cultivate talent where needed. In order to build a more lethal Joint Force, the Defense Department will accelerate the development of cyber capabilities for both war and non-combat malicious state and non-state actors while also simultaneously maintaining flexibility to Joint Force commands to operate smoothly from day to day operations, which includes rapidly adapting to new threats and technologies in cyberspace (Cyber Strategy 2018). Another detail needed to build a more lethal Joint Force is to operate at top speed across different networks to allow analytics to identify malicious cyber activity and ensure tailored specific counter operations (Cyber Strategy 2018). Competing and deterring in cyberspace is a top priority of this department which would conclude that the United States is to use all means available to deter malicious cyber activities and counter cyber campaigns to halt or intercept all cyber threats (Cyber strategy, 2018). Working with the private sector is also a major pillar in deterring cyber-attacks through information sharing on these events that would allow the private sector to evolve in cyber security to defend infrastructures and networks (Cyber Strategy 2018). The Defense Department's plan to strengthen alliances and attract new partnerships in the fight against cybercrime will be brought to fruition in a few ways. The first course of action is centered on a strong focus to build trust with private sector organizations and forming partnerships. These partnerships are to help share and support cyber security activities due to how largely the private sector operates within the United States (Cyber Strategy 2018). Not only will partnerships benefit private companies, but it will also help support norms of responsible behavior and protection in cyberspace to defend infrastructure privately (Cyber Strategy 2018). Due to a seemingly new threat directed at the United States, the Defense Department is undergoing reformation. Thus, this reformation will help enable the Defense Department to adapt to its new cyber space accountability, thereby holding public and private sectors accountable for their actions and seek out solutions that are affordable and reliable (Cyber Strategy 2018).

The final action the DoD will undergoes is cultivating talent within the department. This includes more investment, building a better recruitment for an up-to-date cyber workforce that is constantly ready tackling any cyber-attacks at any time. Primarily, the DoD seeks for filling experienced military service members, civilian employees who are cyber savvy, and contracted service personnel, who have cyber security ability to co-deter cyber events (Cyber Strategy 2018). As pointed out by DoD, deterrence is a major part of the DoD's defensive strategy by using early warning capabilities and fast response time to fend off cyber-attackers.

Driving the Department of Defense to develop a new cyber protection strategy and increase cyber security resilience is seen through three major pillars. The first is to increase cyber security in terms of the Department of Defense's database. The database is one of the largest networks in the world and is in need of aggressive steps to secure its data (Fact Sheet 2015). The second pillar is that the Department of Defense must coordinate a new cyber protection strategy plan; according to the President Obama before he left office, such a strategic plan provides directions to defend the nation from cyber-attacks of major significance (Fact Sheet, 2015). The last driving pillar is the push that the DoD needs to create the Cyber Mission Force (CMF). Initially established in 2012, this newly create tenet of the DoD carries out crucial cyber performance protection (Fact Sheet 2015).

Another federal agency, the United States Department of Homeland Security (DHS) is also involved in the fighting against cyber insecurity. The DHS lends significant assistance to help protect critical infrastructures' information networks and investigates the causes and impacts of cyber breach incidents. The DHS is not alone but works in close coordination with many other government agencies (U.S Department of Homeland Security 2018).

As outlined in the 2017 NSS, a major state actor who has been directing cyber-attacks towards the United States is North Korea. Since the 1950s North Korea has been actively engaged in to a variety of hostile acts against the United States. New to the world of potential threats, however, is its relentless cyber realm. Recently, North Korea has used a malware virus known as WannaCry for attacking. An attack using this program infected hundreds of thousands of computers (Jasper 2017). The virus rendered many of these computers useless, which includes the likes of hospitals, schools, businesses, and homes in as many as over 150 countries (Brady 2017). As one of major victims of such attacks, the United States truly felt the impact of this malware's capability on power grids, electric companies, banks, hospitals, schools, and personal homes. In particular, Sony Entertainment was one of the hard-hit victims from North Korea. Some of the workstations that were targeted were damaged beyond repair and they had to be replaced (Congressional Research Service 2017). Another characteristic of cyber-attacks by North Korea is that most of the previous cyber-attacks from North Korea were more disruptive than destructive (Congressional Research Service 2017). Knowing this characteristic was important to the United States because the U.S. now knows that North Korea has the capability of using destructive cyber-attacks rather than disruptive attacks which thereby prod the United States to take immediate actions to shoring up defenses of the power grids, banks, financial system, and hospitals. Government officials also need to know how through specific acts the U.S. could best respond to both disruptive and destructive cyber-attacks.

The Sony Entertainment attack was a wake-up event for the United States. President Obama and the Federal Bureau of Investigation (FBI) immediately traced the root cause to the state of North Korea. The U.S.

government first tried to repress publicity of the attack, but when the attackers started making threats of violence, it was made public and subsequently alarmed the community at large (DeSimone & Horton 2018). Later, Sony pulled the movie from the theaters to stop the impact of such attacks. Although the attack on Sony Entertainment did not cause significant operational disruption, the attack directly led to an estimated loss of $41 million (DeSimone & Horton 2018).

Another state actor that is hostile to the U.S. is Russia and its cyber divisions have not been out of the U.S. cyber security's radar screen. Russia's cyber divisions have been building complicated software that can attack large companies for their extremely large sums of money, for example, block chain technology, which is capable of wreaking havoc in unimaginable ways. The Main Intelligence Directorate (GRU), associated with the Russian military intelligence organization, is one member of such division that has been on the radar of the U.S. counterintelligence agencies. Two GRU officials were charged with interfering with the 2016 U.S. elections, and were also found to be involved with the NotPetya attack in 2017 (The Treasury Department 2018). More surprisingly, the GRU officials were also found to be complicit in using social engineering methods and tradecraft that everyday cybercriminals use. This further proves that hackers with a multitude of motives continue to target human-centered cyber facilities as their knowledge of easy access and least resistance of social media can be exploited (Jewett 2018). Therefore, it is necessary for the American government to focus its attention and efforts towards education of cyber security and raise public awareness.

A rather low-level of cyber security awareness is not an understatement. Kevin Mitnick, KnowBe4's Chief Hacking Officer, stated that he was surprised to see that Russians were using the same methods his company uses in order to test their clients' security. He also stated that his engineers never seem to fail when they use simple techniques like what the Russians use, such as spear-phishing (Jeweet 2018). Collectively, the United States may be making progress towards cyber-security; however, this nation's adversaries are constantly searching for the loopholes and weak spots to penetrate in to the U.S.' cyber space. Being one of the world's largest countries, it is difficult to have the entire U.S. cyber infrastructure protected at any one moment. Such challenges can be best exemplified by the spear-phishing predatory stalking by Russia. Evolving from the original technique of mass-mail phishing, spear-phishing targets single, high-level employees with bait emails; once the individual falls for the bait, the hacking group is then able to access the entire mainframe of any company's network through their account causing destruction (Parmar 2012). The same tactic, however, cannot be protected against by using advanced firewalls and other security measures, rather it underscores how human error can create vulnerabilities.

Most recently, twelve Russian GRU members were charged with interfering with the 2016 U.S. election. The officers were spear-phishing volunteers and employees of the presidential campaign of Hillary Clinton, including the campaign's chairman. They were able to hack into the computer networks of the Democratic Congressional Campaign Committee (DCCC) and the Democratic National Committee (DNC) and steal emails and documents, covertly monitor the computer activity of dozens of employees, and implant hundreds of files of malicious computer code to steal passwords and maintain access to these networks. The officers then released the stolen information on websites such as DCLeaks.com, and created fake Twitter and Facebook accounts to promote the prosperity of their page. They claimed to be "American hacktivists," and later espoused to have also exploited the computers of state boards of elections, secretaries of state, and U.S. companies that supplied information related to voter data stored on specific computers (The United States Department of Justice 2018). This correlates to the beginning of this section on Russia, that the hackers are not using any highly advanced codes to break into systems, rather are using such low forms of hacking and it would seem implausible that they would ever work. Some preventative measures might be able to be taken such as putting an unrecognized email immediately in the "trash" or "spam" folder of an email, but that has to be the extent of technological capabilities against such an attack.

If that was not enough, a group known as the Internet Research Agency (IRA) LLC, was personally named in the meddling of the 2016 U.S. election. They are known for creating a plethora of fake online profiles by using legitimate citizens such as interest groups and state and local political parties on social media. In doing so, the IRA posted thousands of ads reaching millions of people online influencing their vote casting. With illegally acquired personally identifiable information from U.S. citizens, the IRA opened financial accounts and aided their activities (The Treasury Department 2018). Such incidents raised serious national security questions because of the attack's success without revealing true personal identity until way after the election was over. According to the Treasury Department, the IRA did not act alone; they were also aided by companies and persons such as: Yevgeniy Viktorovich Prigozhin, Concord Management and Consulting LLC, Concord Catering, Dzheykhun Nasimi Ogly Aslanov, Anna Vladislavovna Bogacheva, Maria Anatolyevna Bovda, Robert Sergeyevich Bovda, Mikhail Leonidovich Burchik, Mikhail Ivanovich Bystrov, Irina Viktorovna Kaverzina, Aleksandra Yuryevna Krylova, Vadim Vladimirovich Podkopaev, Sergey Pavlovich Polozov, Gleb Igorevich Vasilchenko, and Vladimir Venkov (The Treasury Department 2018). All of these individuals and companies were involved in some fashion whether it was providing systems and technology for the IRA to use, materials, funding for their program so it could continue, worked in masking the software used to administer the propaganda, created and distributed the propaganda itself, or worked simply as translators for the project to function (The Treasury Department 2018). Similarly, to the persons and companies that aided the IRA, the GRU is said to have knowingly engaged in significant activities that undermine cyber security. The GRU was not only directly involved in meddling with the 2016 U.S. election, but was also directly responsible for the NotPetya cyber-attack in 2017 (The Treasury Department 2018).

Similar to the WannaCry attack of 2017, NotPetya was an attack where over 200,000 computers in 150 nations were infected with a malware that locked users out and would not allow them to function unless they paid a ransom or infected at least two other people with the same virus (Brady 2017). WannaCry devastated the United Kingdom's healthcare system, cancelling hundreds of surgical procedures due to the hospitals' computers being encrypted with the malware (Jasper 2017). Another geographic location, in Ukraine, an attack by a malware known as BadRabbit occurred.

This unfolded when Russian hackers under the NotPetya case used the Mimikatz tool to help steal valuable login information that allowed them to access to enter local systems (Jasper 2017). The differences between the two attacks are that BadRabbit extorted money while NotPetya encrypted files. The intentions of BadRabbit are not clear yet to U.S. investigators, however, researchers believe it was a smokescreen for other attacks to take place and possibly so in this country (Jasper 2017). It is believed that NotPetya intended to disrupt energy, telecom and commercial industries in Ukraine by spreading panic among the people; it also affected many other countries causing collateral damage (Jasper 2017). The shipping giant Maersk and FedEx TNT Express surfaced serious concerns about their falls in their volume of business by almost three hundred million dollars each. Maersk was forced to use WhatsApp on personal telephones once email services went down and Merck also incurred costs because of shutting down production of adult and pediatric vaccines, which may cause loss of innocent life (Jasper 2017). The finding of that NotPetya followed the WannaCry attack by North Korea in 2017 have similar coding and systems that were used between the two malwares, showing a relationship of data sharing between the two countries, the two-cyber hacking cells, or some variation of both (Jasper 2017). The NotPetya crisis, however, was resolved, but now Russian hackers constructed a new version of NotPetya called BadRabbit that has secondary impacts in terms of companies not being able to perform their adequate duties, such as providing crucial vaccines to people in need (Jasper, 2017). Hackers are constantly updating their computer codes and changing their tactics and capabilities, and are developing new tools to improve their hacking ability to ensure successful hackings.

Circling back to Ukraine, geographically close to and strategically located to adjacent to Russia, back in 2015 Ukraine's power grid was hacked and tampered with causing nationwide disruption. Ukrainian Kyivoblenergo, a regional electricity distribution company, reported service outages to customers that was caused by a third party's illegal entry into the company's computer and security systems (Defense Use Case 2016, iv). In the hacking incident, they had to shut down two substations for three hours each, and forced other operations of the power grid to switch to manual mode. The total loss of power to customers was later estimated to include approximately 225,000 residents rather than the previously estimated 80,000 (Defense Use Case 2016, iv). The U.S. DHS issued a report on February 25, 2016, disclosing that three Ukrainian power companies were victims of coordinated cyber-attacks, all within 30 minutes of one another by identifying that the attacking software was KillDisk (Defense Use Case 2016, iv). KillDisk is a malware which erases selected files on targeted systems and corrupts the master boot record rendering the system inoperable. This attacking software also rendered Serial-to-Ethernet devices at substations inoperable by corrupting their firmware. Moreover, the attacking actors reportedly scheduled disconnects for server Uninterruptible Power Supplies (UPS) via the UPS remote management interface (U.S. Department of Homeland Security 2016). It is also reported that other companies had also been infected with a malware known as BlackEnergy, although not confirmed at the time of the report; it was suspected the malware was delivered via spear-phishing (U.S. Department of Homeland Security 2016).

To counter Russia' vicious cyber activities against the U.S., the Federal Security Service (FSB) acted swiftly in the alignment of close watching with other state agencies. Together, these state agencies utilize cyber tools to target Russian journalists and important opposition politicians of the Russian government by including Russian citizens and government officials, former officials from countries bordering Russia, and U.S. government officials, and includes the counterpart of the U.S. (The Treasury Department 2018). Such comprehensive monitoring systems achieved first success in 2017 when the U.S. Department of Justice indicted two FSB officers in their aid in hacking Yahoo which resulted in millions of this company's accounts to be compromised (The Treasury Department 2018). This is necessary in that close internal monitoring can be quite effective preventing information leakage and self-employee's involvement.

The U.S. Treasury Department stands at the forefront of protecting U.S. financial systems. For example, this department has imposed new sanctions against the Russian government and their access to the United States' financial system. It stands firmly that the U.S. holds anyone who launches cyber-attacks accountable for the nefarious acts against the United States (The Treasury Department 2018). It is The Countering America's Adversaries through Sanctions Act (CAATSA) introduced on June 24, 2017 from where these new sanctions emanate. Russia's later behavior in the 2016 U.S. elections further angered the United States because such cyber interference severely undercut American democracy. What is more alarming from this political meddling is that Russian cyber-attacks direct linkage to its state government and high level of vulnerability that the U.S. cyber-based operations and management have ranging from government entities, and multiple critical infrastructure sectors including energy, nuclear, commercial facilities, water, aviation, and manufacturing (The Treasury Department 2018). Again, understanding how the U.S. can best respond to these attacks to protect U.S. companies remains as the single biggest challenge today.

RESEARCH QUESTIONS

In conjunction with the listing of cyber security as the top issue in Joint Publication 1-02 (112) and as previously discussed in the Literature Review, two primary research questions ought to be asked and they are:

Q1: How have Russia and North Korea carried out their cyber-attacks to weaken the position of the United State in the framework of the YIRTM? Will they continue to launch such attacks to weaken the dominant role of the United States in the years to come? And how so?

Q2: Why do Russia and North Korea use cyber-attacks to weaken the hegemony of the United States?

LOGIC MODEL

The authors applied a logic model to frame the issue of the study because it is useful to help decipher potential activities and actions by the United

States' adversaries. The model conceptualized national power in the four spatial dimensions of: diplomacy, information, military, and economic. The instruments are commonly known as the D.I.M.E. (Weaver 2015).

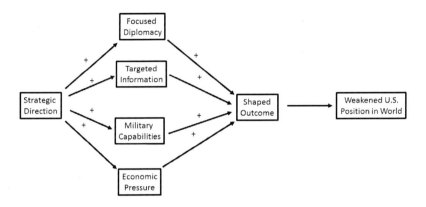

Figure 1. YIRTM (Weaver 2015).

The authors also used the York Intelligence Red Team Model (hereafter the YIRTM), shown in Figure 1. This model provides directionality of cause-effect relationships complementing the D.I.M.E. instruments. Such directionality linkages are suggestive of what likely strategic direction the state or non-state actor is going to or should move toward. As illustrated on the flow diagram, the shaped outcome which leads to weakened U.S. position is the final outcome of the adversary's activities. Conversely, what the United States should take measures to deter and counter malicious cyber-attacks can be inferred. The essence of the YIRTM is the provision of important questions with regard to "who," "what," "when," "where," "why," and "how" and that is exactly what the research questions asked (Weaver1 2015).

The very first dimension of national power is diplomacy. Diplomacy involves a leader that fosters conditions favorable to their cause. Yet, when assessing the impact of a diplomatic movement, one should look at a broader scope, for example, either regionally or globally. A cyber capability is a unique entity of a state that is intricately woven through all aspects, sections, and throughout multiple levels in a society. What long-term consequences it may have must be assessed comprehensively.

Information is the second dimension of national power. More precisely, information is an instrument that could greatly benefit and strengthen a country's power or throw a country to an extremely vulnerable situation weakening its national power. With a diversity of platforms where information is embedded, this instrument is a double-edged sword. Russian hackers obviously are quite experienced using this instrument as was seen in the 2016 U.S. presidential election by creating fake Facebook accounts and false profiles to advance their political interests undercutting the U.S.' democracy (The U.S. Treasury Department 2018). In a much more globalized world today where the average broadband speed has increased five times than that seen of the last decade, individual citizens and organizations are least likely off-line which makes the U.S. collectively much more vulnerable to the country's adversaries.

The military dimension is the use of armed forces as an instrument for national power. This instrument looks at the wide range of militarily manifestations ranging from overseas peacekeeping operations, military combat operations, and field exercises because they project visible strength of a country's military development and capability. The same thing can be said for an adversary of a country.

When turning to economics, this instrument has been increasingly used to analyze a nation's power. A state actor can spend their funds on their economic sectors and fronts creating incentives (economic alliance agreement) or sanctioning another state cutting off those economic ties supporting, for example, the military dimension. In today's much interdependent globalized world, this can be a great catalyst or detrimental blow. Beyond the regional scale, the economic instrument often carries a global effect. On the negative side, chaos over the disruption of the flow of goods and products could easily take place. Financial systems can be interrupted. Capital flows can be stopped. When looking at how the United States could avoid the detrimental effect from its adversaries who uses the economic instrument as their weapons against the U.S., the U.S. needs to be mindful with large economic alliances, for example, China-Russia or other regional economic agreements.

Collectively, these four instruments showcase and project national power. Depending on how they are used in a synthesized fashion, a shaped outcome could be inevitable. By analyzing world issues through the eyes of the U.S.' adversaries, better understanding of the relationships between the involved state actors is the key as they are a critical piece of a better understanding of future conflict.

METHODOLOGY

Given the nature of the two research questions, a qualitative research methodology is most suitable because the essence of a qualitative research is to produce an in-depth understanding of a given issue, not just about empirical statistical analysis. All data used in the study came from openly available secondary sources due to their easy accessibility. When conducting data collection, the Federal Qualitative Secondary Data Case Study Triangulation Model (hereafter the Federal Model) was used to ensure that, first, data came from a variety of sources instead of single source; and second, only those high credible – most authoritative sources were included. In doing so, a high quality of analysis was achieved.

As illustrated on Figure 2, case study stands at the core of the model. A case study affords an opportunity challenging current theoretical assumptions. Triangulation was used multiple times to further ensure the quality of data extraction and coding process. This model works to best balance multiple sources for least biased and most accurate interpretations developing a well-rounded research (Weaver1 2015). The categories of documents, legislation, and policy best represent government's viewpoint and strategies. Documents and reports further provide more details about the official points of view and national strategies. Peer reviewed publications are independent scholarly works mitigating the biases coming from pure governmental sources. Together, these specific tools were used to minimize the potential biases.

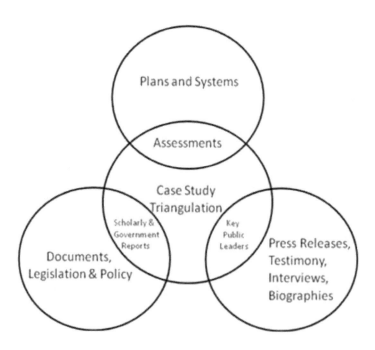

Figure 2. Federal Qualitative Secondary Data Case Study Triangulation Model (Weaver2, 2015).

A second component of the FQSDCSTM is the plans and systems section. This sectional category looks at specific procedures and detailed processes regarding tactics combating potential threats, which is important in identifying gaps and closing loopholes in the existing arena.

The final categorical component is press releases, testimony, interviews, and biographies. With these sources, data from some of the most important individuals can be obtained further filling the gaps from governmental sources. These mostly oral accounts come from individuals who holds high rank or political appointment and were personally involved for a long time and thus holding longitudinal understanding the issue, so they are qualified as key informants with first-hand information regarding the topic at hand.

To sum, a collection of aforementioned methodological tools best balance what a piece of data is, where a data comes from, how that piece of data is being verified, should it be included or excluded, how a data is and/or should be coded, and how it is being interpreted to avoid all possible biases, ambiguities, and inaccuracy to achieve a strong basis of validity. By having a strong validity, high quality analysis that is accurate and confirmative could only be guaranteed in an important issue this research project investigates.

LIMITATIONS

A qualitative research approach has some limitations that must be appropriately addressed. No primary data was used including surveys, questionnaires, interviews, focus groups and the like due to time and cost constraints. The next limitation is a rather short temporal scope (generally a five year period ending in 2018) which excluded a lot of data out of the study outside of the time period considered. Thirdly, using the D.I.M.E. instruments and the YIRTM in Figure 1 could leave other variables out. Lastly, the analysis cannot be generalized as no statistical experiments were conducted for significance (Creswell 2008).

ANALYSIS

Annex A contains the coded data for this study. In total, there were 17 entries. Through the cross-coding, the original D.I.M.E. logical model has been modified to a variant of an I.E.D.M. model because the frequency of data recording rendered the following list from highest to the least: "I" for 15 times, "E" for nine times, "D" for eight times, and "M" for six times. As such, the variant of D.I.M.E. was used as the basis of this analysis.

The two state actors, North Korea and Russia, have earned notable positions for their past and frequent cyber-attacking events that occurred during this study's temporal period. These attacks were launched hitting significant economically important sectors and critical companies in both disruptive and destructive ways. Data from these two state actors' statements posit that these two countries are the homeland's greatest threat at present.

Looking forward to the near future, they most likely will continue to develop newer and more sophisticated technologies and launching subsequent cyber-attacks undercutting the U.S.' economic position which is the most vulnerable at present.

Russia alone is a great threat to the United States because its broad scope of attacks not only in the U.S. homeland but also among foreign allies who are aligned with America. The event where Russia attacked Ukraine's power grid in 2015 was an excellent example disrupting thousands of ordinary Ukrainian citizens' lives (Defense Use Case 2016). Recent malware attacks still are directed against Ukraine but this time shifted to its critical infrastructure sector of energy, telecom, and commercial industries attempting to cripple the basic economic function of the country (Jasper 2017, 1). The U.S. has felt the impact of such cyber-attacks. Although they can be counted as the secondary effects, they still raise a red flag to the U.S. warning of imminent cyber threats that could directly hit it. Many other examples further confirmed Russia' objective which is to limit and/or weaken the U.S.' dominant power on the global stage.

To counter such threats coming from cyber platforms, the United States has recently conducted internal measures designed to shore up cyber defenses and pursue those willing to do harm to this nation. Two FSB officers from Russia, for their involvement in the hacking of Yahoo in 2017, were indicted. To extend the efforts, the U.S. has charged 12 GRU members of Russia in their involvement in the meddling of the 2016 Presidential election. Both show that the U.S. is fully aware of the backseat driver of these cyber-attacks which is Russia. Russia's meddling in the 2016 U.S. presidential election was marked by great discontent from the U.S. government. Subsequent U.S. responses have restricted Russia' access to America's financial system to some degree (The U.S. Treasury Department 2018).

North Korea is another major state actor that threatens the U.S. cyber space. Similar to what Russia has done, North Korea also successfully launched cyber-attacks in more than 150 countries by damaging their hospitals, schools, businesses, and personal home computers (Brady 2017). North Korea's successful dismantling of Sony Entertainment's security measures is a wake-up call for its heinous cyber activities (DeSimone & Horton 2018). It is worth noting that while the U.S. and other countries direct their focus on North Korea's nuclear power, North Korea secretly acquired a substantial cyber capability launching cyber threats from a different front challenging and weakening the U.S. power. How to balance the monitoring of North Korea's ongoing nuclear weapon systems and its cyber development remains disconnected by the United States.

The first instrument of national power, diplomacy which is reflected by Annex A eight times, was used effectively by both North Korea and Russia. As the key to the success of a nation's international relationship, both state actors diplomatically manipulated and established favorable official channels in support of their own state agendas and interrupted when there are nefarious acts in the background, and prevented the success of the United States in trying to counter them. Either from a point of view of being a direct victim of both state actors' cyber-attacks shows that the U.S. was clearly a target. Hacking into the computers and databases of Hillary Clinton's campaign (The United States Department of Justice 2018) and intentional use of Facebook and other social media accounts and posting propaganda specific to one political party leading skewing vote casting (The Treasury Department 2018) cannot be tolerated in the future.

Information, the most used instrument of national power and recorded over fifteen times as reflected on Annex A, was embedded and utilized through every cyber-attack conducted by North Korea and Russia. In these attacks, sensitive data was exploited and illegally acquired by Russia and North Korea. Economic sectors suffered significant losses. Critical infrastructures in energy, public health, and utilities were under attack. Malicious malware such as spear-phishing penetrated in to this nation's interconnected cyber networks. With undertrained staff, the U.S. will only endure more cyber disruptions and network destructions as Russia's and North Korea's rapid technological sophistication continues to grow.

The instrument of economics was used in conjunction with information has been exerted by both countries using these instruments of national power weakening the United States. By carrying out cyber-attacks on the U.S.' allies' economic apparatus, Russia and North Korea manually created financial hardships for Maersk and FedEx TNT Express (Jasper 2017, 1). In response, the United States exchanged formal messages with Russia condemning its misbehavior (DeSimone & Horton 2018). As implied in the North Korean hackers' revelations, North Korea did not care who was impacted by the attack; they just wanted money. Numerous statistics suggest cyber security must be implemented at multiple levels to fend off attacks from Russia and North Korea alike. Conversely, the economic pressure exerted by the U.S. can protect U.S. citizens, private companies, and public sectors to be immune from future North Korea's cyber-attacks.

In spite of the instrument of the military being ranked for its lowest frequency in Annex A, military this dimension cannot be separated away from a national collective power. When it is in use along with economic sanctions, the military instrument has helped in curbing North Korea's aggressive behavior towards the U.S. (House of Commons Defense Committee 2018). The idea of the sanctions is to make the testing costlier than it would be beneficial for North Korea (House of Commons Defense Committee, 2018) warning North Korea's allies (House of Commons Defense Committee 2018). Scholars have been arguing these sanctions that are in place have reached the original goals. Given the short time and lack of inside information, it is not possible to draw a conclusion about these sanctions.

To sum, the variant model of the I.E.D.M. revealed the U.S.' adversaries of two state actors, Russia and North Korea, have taken advantage of the national power's four instrument to create favorable condition for their own agenda which is the cost of eroding the U.S. influence. They were able to manipulate multiple platforms as the means of cyber-attacks disrupting and destructing their adversaries creating greater insecurity.

FINDINGS AND CONCLUSION

During the study' temporal period, victims of foreign cyber-attacks included both individual citizens and collective organizations. Considering the impact of malicious cyber-attacks, the U.S.' critical infrastructures and federal information systems from civilian sectors to national agencies were targeted heavily by adversaries such as Russia and North Korea who intentionally used cyber platforms as a counter means exploiting the information from the U.S. and later used such to damage this country's internal assets. It is clear that, in the foreseeable future, nothing will change. That is, the U.S. will remain as a primary target of foreign cyber-attacks and such cyber-based events will be more frequent and more malicious.

To answer the first research question that was intended to address the "how" aspect of the state actors of Russia and North Korea and what they are doing to weaken the position of the United States, it is concluded that through the means of the information instrument, both countries possessed effective cyber-strategies weakening the United States. In combination with using economic and diplomatic instruments, both countries have taken absolute advantages of cyber-attacks as a means of spreading propaganda, damaging and influencing their adversary country, the U.S., to the direction of what they intended. With their employment of using the diplomatic instrument with their own allies, they were able to create instability, disruptions, and destructions to their adversaries in domestic and foreign nations. Russia's recent focus of its efforts towards the diplomatic instrument of national power and undermining U.S. and foreign elections, they advanced their own agenda by pursuing measures to put favorable candidates in office. This suggests the possibility that they are attempting to make a world regime of leaders that are more favorable to Russia and its cause. Additionally, this destabilizes the American democratic governmental system that has been in place for many years, causing turmoil among the American people. By North Korea focusing on hacking Equifax to steal people's social security numbers, names, and addresses, this allowed them to gain more power as American companies lost credibility at home. Americans were in a state of unease because their personal information had been stolen and it shut down certain services in the U.S. while they tried to resolve the problem. North Korea knows that they have tremendous influence and if they can lessen the power in the United States by hacking businesses like Equifax, as it will help them gain prominence as a major actor. This will also allow for North Korea and Russia to grow stronger together as the U.S. slowly falls as its companies' credibility falters and lose power.

With regard to answering the second research question which is on "why," as the direction illustrated in the YIRTM suggested, Russia and North Korea's state leaders have a clear and hostile agenda of their own and aggressively materialized their attempts to create a global climate favorable to their own intentions. As their intentions are built upon being a global regime of leaders that are favorable to their cause, they have used cyber-attacks to create less competition. At a broader scope, they hold economic companies hostage of their own state agenda by creating panic and havoc destroying computers and networks where today's nations are fundamentally built on. A wide geographic scope of cyber-attacks' impact has helped the adversaries to strengthen their national power while simultaneously reducing that of the United States. With the agenda of retribution of sensitive information from the U.S. to their own hands, they well demonstrated their presence on the global stage and their technological capabilities.

To conclude, the state actors including Russia and North Korea have demonstrated their technological advancement and capabilities in launching cyber-based attacks weakening their adversary's national power, and more pointedly in this case, the U.S.' hegemony. Although these weakening effects may be more apparent in one dimension over other dimensions, it would be naïve if one assumes fighting against cyber insecurity should be focused on one instrument and is only about implementation of only antivirus programs or any other low-level technological pursuits. To best combat the danger and prevent future cyber-based attacks, the U.S. must address cyber security awareness through seamless coordination among the intelligence community and pursue wider and better education at all levels and span beyond government to private industry and citizens as well. In addition, the U.S. intelligence community members must overcome the shallow perception of cyber security as only putting antivirus mechanism into a computer station. More systematic and network wide security assurance measures that are at a more sophisticated level, particularly in

ANNEX A

How/Why	D.I.M.E	Source	Source Type	Date	Page (if applicable)
Increases to sophistication and severity of cyber threats	I,M	Fact Sheet	Government Document	Apr-15	1
Security incidents increase from 5,500 to 67,000 in eight years	I,M	GAO-15-758T	Testimony	Jul-15	N/A
Over 4,000,000 OPM records hacked	I,E	GAO-15-758T	Testimony	Jul-15	8
100,000 IRS tax records accessed	I,E	GAO-15-758T	Testimony	Jul-15	8
Cyber intrusion into postal workers records	I,E	GAO-15-758T	Testimony	Jul-15	9
Russia cyber-attack that shut down Ukrainian electrical grid	I	Defense Use Case	Government Document	2016	NP
worldwide effects of cyber security	I,E,M	Center For Strategic & International Studies	Online Article	2018	NP
Equifax failures	I	Federal Trade Commission	Government Document	2017	
United States summary of cyber security defense	D,I,M,E	Department of Defense Cyber Strategy	Government Document	2018	1-6
Known Russian involvement in U.S. 2016 election	D,I	The U.S. Department of Justice	Government Document	2018	NP
Use of spear-phishing on high ranking employees to gain entry to company/business mainframe, records, and data through the victim's credentials	I	Parmar	Peer Reviewed Publication	2012	1,2

Annex A. (Continued)

How/Why	D.I.M.E	Source	Source Type	Date	Page (if applicable)
Use of spear-phishing on high ranking employees to gain entry to company/business mainframe, records, and data through the victim's credentials	I	Parmar	Peer Reviewed Publication	2012	1,2
U.S. cutting off Russia's access to U.S. financial system	D, E	The U.S. Treasury Department	Government Document	2018	NP
U.S. indicted two Federal Security Service employees for their aid in hacking Yahoo in 2017	D, I, E	The U.S. Treasury Department	Government Document	2018	NP
12 Russian GRU members charged with interfering with 2016 election. Spear-phishing Clinton's campaign, steal emails and documents, monitor activity, released information to public	D, I	The U.S. Department of Justice	Government Document	2018	NP
NotPetya cyber-attack accredited to Russia against Ukraine in 2017, focused on disrupting energy, telecom, and commercial industries	D, I, E	Jasper	Peer Reviewed Publication	2017	1,2
Ukrainian government election support by Russia to put favorable candidate in power	D,I,M,E	Stanford University	Peer Reviewed Publication	2018	3,4
Rash or Rational? North Korea and the threat it poses	D,M	House of Commons Defense Committee	Peer Reviewed Publication	2018	12

networking, computing, sensing, and control systems, must be quickly developed and implemented. In addition, better risk ranking of cyber data and network systems might help the U.S. intelligence community set the tiers of priority management hierarchies.

REFERENCES

Bair, Jonathan, Steven M. Bellovin, Andrew Manley, Blake E. Reid, and Adam Shostack. 2017. "That was close! Reward reporting of cyber security "near misses"." *Colorado Technology Law Journal.* 16:327-364.

Bierman Noah. 2017, December 20. *"Press Briefing on the Attribution of the WannaCry Malware Attack to North Korea."* The White House: Infrastructure and Technology. https://www.whitehouse.gov/briefings-statements/press-briefing-on-the-attribution-of-the-wannacry-malware-attack-to-north-korea-121917/

Center for Strategic & International Studies. 2018. *"Significant Cyber Incidents."* https://csis-prod.s3.amazonaws.com/s3fs/public/180910_Si gnificant_Cyber_Events_List.pdf?IjP3fnWfsOPcRjUBLQ2XXM9lqqti CHiE

Chen, Qian & Robert Bridges. 2017. *"Automated Behavioral Analysis of Malware a Case Study of WannaCry Ransomware."* Accessed on September 22, 2018. *arXiv preprint arXiv:1709.08753.* p. 1-9.

Congressional Research Service. 2017, August 7. *"North Korean Cyber Capabilities: In brief."* Congressional Research Service. Accessed on September 23, 2018. https://fas.org/sgp/crs/row/R44912.pdf.

Creswell, John W. 2008. *Research Design; Qualitative, Quantitative, and Mixed Methods Approaches.* Thousand Oaks, CA: SAGE Publications

Cyber Strategy. 2018. "The Department of Defense Cyber Strategy." Accessed on September 23, 2018. https://media.defense.gov/2018/ Sep/18/2002041658/1/1/1/CYBER_STRATEGY_SUMMARY_FINA L.PDF.

Defense Use Case. 2016. "*Analysis of the Cyber-attack on the Ukrainian Power Grid.*" Accessed September 23, 2018. Electricity Information Sharing and Analysis Center (E-ISAC). p. Iv-23.

DeSimone, Antonio, & Nicholas Horton. 2018. "*Sony's nightmare before Christmas the 2014 North Korean Cyber-attack on Sony and Lessons for U.S. Government Actions in Cyberspace.* National Security Report. Retrieved from http://www.dtic.mil/dtic/tr/fulltext/u2/1046744.pdf.

Fact Sheet. 2015. "*Fact Sheet: The Department of Defense (DOD) Cyber Strategy April 2015.*" http://archive.defense.gov/home/features/2015/0415_cyberstrategy/department_of_defense_cyber_strategy_fact_sheet.pdf.

Federal Trade Commission. 2017. *The Equifax Data Breach.* Accessed September 23, 2018. https://www.ftc.gov/equifax-data-breach.

GAO-15-758T. 2015. *Information Security Cyber Threats and Data Breaches Illustrate Need for Stronger Controls across Federal Agencies.* Accessed on October 12. 2018. https://www.gao.gov/assets/680/671253.pdf.

Hathaway, Oona, and Rebecca Crootof. 2012. "The Law of Cyber-attack." *California Law Review*, 100(4): 817-885. http://www.jstor.org/stable/23249823.

House of Commons Defense Committee. 2018. "*Rash or Rational? North Korea and the Threat It Poses.*" https://publications.parliament.uk/pa/cm201719/cmselect/cmdfence/327/327.pdf.

Jasper, Scott. 2017. "*Russia and Ransomware: Stop the Act, Not the Actor.*" Calhoun: The NPS Institutional Archive Space Repository.

Jewett, Jennifer. 2018, July 17. *The Business JournalsKnowBe4 analysis: Lack of Security Awareness Training Allowed Russians to Hack American Election.* Accessed October 23, 2018. https://www.bizjournals.com/prnewswire/press_releases/2018/07/17/FL55419.

JP 1-02. 2010, November 8. Department of Defense Dictionary of Military and Associated Terms. *Joint Publication 1-02*.

NSS. 2017, December. *The National Security Strategy of the United States of America.* Accessed September 24, 2018. http://nssarchive.us/wp-content/uploads/2017/12/

Parmar Bimal, Faronics. 2012. "Protecting against Spear-phishing." *Computer Fraud & Security.* Accessed on October 23, 2018. https://www.faronics.com/assets/CFS_2012-01_Jan.pdf.

Sigholm, Johan. 2013. "Non-State actors in cyberspace operations." *Journal of Military Studies.* 4. 1-37. 10.1515/jms-2016-0184.

The Treasury Department. 2018, March 15. *"Treasury Sanctions Russian Cyber Actors for Interference with the 2016 U.S. Elections and Malicious Cyber-attacks."* Accessed September 23, 2018. https://home.treasury.gov/news/press-releases/ sm0312.

The White House. 2017, May 12. The White House. *"National Security Strategy of the United States of America."* Accessed October 23, 2018. https://www.whitehouse.gov/wp-content/uploads/2017/12/NSS-Final-12-18-2017-0905.pdf.

Tomz, Michael, & and Jessica L. P. Weeks. 2018, August. *Public Opinion and Foreign Electoral Intervention.* Stanford University. Accessed October 23, 2018. https://web.stanford.edu/~tomz/working/Tomz Weeks-ElectoralIntervention-2018-08-24.pdf.

Trump, Donald. 2017, May 12. *President Trump Protects America's Cyber Infrastruc-ture. The White House: Infrastructure & Technology.* Accessed on October 23, 2018. https://www.whitehouse.gov/briefings-statements/president-trump-protects-americas-cyber-infrastructure/

U.S. Department of Homeland Security. 2016. *Cyber-attack against Ukrainian Critical Infrastructure.* Industrial Control System Cyber Emergency Response Team (ICS-CERT). Accessed September 23, 2018. https://ics-cert.us-cert.gov/alerts/IR-ALERT-H-16-056-01.

U.S. Department of Homeland Security. 2018. Cyber Incident Response. *Cybersecurity.* Accessed September 23, 2018. https://www.dhs.gov/cyber-incident-response.

U.S. Department of Justice. 2018, July 13. *Grand Jury Indicts 12 Russian Intelligence Officers for Hacking Offenses Related to the 2016 Election.* Office of Public Affairs. Accessed on September 23, 2018. https://www.justice.gov/opa/pr/grand-jury-indicts-12-russian-intelligence-officers-hacking-offenses-related-2016-election.

Weaver, John M. (2015). The Perils of a Piecemeal Approach to Fighting ISIS in Iraq. *Public Administration Review.* 75(2):192-193.

Weaver 2, John M. 2015. The Enemy of My Enemy is My Friend...Or Still My Enemy: The Challenge for Senior Civilian and Military Leaders. *International Journal of Leadership in Public Service.* 11(3-4).

Weaver 3, John M. 2015. The Department of Defense and Homeland Security relationship: Hurricane Katrina through Hurricane Irene. *Journal of Emergency Management.* 12(3): 265-274.

In: Global Intelligence Priorities
Editors: John Michael Weaver et al.
ISBN: 978-1-53615-836-6
© 2019 Nova Science Publishers, Inc.

Chapter 12

CHALLENGES OF THE U.S. NATIONAL SECURITY AND MOVING FORWARD

Jennifer Yongmei Pomeroy, Ph.D.
York College, York, Pennsylvania, US

The National Security Strategy (NSS) is a mandatory document required by Congress to provide strategies to the U.S. national security. The "America First" policy stated in the 2017 Trump Administration's NSS shifts to a domestic economic growth and a strong border setting a different strategic direction than the previous administrations have. The release of it in Trump's first year of his presidency gets much attention and has been debated. For example, Cordesman (2017) thinks that the document is too vague because there is no actual strategy provided, though it does carry on those traditional themes of a U.S. strategy. Feaver (2018) argues that, although the 2017 NSS is not as good as it could be, it does contain a workable foundation by providing "an effective framework for American engagement around the world" and "by choosing to abide by his own commitments, Trump could restore America's global influence."

While it may be too soon to assess the impact of this critical document, this book focuses on the cross-sections of nine "hot spots" identified in this document and conducted systematic assessments on national power. Mostly, these systematic assessments are conducted in the dyad form - the U.S. against either a state-actor such as North Korea, Russia, Iran, and Turkey, or a non-state actor including the Islamic State (ISIL) and cyber space, except in Chapter 11 where the author investigated the trilateral relationships among U.S.-China-India. Collectively, all authors use diplomacy, information, military, and economic instruments, also known as the D.I.M.E. in conjunctions with the York Intelligence Red Team Model, known as YIRTM, as the conceptual framework and investigated how those state actors and non-state actors have been using the four instruments creating and projecting their power. All authors together also addressed another central overarching question which is why those adversaries of the U.S. have undermined the U.S. hegemony in global affairs in the context of the YIRTM and will continue to do so.

Starting from the homeland, each chapter generated a variant model of the D.I.M.E. logic model. These models were derived from extensive data extraction and cross-coding of frequency. Table 1 shows these models. If an actor has the same frequencies for two instruments, then this actor is characterized with additional models – see the columns of "Model 2," "Model 3," and "Model 4." For example, in the case of China, the coding frequencies for diplomatic and information are the same, therefore, China has been emphasized using these two models for its national power building.

Using this approach, all regions studied in this research yield variant models by prioritizing different instruments in their own unique context. As shown in Table 1, all nine cross-section actors as a whole have 194 data sources through the Federal Model. From the highest to the lowest, a model of the I.D.D.E. is derived. This model means all identified U.S. adversaries prioritize information as the first and most central instrument to create their national power against their national adversaries, which is predominately oriented at the United States. Diplomacy is used as the second instrument. Military is the third and economic is the fourth. Such models verify that all actors, including state and non-state actors, clearly know the role of information and technology in today's world and have been able to successfully use it to help each of them to accomplish their national goals and objectives.

The homeland chapter developed the model of I.M.E.D. through their analyses. National power can be simply considered as a sum of all resources and the collective ability to pursue leader goals. The I.M.E.D. model suggests that the U.S. has been on par with the information technology instrument to encounter its adversaries for a safe, prosperous, and free nation. The U.S. government continues to make significant investment to continue to modernize its information sector. Yet, the U.S. information infrastructure and cyber space network have been vulnerable and thus becoming an easy target by the state actors including Russia, North Korea, and China. The military instrument is used secondarily. According to the Heritage Organization (heritage.org 2018), the U.S. military power is sizable in the world and equipped by the most advanced weapons, tanks, ships, airplanes, and all other supporting combat tools. Its 2018 military strength report also states that the U.S. government has historically been able to allocate and balance defense costs. It concludes that the U.S.' 2019 aggregated military power is most likely capable of satisfying an involvement of a regional conflict. The economic instrument is ranked in the third place as it applies to U.S. economic power. According to Frank Gaffney (2004), the effectiveness of the economic instrument of national power has been mixed at best. Diplomacy is the least used instrument by the United States. Collectively, current cyber activities by the U.S. adversaries have eroded the U.S. military advantages and negatively impacted the U.S. economic prosperity.

Interestingly, the non-state actor, ISIL, is the only one out of the nine regional actors who exhibits the exact same model as that of the Homeland, which is the I.M.E.D. model. Also using the information instrument, ISIL effectively spread their anti-Western views, recruited their followers and soldiers, and facilitated their financial support network spreading their influence territorially and ideologically. Compare the frequency numbers of the U.S. and ISIL models, one sees that ISIL's frequency values are lower than that of the United States. This suggest that although the non-state ISIL possesses modern information and communication technology knowledge and skills, they do not possess the same level of advancement. Through the assessment, it is suggested that ISIL will likely continue to use the information tool to strengthen its organizational power by launching terrorist attacks, whether by a sleeper cell, lone wolf, or suicide bomber. It is fair to assess that the forms and locations of ISIL-backed attacks will be in greater variety and expanded because of high level of mobility today until it achieves a statehood.

Table 1. Summary of the D.I.M.E. Models Used by All Actors

Region	N	D	I	M	E	Model	Model 2	Model 3	Model 4
Homeland	24	10	19	14	11	IMED			
China	13	6	6	7	11	EMDI	EMID		
Cyber	17	8	15	6	9	IEDM			
Iran	18	14	6	14	13	DMEI	MDEI		
ISIL	14	6	11	10	7	IMED			
N. Korea	19	16	14	16	14	DMIE	MDIE	DMEI	MDEI
Russia	17	8	8	5	10	EDIM	EIDM		
Syria	15	12	8	8	3	DIME	DMIE		
Turkey	27	16	12	15	5	DMIE			
Column Total	164	96	99	95	83	IDME			

Source: Data from the Annexes of all chapters.

Other interesting models derived are China's E.M.D.I. and E.M.I.D. models and Russia's E.D.I.M. and E.I.D.M. models. What is common between these two state actors is that China and Russia have been using the economic-centered instrument as the best way to thrust the building and projecting of their national power. As state actors, they both have formal representation power on behalf of their citizens developing bilateral and/or multilateral international relations through the use of the diplomacy instrument. For example, China' BRI and Russia' energy export to Europe. In the case of China, the use of diplomacy is also important in that China shares its border with fourteen neighbors and having good bilateral international relations is crucial to its own national security. Both state actors fully recognize the essential position of information and strategically employ it as needed. What is different between these two state actors is that China uses the military instrument as a secondary tool while Russia alternates information and diplomatic tools. Regarding the fourth dimension, China focuses on either information or diplomacy while Russia exercises the military instrument in the example of its aggressive Crimea annexation action and subsequent invasion into the eastern sector of Ukraine.

North Korea in the East Asia region has made to the top of the list threatening the United States. Not surprisingly, as shown in Table 1, there are four models used and they are: the D.M.I.E., the M.D.I.E., the D.M.E.I., and the M.D.E.I. The models of M.D.I.E. and M.D.E.I. center on the military instrument. The models of D.M.I.E. and D.M.I.E. have the military instrument as secondary one for its national power. Maybe, the first two models can explain North Korea's global influence through its military instrument as Pyongyang sees nuclear weapons as the key to its regime survival and last two models are for its regional international relations.

Other U.S. adversaries including Iran and Syria in the Southwest Asia do not have consistent model demonstrations. Iran seems toggle back and forth between the diplomacy and military instruments for the first and second dimensions of its national power but maintains the economic and information instruments at the third and fourth dimensions. On a contrary note, Syria places the military instrument for the first dimension; it switches back and forth between information and the military instruments.

Although the data collected by all authors is somewhat limited, the evidence of disparate forms of the D.I.M.E. shows a unique topology of national power that each hot spot employs. Such diverse strategies from each adversary confirm a plethora of challenges lying ahead for the U.S.' global hegemonic position. These challenges include the prevailing occurrence of transnational terrorism fundamentally exacerbated by anti-Western views, increasingly intense economic competition in a less predictable global economic environment, vulnerabilities in cyber space, and rival near-peer actors. Challenges also present opportunities because they are the drivers of change. Seamless synchronization and realignment of the I.M.E.D. model to maximize the effect of each instrument can only make the U.S. more secure and continues to retain its position as the only global hegemony. Such synchronization and realignment must recognize that each instrument of national power needs to be optimal and must be used in the best combination to achieve its intended strategic advantage not only in the current power competition but also with regards to future competition.

As a "fifth domain," U.S. cyber security safeguards must be built upon three pillars: technology, process, and people (Dutton 2017) and greatly expanded and improved for sophistication. Some technical prevention mechanisms would include frequently running antivirus software for spotting phishing emails and the use of antispyware on all computer stations, installation of firewalls for internet connections, backing up critical databases, and securing Wi-Fi networks. Educating individual users and their behaviors will reduce risk of being victimized. Cross-domain checks like the Domain Name System (DNS) Risk Index that is a quantified metrics by the 2018 Ponemon could help defense contractors learn their gaps, inadequacies, and improve resilience (Infoblox 2018). In combination with artificial intelligence and machine learning, tackling these challenges is not insurmountable.

Cyber security issues are often inherently technical but other challenges are people related (Dutton 2017). The theories of cyber threat and cyber threat inflation are still valid because the cyber-attack patterns during the study period continue to shift from government offices/buildings to more non-government public spaces to disturb and disrupt ordinary Americans' daily lives. Such characteristics presents significant challenges to the U.S. national security community to perform detection and prevention. This is because Americans' economic and societal functions are practically connected with U.S. military, intelligence and the governmental information web. Such interconnectedness fosters a fuzzy boundary between the public-private partnership in terms of the allocation of responsibility and accountability of cyber security (Carr 2016). In order to disjuncture of such confusion among the public-private partnership, Carr suggests with that acknowledging this disjuncture in the partnership is a first critical step towards moving to the solution. As discussed previously, another solution to the interconnectedness would be timely accurate risk analysis and sound assessments as they can effectively cut down the disturbances and disruptions of foreign cyber-attacks.

Reid and Niekerk (2014) make the argument which is that an information security solution should be a precursor of cyber security. Niekerk along with Solms (2013) divide cyber infrastructure into a two-tier structure and an ultimate solution for security would have to be information security at his/her level and must add an extra dimension which is a wider societal network for collective responsibility. CISO Platform is a social network for CISO (Chief Information Security Officers) echoes that understanding the differences between the two is important. Only when information security management is more holistic can true cyber security be achieved (Soomro et al. 2015).

Traditional military defense ability is made up of direct military actions upon other states by sea, on land, and in air for the defense and survival of a sovereign state. Although modern military power has shifted to high-tech military capabilities, the hardcore of military power remains. What is being added to the traditional spectrum of military power, computers and access to the internet reinforce an actor's military might. Moving forward, the U.S.' military power is not in a vulnerable situation, rather, it is large and strong (Farley 2018).

Today, it is indisputable that the U.S. retains its top spot of land, air, and sea forces to protect Americans abroad, its allies, and the freedom to use international air, water, and space. According to Chinese President Xi, he wants Chinese military power to be equivalent to the U.S. by 2050 (Ward 2018). The U.S.-China Economic and Security Review Committee of the U.S. Congress in its 2018 annual report states that China had made major improvements in hypersonic weapons, cyber abilities, and space defense (Ward 2018). Russia, in 2018, made several high-profile development and procurement programs helping Russia achieve success in recent conflicts in Crimea and Syria grabbing naval and air bases but its overall high-tech equipment is still much less capable when compared to that of the United States. The U.S.' government and intelligence community fully recognize the unique place and power from the information instrument of national power and national security in today's world. In order to reduce the U.S.

cyber security's vulnerability, the Trump Administration in September 2018 laid four specific cyber security strategies in *the National Cyber Strategy of the United States of America* as the pillars of specific implementation strategy for the information instrument. As explained by the President Trump, the four pillars are:

- Defend the homeland by protecting networks, systems, functions, and data;
- Promote American prosperity by nurturing a secure, thriving digital economy and fostering strong domestic innovation;
- Preserve peace and security by strengthening the ability of the United States – in concert with allies and partners – to deter and, if necessary, punish those who use cyber tools for malicious purpose; and
- Expand American influence abroad to extend the key tenets of an open, interoperable, reliable, and secure internet.

These pillars demonstrate the Trump Administration's interagency process to further empower the U.S. military instrument in a manner that stresses the integration between the Armed Forces and other departments and agencies to develop best possible capability to protect and advance the U.S.' national interests and to engage in global affairs.

The economic instrument cannot be separated from national power. A healthy growing U.S. economy is the engine of the general welfare of the United States because it provides fair financial support in its pursuit of national goals. Explicit economic policies such as trade policies, fiscal and monetary policies, embargoes, tariffs, and assistance are important means to enable the U.S. to avoid direct physical military encounters and cut down on risk and vulnerability. While the U.S. GDP grows at a small rate, it has shown a steady increase. As of 2017, the U.S. GDP was $19.39 trillion counting for an approximate share of 20% of global total. The GDP per capital was $54,800. Furthermore, the U.S. dollar is used for international business transactions and elevates this country's economic power. Last but not the least, the U.S. is naturally endowed by abundant natural resources. With such natural endowment, the economic power will mostly grow.

However, when the economic instrument is in use by itself, the effectiveness is limited. When it is joined with other instruments, for example, with information, the effectiveness of two could be maximized. The joint power from two instrument has been noted by the adversaries. Padgett et al. (2018) point out that the adversaries of the U.S. see the U.S. military power as the strongest so "it is rare to be challenged. Most adversaries have shifted their focus on countering U.S. military power by attacking the U.S. using other elements of national power."

As discussed earlier, rival states and non-state actors equally recognize the power of the information instrument in today's geopolitics and they clearly know the effectiveness when it is combined with other instruments for national power competition games. These state actors will continue to launch cyber warfare targeting at the U.S.' critical infrastructure networks (Pomeroy 2018, 299). Increasingly more sophisticated techniques are used to hack and hijack firms, companies, banks, and schools. Notable examples include malware (malicious code/programs) hackings at the U.S. Federal Reserve and website defacement, meddling in the 2016 presidential election by Russia, and Park Jin Hyok's cyber perpetration against the National Health Service and more (Hymas 2018). Keohane and Nye (2012) argue that there are no hierarchies of military and economic instruments in today's interdependent world; structural realism remains an essential role in creating and implementing the military instrument when considering a national power in their view. The information instrument becomes the backbone of all instruments.

Diplomacy combined with the economic instrument can also be successful in a regional context. The European Union (hereafter EU) employs economic diplomacy playing a major role in the global community today. The EU's concentration on economic diplomacy is what the EU provides its regional leadership negotiating better trade deals with other countries and/or regional organizations exerting greater power (Woolcock 2016).

Power is multidimensional and needs to consider all facets and context. Diplomacy is a critical platform for information, economic, and other tools operationalizing military power. All nine actors rely on military tactics and actions to fight against their enemies. Diplomacy is the art of foreign policy for a sovereign state and an important aspect of national power. To many, diplomacy is seen as a "soft" power which is a way for a country to persuade others to follow one's goals. Diplomacy plays an essential role as international decisions and actions must be taken within a multilateral framework.

At a global scale, cyber security has risen to a norm as the proliferation of IT devices and internet services occurs; however, systematic, society-wide digital insecurity at a global scale is in existence. Violation of cyber security by state actors such as Syria's chemical attacks ordered by the President Assad using information technology on its civilians and the Putin-backed power grid hacking on Ukrainians. Such state-sponsored international cyber violation is increasing. The UN General Assembly codifies state cyber behavior as "states should not knowingly allow their territory to be used for internationally wrongful acts using ICTs (information and communication technologies); states should take appropriate measures to protect their critical infrastructure from ICT threats, taking into account General Assembly resolution 59/199 on the creation of a global culture of cybersecurity and the protection of critical information infrastructures, and other relevant resolutions" [2015, para. 13(c)(f)(g)]. Recognition of ordinary citizens as a crucial part of national security is important. In this regard, to protect private citizens' and consumers' personal data must be educated by communicating the interrelation between security individuals, personal devices, and national security (Donahoe 2017, 31). Citizen co-production of security could be most self-helpful for vigilantes combating cybercrime (Change et al. 2016).

To conclude, in today's interdependent world, the center of global power has shifted from the Atlantic's Western Europe and North America to Pacific Asia where emerging powers such as China and India are located and are in competition for power. Khong (2019) points out that power is a resource, power has the ability to obtain preferred outcomes, and prestige as the reputation for power. He continues to argue that "the state with the greatest reputation for power gets to govern the region; it will attract more followers, and regional powers will defer to and accommodate it, and it will play a decisive role in shaping the rules and institutions of international relations (Khong 2019). A state-centric perspective no longer works in an era of globalization. Rather, geocentric or global politics is a more appropriate characterization of the reality. For the U.S. as it works to remain as the hegemonic power for the years to come, it may need to consider to modify the current national power model to the variant model of I.D.E.M., which is anchored by the information instrument, diplomacy as second, the economic tool as third, and lastly the military instrument; when these tools are implemented in synergetic applications, the U.S. can forge ahead to promote its national values, protect its interests, and protect itself and its allies from those hybrid threats.

REFERENCES

Bachmann, Sascha-Dominik. & Hakan, Gunnerisson. (2015). "Hybrid Wars: the 21st-Century New Threats to Global Peace and Security. *Scientia Militaria: South African Journal of Military Studies, 43*(1), 77-98.

Carr, Madeline. (2016). "Public-Private Partnerships in National Cybersecurity Strategies". *International Affairs, 92*(1), 43-62.

Chang, Lennon Y. C., Lena, Y. Zhong. & Peter, N. Grabosky. (2016). "Citizen Co-Production of Cyber Security: Self-help, Vigilantes, and Cybercrime." *Regulation & Governance, 12*(1), 101-14.

Cordesman, Anthony H. (2017). Devember 17. "President Trump's New National Security Strategy." Center for Strategies and International Studies (CSIS). Accessed January 12, 2019, 2019. https://www.csis.org/analysis/president-trumps-new-national-security-strategy.

Csurgai, Gyula. (2017). "The Increasing Importance of Geoeconomics in Power Rivalries in the Twenty-First Century." *Journal of Geopolitics, 23*(1), 38-46.

DeDominicis, Benedict E. "Back to the Future: Post-Cold War US National Security Strategy and American Hegemony under the Trump Administration." *The Global Studies Journal*, *11*(3), 1-25. Accessed January 15, 2019. https://web-b-ebscohost-com.ezproxy.ycp.edu:8443/ehost/pdfviewer/pdfviewer?vid=11&sid=1fa0468c-ade2-429e-90bc-9bec537de9a2%40sessionmgr103.

Dutton, Julia. (2017, September 26). "Three Pillar's of Cyber Security." Accessed January 31, 2019. https://www.itgovernance.co.uk/blog/three-pillars-of-cyber-security.

Farley, Robert. (2018, July 5). "Yes, the U.S. Military Is in Decline. And There Is No Need to Panic." The National Interest. Accessed January 31, 2019. https://nationalinterest.org/blog/buzz/yes-us-military-decline-and-there-no-need-panic-25057.

Feaver, Peter. (2018, December 18). "Elephant in the Room: Five Takeways From Trump's National Security Strategy." *Foreign Policy*. Accessed January 12, 2019. https://foreignpolicy.com/2018/01/24/trump-should-abide-by-his-own-national-security-strategy/.

Gaffney, Frank. Jr. (2004, December 14). "The Economic Element of National Power." Center for Security Policy. Accessed January 31, 2019. https://www.centerforsecuritypolicy.org/2004/12/14/theeconomic-element-of-national-power-2/.

Hampson, Fen Osler. & Michael, Sulmeyer. ed. (2017). Getting Beyond Norms: New Approached to International Cyber Security Challenges - Special Report. Centre for International Governance Innovation. Waterloo, ON, Canada N2L 6C2. Accessed January 6, 2019. https://www.cigionline.org/sites/default/files/documents/Getting g%20Beyond%20Norms.pdf.

Hymas, Charles. (2018, Ictiber 9). "China is Ahead of Russia as 'Biggest state sponsor of Cyber-attacks on the West.'" *The Telegraph*. Accessed January 5, 2019. https://www.telegraph.co.uk/technology/2018/10/09/china-ahead-russia-biggest-state-sponsor-cyber-attacks-west/.

Infoblox, Next Level Networking. (2018). Assessing the DNS Cyber Attack Security Risk: 2018 Ponemon report on DNS and Cyber Attack Risks. Accessed January 5, 2019. https://info.infoblox.com/WW-PPCFY19

PonemonDNSCyberAttackRiskReport.html?ss=google&st=cyber%20a ttack&gclidCj0KCQiAJXiBRCpARIsAGqF8wX1fZzmRIkiKodsg51j8 CjzydoOGPW3gBcLs7duQPh5UIt3xVqxpCsaAqwSEALw_wcB.

Jain, B. M. (2015). *Rethinking Asia and International Relations: India-U.S. Relations in the Age of Uncertainty – An Uneasy Courtship.* London and New York: Routledge Taylor & Francis Group.

Keohane, Robert O. & Joseph, Nye. (2012). Power and Interdependence. New York: Longman.

Khong, Yuen Foong. (2019). "Power as Prestige in World Politics." *International Affairs*, 95(1), 119-42.

Kofman, Michael. & matthew, Rojansky. *A Closer Look at Russia's "Hybrid War'".* Wilson Center. Accessed January 6, 2019. https://www.files.ethz.ch/isn/190090/5-KENNAN%20CABLE-ROJANSKY%20KOFMAN.pdf.

Lissner, Rebecca F. (2017, December 19). "*The National Security Strategy Is Not a Strategy.*" Foreign Affairs.

Masterpeter, Craig. (2008 December). *The Instruments of National Power: Achieving the Strategic Advantage in a Changing World.* Thesis for Master of Arts in Homeland Security and Defense at Naval Postgraduate School. Monterey, California. Accessed January 18, 2019. https://apps.dtic.mil/dtic/tr/fulltext/u2/a493955.pdf.

Nye, Joseph S. (1976). "Independence and Interdependence." *Foreign Policy, 22* (Spring 1976), 130-61.

O'Hanlon, Michael E. & Alice, M. Rivlin. (2017, April 4). "Trump Must Recognize that National Power Goes beyond the Military." The Brookings Institute. Accessed January 31, 2019. https://www.brookings.edu/blog/order-from-chaos/2017/04/04/trump-must-recognizethat-national-power-goes-beyond-the-military/.

Padgett, Michael., John, Kummer. & Brent, Ramsey. (2018, July 12). *Increasing Economic Power as an Instrument of National Power.*" RealClear Defense. Accessed January 6, 2019. https://www.realcleardefense.com/articles/2018/07/12/increasing_economic_power_as_an_instrument_of_national_power_113598.html.

Reid, Rayne. & Johan, Van Niekerk. (2014, November 10). "From Information Security to Cyber Security Cultures." *Conference Paper at the 2014 Information Security for South Africa*. Accessed January 31, 2019.

Solms, Rossouw von. & Johan, van Niekerk. (2013). "From Information Security to Cyber Security." *Computer and Security*, 38, (October 2013), 97-102.

Soomro, Zahoor Ahmed., Mahmood, Hussain Shah. & Javed, Ahmed. (2015). "Information Security management Needs More Holistic Approach; A Literature Review. *International Journal of Information Management*, 36(2), 215-225.

The White House. (2018, September). *"National Cyber Strategy" of the United States of America."* Access January 20, 2018. https://www.whitehouse.gov/wp-content/uploads/2018/09/National-CyberStrategy.pdf.

"The United States Military's Contribution to National Security." (2015 June). Accessed January 10, 2019. https://www.jcs.mil/Portals/36/Documents/Publications/ 2015_National_Military_Strategy.pdf.

Ward, Alex. (2018, November 14). *"China's Military Power Could Match America's by 2050.* Vox. Accessed January 6, 2019. https://www.vox.com/world/2018/11/14/18091800/china-military-power-congress-commission-report-2050.

Wood, Dakota L. ed. (2018). *2018 Index of U.S. Military Strength, Davis Institute for National Security and Foreign Policy.* The Heritage Foundation. Accessed January 31, 2019. https://www.heritage.org/sites/default/files/2017-10/2018_IndexOf USMilitaryStrength-2.pdf.

Woolcock, Stephen. (2016). *European Union Economic Diplomacy: The Role of the EU in External Economic Relations.* London and New York: Routledge Taylor & Francis Group.

ABOUT THE EDITORS

Jennifer Yongmei Pomeroy, PhD
York College, York, Pennsylvania, US

Jennifer Pomeroy is an Assistant Professor of Geography at York College of Pennsylvania (USA). She teaches physical geography, human geography, and geo-spatial technology (Geographic Information Systems) courses. Prior to join York College, she was an Assistant Professor (tenure track) of Chinese Mandarin at Defense Language Institute of Department of Defense, Monterey, CA. She earned her PhD in Geography in 2012 from the Department of Geographical Sciences of University of Maryland, College Park, received her M.A. in Geography/Planning in 1999 from the University of Akron, OH. Being a Chinese-American, she developed an interest in applying geographical approach studying international relations and intelligence analysis.

John M. Weaver, DPA
York College, York, Pennsylvania, US

John Weaver is an Assistant Professor of Intelligence Analysis at York College in Pennsylvania (USA), a retired DOD civilian from the United

States' Intelligence Community, and has served as an officer in the U.S. Army (retiring at the rank of lieutenant colonel). Since entering active duty, he has lived and worked on four continents and in 19 countries spending nearly eight years overseas (on behalf of the U.S. government). His experience includes multiple combat deployments, peace enforcement, peacekeeping, humanitarian relief and disaster assistance support in both conventional and unconventional/non-traditional units. John earned a Bachelor of Arts degree in business management from Towson University in 1990, graduated from Central Michigan University with a Master of Science in Administration degree in 1995, earned a Master of Operational Arts and Science degree from the U.S. Air Force's Air University in 2004, and graduated from the University of Baltimore with a Doctorate in Public Administration in 2013.

INDEX

A

Afghanistan, 114, 150, 247, 304
Africa, 59, 74, 77, 78, 84, 85, 87, 94, 108, 120, 265, 276, 319
al Qaeda, 131, 158
al-Assad, Bashar, xv, 199, 204, 205, 206, 209, 218
al-Masri, Abu Ayyub, 303
al-Qaeda in the Arabian Peninsula (AQAP), 149
al-Zawahiri, Ayman, 302
Ankara, 226, 229
antispyware, 371
antivirus, 356, 371
Armistice, 180
Arthashastra, 289
artificial islands, 61, 76
Asian Infrastructure Investment Bank (AIIB), 278, 294
Assad Regime, 203, 208, 211, 218, 220
Association of Southeast Asian Nations (ASEAN), 276, 281, 282, 283
asymmetric, 6, 16
Atlanticists, 240

B

Baathist, 305, 322
Baghdadi, Abu Umar al, 303
Bakr, Haji, 305
BRICS (Brazil, Russia, India, China, and South Africa), 94, 107, 120

C

caliph, 303
caliphate, 201, 303, 310, 311, 320, 329
Camp Bucca, 305
chief information security officers, 372
Chief Information Security Officers (CISO), 372
China, v, vi, xii, xvi, xix, 4, 5, 17, 22, 26, 39, 40, 57, 58, 59, 60, 61, 62, 63, 64, 65, 66, 68, 69, 70, 71, 72, 73, 74, 75, 76, 77, 78, 79, 80, 82, 83, 84, 85, 86, 87, 88, 89, 90, 92, 94, 107, 109, 110, 112, 113, 120, 136, 137, 167, 175, 176, 177, 181, 185, 189, 195, 263, 264, 265, 266, 267, 268, 269, 270, 271, 272, 275, 276, 277, 278, 279, 280, 281, 282, 283, 284, 285, 287, 288, 289, 290, 291, 292, 293, 294, 295,

296, 297, 298, 299, 300, 332, 348, 366, 367, 368, 369, 372, 376, 378, 380
Communist Party of China (CPC), 59, 64, 72, 83, 90
Congressional Record E1090, 238, 252, 257
Congressional Record H3582, 239, 243, 245, 254, 258
Congressional Record S2770, 241, 252
Crimea, 33, 36, 101, 108, 110, 115, 117, 126, 369, 372
critical infrastructure, 21, 23, 39, 40, 42, 46, 50, 51, 136, 151, 152, 155, 335, 338, 345, 351, 353, 354, 374, 375
cyber, vii, x, xi, xiii, xiv, xvii, xix, 2, 3, 4, 6, 8, 11, 15, 18, 22, 25, 32, 39, 40, 44, 52, 58, 61, 65, 83, 88, 92, 96, 102, 106, 116, 130, 131, 132, 133, 136, 137, 138, 139, 140, 142, 151, 152, 153, 155, 159, 160, 163, 165, 168, 169, 170, 172, 182, 184, 187, 192, 194, 329, 333, 334, 335, 336, 337, 338, 339, 340, 342, 343, 344, 345, 347, 351, 352, 353, 354, 355, 356, 358, 360, 361, 362, 363, 364, 366, 367, 368, 370, 371, 372, 373, 374, 375, 377, 378, 379
cyber capabilities, xiii, xiv, 4, 39, 40, 58, 61, 130, 136, 137, 151, 153, 155, 163, 337
cyber command, 336
cyber defenses, 352
cyber security, xvii, 16, 92, 333, 335, 336, 338, 340, 342, 345, 353, 356, 358, 361, 371, 372, 373, 375
cyber space, xi, xix, 3, 334, 337, 340, 352, 366, 367, 370
cyber space and terrorism, xi, 3
cyber terrorism, 132
cyber warfare, 15, 40, 136, 137, 140, 151, 374
cyber-attacks, xvii, 15, 18, 22, 25, 33, 39, 40, 65, 83, 116, 132, 133, 136, 138, 139, 165, 170, 182, 333, 334, 335, 337, 338,
342, 344, 345, 347, 351, 352, 353, 354, 355, 356, 358, 360, 362, 363, 364, 371, 378
cyberspace, 14, 31, 61, 83, 147, 335, 336, 362, 363

D

D.I.M.E. (diplomacy), xvi, xix, 6, 10, 11, 24, 25, 26, 30, 34, 44, 45, 46, 47, 49, 62, 63, 69, 82, 85, 97, 98, 99, 105, 107, 117, 118, 119, 120, 121, 139, 151, 168, 169, 175, 203, 207, 208, 218, 219, 226, 232, 238, 265, 269, 273, 275, 309, 310, 317, 346, 350, 351, 366, 368, 370
Damascus, 202, 221
data, iv, ix, xvi, xix, 9, 11, 23, 24, 26, 27, 28, 29, 41, 44, 52, 53, 58, 66, 68, 69, 70, 71, 77, 86, 96, 100, 101, 102, 103, 104, 105, 117, 118, 119, 123, 136, 138, 143, 144, 145, 146, 153, 155, 159, 164, 171, 172, 173, 174, 175, 178, 206, 207, 208, 209, 214, 221, 225, 234, 235, 236, 237, 238, 244, 257, 260, 264, 273, 274, 313, 314, 315, 316, 324, 338, 341, 343, 348, 349, 350, 351, 353, 359, 361, 362, 366, 369, 370, 373, 376
debt-trap diplomacy, 278
Defense and Economic Cooperation Agreement (DECA), 228
Defense Department, ix, xi, 3, 61, 68, 187, 282, 337
Demilitarized Zone, 179
Demilitarized Zone (DMZ), 179, 180
Democratic People's Republic of Korea (DPRK), xiv, 4, 163, 165, 166, 168, 182, 184, 185, 188, 197
denuclearization, 32, 166, 171, 180, 190, 191
Department of Defense (DOD), xi, 3, 8, 11, 12, 46, 47, 54, 89, 131, 133, 138, 153,

Index

158, 159, 161, 167, 168, 197, 200, 220, 221, 222, 223, 296, 315, 336, 338, 358, 362, 363, 364, 381
Department of Defense Cyber Strategy, 336, 358, 362
Department of State (DOS), xi, xvi, 3, 27, 35, 46, 48, 51, 52, 59, 98, 101, 106, 122, 126, 132, 133, 134, 136, 137, 148, 153, 161, 166, 183, 184, 189, 194, 200, 221, 225, 226, 248, 250, 251, 252, 260, 318, 330, 332
Departments of Homeland Security, xi, 2, 3
destabilizing force, xiii, 129, 152
diplomacy, xv, xvi, xix, 6, 8, 23, 24, 25, 28, 30, 34, 35, 36, 37, 41, 44, 46, 47, 48, 62, 63, 64, 71, 80, 97, 98, 105, 109, 139, 140, 141, 148, 149, 151, 153, 157, 161, 165, 168, 169, 170, 180, 185, 187, 188, 200, 203, 204, 211, 212, 215, 217, 226, 232, 233, 237, 238, 250, 251, 256, 265, 269, 270, 275, 289, 290, 294, 299, 309, 310, 311, 322, 329, 346, 347, 352, 366, 367, 369, 370, 375, 376, 380
Duterte, President Philippine Rodrigo, 277

E

Economic Exporting Zones (EEZs), 269, 280
Emni, 305, 306, 320, 321, 327, 331
encrypted, 201, 314, 342
environmental exploitation, xiv, 130, 147
Erdoğan, President Recep Tayyip, xvi, 226, 227, 233, 239, 241, 242, 243, 245, 246, 248, 249, 250, 251, 254
Ethio-Djibouti Railways, 276
EU, 34, 126, 228, 231, 375, 380
Eurasianists, 240
European Union, 34, 120, 126, 228, 231, 266, 297, 308, 375, 380

F

Facebook, 31, 33, 242, 320, 324, 341, 347, 353
Federal Bureau of Investigation, 37, 53, 339
Federal Qualitative Secondary Data Case Study Triangulation Model, xii, xvii, 9, 10, 11, 13, 26, 28, 29, 41, 66, 67, 68, 69, 71, 86, 100, 101, 103, 104, 105, 118, 119, 143, 144, 145, 146, 152, 172, 173, 188, 207, 208, 217, 221, 235, 236, 238, 239, 246, 272, 273, 314, 333, 348, 349
firewalls, 65, 341, 371
foes, 7, 40
Freedom of Navigation Operations (FONOP), 281

G

gang violence, xii, 13, 39
Geographic Analysis, 105, 147, 175

H

Hamas, 135, 136, 149, 213
hegemony, v, xii, xiii, xiv, xvi, xix, 6, 13, 42, 51, 57, 58, 61, 62, 74, 77, 79, 86, 88, 92, 129, 139, 141, 153, 154, 164, 169, 182, 185, 187, 188, 203, 213, 226, 232, 247, 248, 256, 263, 266, 269, 270, 273, 282, 286, 290, 309, 310, 325, 346, 356, 366, 370, 377
Hezbollah, xv, 132, 135, 149, 200, 209, 210, 213, 214, 217
homeland, xii, xvi, xix, 3, 13, 14, 15, 17, 18, 21, 23, 24, 25, 27, 28, 29, 30, 32, 36, 38, 39, 41, 42, 44, 46, 47, 48, 51, 53, 55, 58, 74, 92, 131, 157, 164, 165, 201, 205, 226, 271, 321, 322, 325, 336, 351, 366, 367, 373

homeland security, xii, 13, 14, 21, 24, 27, 28, 29, 32, 36, 39, 41, 42
Homeland Security Investigations, 20, 21
hostile nation states, xii, 13, 16, 34, 39, 42, 51
Houthis, 134
human rights abuses, xiv, 31, 130, 137
Hussein, Saddam, 305
hypersonic, 372

I

illicit financial activity, xiii, 130, 147
Incirlik Air Base, 249
India, vi, xvi, xix, 5, 94, 107, 263, 264, 266, 270, 272, 275, 282, 283, 284, 285, 286, 287, 288, 289, 290, 291, 292, 293, 295, 296, 297, 298, 300, 366, 376, 378
Indo-Pacific region, xvii, 5, 32, 61, 76, 80, 264, 270, 275, 278, 281, 282, 283, 285, 286, 287, 288, 289, 290, 291, 292, 294, 297, 299
instruments of national power, xii, xiii, xiv, 6, 14, 23, 24, 34, 63, 69, 86, 92, 97, 98, 99, 109, 117, 118, 129, 139, 140, 142, 153, 163, 169, 207, 209, 214, 215, 232, 273, 353
integrated country strategy, xv, 225, 250, 251, 252, 260
intellectual property, 40, 60, 72
Intelligence Community (IC), ix, xi, 2, 3, 14, 15, 16, 35, 44, 47, 48, 49, 51, 52, 54, 63, 68, 96, 123, 125, 256, 315, 334, 356, 361, 373, 382
Intercontinental ballistic missile (ICBM), 17, 166, 171, 189, 190, 196
International Atomic Energy Agency (IAEA), 130, 134, 162
Iran, vi, xiii, xv, xvi, xix, 4, 5, 16, 17, 23, 30, 31, 34, 40, 41, 42, 48, 53, 54, 92, 108, 120, 126, 129, 130, 131, 132, 133, 134, 135, 136, 137, 138, 139, 140, 141, 142, 143, 144, 146, 147, 148, 149, 150, 151, 152, 153, 154, 155, 156, 157, 158, 159, 160, 161, 162, 165, 200, 202, 205, 206, 208, 209, 211, 213, 214, 216, 217, 218, 219, 220, 222, 226, 229, 240, 244, 245, 248, 250, 254, 260, 292, 366, 368, 370
Islam, 209, 231, 305, 317, 319
Islamic ideology, 130, 155
Islamic Revolutionary Guard Corps, 142, 213
Islamic Revolutionary Guard Corps (IRGC), 142, 213
Islamic State of Iraq (ISI), xv, xvii, 19, 131, 200, 301, 302
Islamic State of Iraq and Syria (ISIS), xv, 12, 131, 132, 158, 200, 201, 210, 218, 223, 234, 244, 253, 258, 329, 330, 331, 332, 364
Islamic State of Iraq and the Levant (ISIL), vi, xvii, xix, 19, 135, 301, 302, 303, 304, 305, 306, 307, 308, 309, 310, 311, 312, 314, 315, 316, 317, 318, 319, 320, 321, 322, 323, 324, 325, 326, 327, 328, 329, 366, 368
Islamophobia, 305

J

Japanese Prime Minister Shinzo Abe and India's Prime Minister Modi, 275
Jihadist, xvii, 201, 205, 301
jihadist ideology, 132
Jinping, President Xi, 59, 64, 65, 71, 80, 83, 266, 271, 277, 281
Joint Comprehensive Plan of Action (JCPOA), xiii, 16, 31, 34, 52, 130, 133, 134, 137, 139, 141, 144, 148, 152, 156, 157, 158, 160, 162

joint strategic plan, xi, xii, 3, 11, 13, 16, 17, 27, 46, 54, 61, 83, 89, 134, 136, 157, 161, 166, 189, 195, 196, 315, 332
Jong-un, Kim, 4, 165, 167, 170, 172, 180, 182, 185, 187, 190
Juche, 180
July 2016 military coup, 241, 242
Justice and Development Party (AKP), 242

K

Khamenei, Ali, 130, 141
Khuzestan, 150
Kurdistan Workers Party Rebels, 234

L

Laden, Osama bin, 302
Liaoning, 74
liberate, 206, 220, 307, 308, 317, 327, 330
Libya, 206, 304, 319
Line of Actual Control (LAC), 288
lone wolf style attacks, xii, 13, 18, 37, 38
Lykketoft, President Mogens, 227

M

Middle East, vi, xiii, xv, 4, 5, 16, 93, 126, 129, 131, 132, 133, 135, 136, 140, 142, 147, 148, 149, 151, 152, 154, 158, 160, 203, 205, 208, 209, 210, 212, 213, 214, 215, 216, 217, 225, 226, 228, 229, 234, 244, 245, 246, 247, 248, 249, 250, 251, 301, 313, 317, 323, 329
MS-13, 20, 21, 26
multilateral, 286, 288, 369, 375
Muslims, 302, 303, 305, 320

N

National Defense Authorization Act, 27, 54, 58, 84, 87, 131, 133, 153, 158, 161, 167, 189, 196
National Defense Authorization Act (NDAA), 27, 54, 58, 84, 87, 131, 133, 152, 158, 161, 167, 181, 189, 196
National Defense Strategy (NDS), xi, 3, 9, 12, 47, 61, 85, 131, 153, 157, 165, 182, 192, 195, 282
National Intelligence Priority Framework (NIPF), xi, 3
National Security Act, 6, 170, 232, 260
National Security Act of 1947, 6, 170, 232, 260
National Security Council, ix, 73, 171, 256
National Security Strategy (NSS), x, xi, xii, xiii, xiv, xv, xviii, 2, 3, 9, 12, 13, 14, 15, 17, 32, 41, 42, 47, 55, 56, 58, 63, 72, 73, 75, 76, 77, 78, 82, 89, 91, 92, 98, 100, 103, 117, 126, 130, 131, 135, 148, 152, 157, 160, 161, 162, 163, 164, 165, 183, 191, 192, 196, 199, 200, 201, 204, 205, 218, 222, 232, 264, 270, 275, 279, 282, 286, 298, 314, 331, 336, 338, 363, 365, 377, 378
NATO, xv, 5, 34, 46, 53, 95, 117, 132, 206, 209, 218, 225, 226, 229, 240, 246, 248, 250, 259, 330
naval threats, xiv, 130
Nigeria, 304
non-alignment, xvi, 264, 283, 284, 285, 290
nord stream pipeline, 93
North Atlantic Treaty Organization (NATO), xv, 5, 34, 46, 53, 95, 117, 132, 206, 209, 218, 225, 226, 227, 229, 240, 246, 248, 250, 259, 330
North Korea, vi, xiv, xviii, xix, 4, 16, 17, 23, 30, 31, 32, 34, 40, 41, 42, 52, 62, 83, 92, 110, 163, 164, 165, 166, 167, 168,

169, 170, 171, 172, 173, 174, 175, 176, 177, 178, 179, 180, 181, 182, 183, 184, 185, 186, 187, 188, 189, 190, 191, 192, 194, 195, 196, 197,334, 336, 338, 339, 343, 345, 351, 352, 353, 354, 355, 356, 360, 361, 362, 366, 367, 369
nuclear capabilities, xiv, 16, 30, 59, 130, 151, 152, 164, 182, 184, 186
Nye Jr., Joseph, 60, 83

O

Office of the Secretary of Defense, 62, 74, 88, 222
One China, 75
Ottoman Empire, 228, 239, 244, 259

P

Pahlavi, Mohammad Reza, 148
Paracel Islands, 268
People's Republic of China (PRC), 63, 75, 182
Petya, 335
phishing, 340, 371
price scissors, 93
proliferated aggression, xiv, 130, 152
propaganda, 25, 71, 80, 119, 142, 151, 154, 271, 304, 305, 308, 323, 324, 330, 342, 353, 355
public-private partnership, 371
Putin, Vladimir, 18, 35, 97, 115, 122

Q

Quadrilateral Strategic Dialogue (the Quad), 286, 292, 300
qualitative, ix, xii, xiii, xiv, xv, xvi, 9, 26, 29, 58, 63, 66, 70, 91, 97, 98, 100, 101, 102, 105, 116, 143, 146, 163, 171, 172, 174, 200, 208, 235, 237, 264, 265, 273, 274, 315, 348, 350
qualitative techniques, 9, 66, 143, 172
Quds Force, 142

R

Raqqa, 303, 332
Republic of Turkey, 228, 231, 239, 254, 259
research and development (R & D), 72, 95, 107
Rouhani, President Hassan, 130, 141, 155
Russia, x, xiii, xv, xvi, xviii, xix, 2, 3, 5, 16, 17, 18, 22, 30, 32, 33, 35, 39, 41, 42, 45, 48, 56, 85, 91, 92, 93, 94, 95, 96, 97, 98, 99, 100, 101, 102, 103, 104, 105, 106, 107, 108, 110, 111, 112, 113, 114, 115, 116, 117, 118, 120, 121, 122, 123, 124, 125,126, 175, 176, 200, 202, 204, 205, 206, 208, 209, 210, 211, 212, 213, 214, 215, 216, 218, 219, 220, 222, 226, 229, 240, 244, 245, 247, 248, 250, 251, 253, 254, 256, 258, 260, 283, 292, 334, 336, 339, 340, 341, 343, 344, 345, 348, 351, 352, 353, 354, 355, 356, 358, 359, 360, 363, 366, 367, 369, 372, 374, 378
Russian Federation, xiii, 91, 92, 93, 95, 96, 97, 98, 100, 103, 106, 107, 108, 109, 110, 115, 116, 118, 119, 121, 124, 125, 176, 202, 219

S

S-400 missile system, 245, 248, 250
Salafi Jihadism, 320
Salafism, 320
sanctions, 4, 30, 31, 32, 33, 34, 35, 51, 73, 99, 101, 108, 110, 117, 126, 133, 141, 142, 148, 149, 153, 154, 156, 157, 166, 167, 168, 180, 181, 182, 184, 185, 186,

188, 189, 190, 191, 196, 206, 210, 218, 220, 222, 235, 246, 345, 354, 363
Saudi Arabia, 4, 113, 134, 147, 158, 159, 160, 216, 322
Scarborough Reef, 268
Shah, 148, 154, 379
Sino-Indo-U.S. relations, 291
South Africa, 94, 107, 376, 379
South China Sea, xvi, 4, 59, 61, 65, 71, 74, 76, 77, 79, 83, 264, 267, 268, 269, 275, 277, 279, 280, 281, 282, 290, 291, 292, 293, 294, 298, 299, 300
spear-phishing, 136, 340, 341, 344, 353, 359, 360, 363
Spratly Islands, 4, 77, 268, 281
State Department, ix, xi, 3, 95, 166, 167, 190, 224, 308, 318, 332
state sponsored terrorism, xiii, 130, 157
Syria, xv, 5, 115, 132, 133, 134, 171, 183, 191, 199, 200, 201, 202, 203, 205, 206, 208, 209, 210, 211, 212, 213, 214, 215, 216, 217, 218, 219, 220, 221, 222, 223, 228, 229, 244, 245, 246, 254, 260, 303, 305, 307, 308, 317, 319, 322, 330, 332, 369, 370, 372, 375

T

tactics, x, xv, xvii, 1, 15, 22, 63, 66, 117, 137, 138, 150, 151, 153, 170, 200, 201, 203, 204, 273, 278, 279, 301, 312, 317, 320, 321, 327, 329, 341, 343, 350, 375
tactics, techniques, and procedures (TTP), x, 1, 8, 66, 152, 154, 273
Taiwan, 60, 62, 64, 72, 75, 84, 268
Taliban, 135, 149
tariffs, 60, 77, 80, 84, 235, 272, 308, 373
techniques and procedures, 170, 204
Tehran, 142, 149, 151, 292
terrorism, vi, x, xiii, 1, 5, 14, 16, 19, 37, 38, 44, 46, 49, 51, 53, 54, 55, 108, 129, 130, 132, 135, 137, 138, 139, 147, 150, 152, 153, 155, 156, 157, 159, 161, 201, 202, 216, 284, 306, 312, 318, 319, 331, 370
terrorism and more specifically the Islamic State, 5
terrorists, xiv, xv, xvii, 15, 18, 20, 23, 25, 36, 37, 38, 40, 46, 116, 130, 131, 132, 133, 135, 138, 147, 148, 149, 152, 154, 155, 158, 165, 199, 201, 205, 211, 213, 217, 301, 302, 304, 307, 311, 312, 316, 318, 319, 320, 322, 323, 324, 325, 326, 330, 368
The Russian Federation's National Security, 92, 121, 125
trade, x, xii, 2, 4, 57, 59, 60, 65, 70, 71, 73, 76, 77, 78, 79, 80, 83, 84, 87, 88, 89, 93, 99, 108, 109, 111, 116, 120, 125, 141, 154, 174, 185, 186, 194, 210, 222, 235, 247, 264, 266, 267, 268, 272, 274, 277, 287, 288, 289, 293, 306, 307, 311, 322, 335, 358, 362, 373, 375
Trump, Donald, x, 1, 14, 17, 32, 58, 60, 72, 105, 106, 164, 165, 170, 180, 182, 191, 192
Turkey, vi, xv, xix, 5, 208, 225, 226, 227, 228, 229, 230, 231, 232, 233, 234, 235, 236, 237, 238, 239, 240, 241, 242, 243, 244, 245, 246, 247, 248, 249, 250, 251, 252, 253, 254, 256, 257, 258, 259, 260, 261, 291, 306, 307, 308, 320, 366, 369
Turkish Defense Ministry, 227, 243, 245
Twitter, 15, 31, 33, 242, 304, 324, 341

U

U.S. Department of State, 11, 53, 54, 59, 89, 134, 157, 191, 196, 248, 295, 307
U.S. Immigration and Customs Enforcement's (ICE), 20, 21, 49, 53
UN Resolution 2254, xv, 200, 210, 219

338 Index

United Nations (UN), xv, 4, 17, 72, 110, 117, 130, 141, 167, 177, 179, 180, 185, 187, 195, 196, 197, 199, 201, 202, 205, 210, 211, 215, 219, 220, 221, 223, 227, 240, 260, 266, 280, 294, 298, 307, 308, 375

United Nations Convention of the Law of the Sea (UNCLOS), 280, 281, 294

United Nations Security Council (UNSC), 4, 110, 201, 202, 205, 212, 223, 307, 308

United States (US), 1, 13, 44, 51, 57, 88, 91, 129, 163, 199, 223, 225, 254, 260, 263, 294, 295, 297, 298, 301, 333, 365, 377, 381

United States Agency for International Development, 279

uranium enrichment, 130, 153, 157

W

Wahhabism, 320

weapons of mass destruction, 135, 140, 147, 148, 157, 165, 166, 210

Weapons of Mass Destruction (WMD), 200

Y

York Intelligence Red Team Model (YIRTM), xii, xiii, 7, 14, 23, 24, 63, 86, 97, 129, 141, 143, 164, 170, 206, 233, 269, 310

Yuen Foong Khong, 62, 82

Z

Zarqawi, Abu Musab al, 302

Related Nova Publications

THE CHIEF PERIODS OF EUROPEAN HISTORY

AUTHOR: Edward A. Freeman

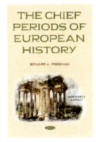

SERIES: Political Science and History

BOOK DESCRIPTION: The Chief Periods of European History is about the birth of modern Europe, tracing the history from the end of the Middle Ages and the Renaissance into the modern era. The book contains six lectures read in the University of Oxford in Trinity Term, 1885. It also contains the essay "Greek Cities under Roman Rule," as an appendix.

SOFTCOVER ISBN: 978-1-53615-723-9
RETAIL PRICE: $95

COLD WAR: GLOBAL IMPACT AND LESSONS LEARNED

EDITOR: Allison L. Palmadessa, PhD

SERIES: Political Science and History

BOOK DESCRIPTION: *The Cold War: Global Impacts and Lessons Learned* offers readers insight into the immediate challenges, the continued obstacles, and the knowledge gained from this tumultuous period riddled with fear that dominates the narrative of 20th century world history.

HARDCOVER ISBN: 978-1-53615-667-6
RETAIL PRICE: $195

To see a complete list of Nova publications, please visit our website at www.novapublishers.com

Related Nova Publications

THE RUSSIAN TURMOIL: MEMOIRS: MILITARY, SOCIAL, AND POLITICAL

AUTHOR: Anton Denikin

SERIES: Political Science and History

BOOK DESCRIPTION: Anton Denikin was an officer in the Russian army stationed in the Western Front during the Revolution. This memoir deals chiefly with the disintegration of the Russian army and its participation in the progress of the Revolution.

HARDCOVER ISBN: 978-1-53615-727-7
RETAIL PRICE: $230

To see a complete list of Nova publications, please visit our website at www.novapublishers.com